New
One-Act
Plays
for
Acting
Students

A new anthology
of complete one-act plays
for one, two, or three actors

edited by
Deb Bert &
Norman A. Bert

MERIWETHER PUBLISHING LTD.
Colorado Springs, Colorado

Meriwether Publishing Ltd., Publisher
PO Box 7710
Colorado Springs, CO 80933-7710

Executive editor: Ted Zapel
Editorial coordinator: Renée Congdon
Cover design: Janice Melvin

© Copyright MMIII Meriwether Publishing Ltd.
Printed in the United States of America
First Edition

Library of Congress Cataloging-in-Publication Data

New one-act plays for acting students : a new anthology of complete one-act plays for one, two, or three actors / edited by Debbie DeAnne Bert and Norman Allen Bert.
    p. cm.
  ISBN 13: 978-1-56608-084-2
  ISBN 10: 1-56608-084-3
1. Acting. 2. One-act plays, American. 3. American drama--20th century. I. Bert, Deb, 1954- II. Bert, Norman A.
  PN2080.N53 2003
  812'.04108--dc21

                          2003002380

                                      CIP

2   3   4   06   07   08

Preface

Welcome to the third volume in our series of short play anthologies. We're grateful to the teachers and students who have been using the earlier two volumes *One-Act Plays for Acting Students* (1987) and *More One-Act Plays for Acting Students* (previously published as *Play It Again!* [1993]), and we're excited about this new collection of scripts. We hope you'll enjoy studying and performing these plays.

We're eager to have you and your students meet the great variety of fine authors in the present volume. Two icons of the American avant-garde, Megan Terry and Robert Patrick, both contributed scripts to the book. Writers like Conrad Bishop and Elizabeth Fuller, Matthew Calhoun, and William Borden, who have contributed so much to regional theatre over the past twenty years and whose plays appeared in earlier volumes of the series, return with new works to the pages of this book. And then many other exciting voices make their debut here with beautiful effect.

We are particularly happy with the variety and usefulness of the scripts in this volume. Along with the heart of the book — fifteen scripts for two actors — there are also five monologs and five three-character plays. The collection provides roles for almost any mix of students in a typical acting class. The plays range in mood from serious and heavy to dark or satiric comedy to farce. Many of the scripts, realistic in style, feature traditional dramaturgy, but several "epic," poetic, and semi-realistic plays provide variety. Issue-oriented problem plays, character studies, fantasies, and even two plays about Vietnam enrich this volume.

As with the first two volumes of *One-Act Plays for Acting Students*, we intend this book to provide a text for acting classes. To that end, we have selected plays of similar length with balanced roles so that all students using plays from the book have approximately the same size of role. The scripts are all complete in themselves rather than presenting portions of longer plays; as a result, the students need not cope with questions of the relationship between their "cutting" and the longer play from which it comes. Most of the characters' ages range in the fifteen-to thirty-year-old age span typical of student actors. The book includes rehearsal plans and other supplementary materials to assist actors with the common problems they face when rehearsing on their own without the continual presence of a director.

The brevity of the scripts and their structural and stylistic variety also make the collection useful in other courses including playwriting, script analysis, scenic design, and introductory drama courses. Students will find these plays short enough to read, analyze, and discuss in a single class period. Exercises based on the plays can effectively conclude class sessions on topics as various as plot or character analysis, dialog writing, structures of didactic drama, and use of color in costume design.

Taken all together, the series of three volumes of *One-Act Plays for Acting Students* provides a wealth of materials for use in classes and for production in competitions, festivals, and other settings. The set presents a combined total of seventy-three plays (twelve monologs, forty-seven dialogs, and fourteen trios). The dialogs include nine scripts for two women, eleven scripts for two men, and twenty-seven scripts for one woman and one man. So if the present volume doesn't have exactly the right script for you, do check out the earlier books; you're sure to find a script that works.

We want to thank Texas Tech's Department of Theatre and Dance for providing Norman with research assistants who helped assemble this book. And special thanks to those research assistants themselves — Patrick White whose sense of theatre contributed to the screening process and Liz Castillo, a fine dramatist in her own right, who pulled together the detailed materials in the book and helped prepare the manuscript for the publisher. Finally, thanks as always to Art Zapel and the others at Meriwether Publishing for their continued support and guidance.

We believe you've got a collection of exciting scripts in your hands — scripts to read, plays to produce. Enjoy!

Norman and Deb Bert, Editors
Lubbock, Texas
2002

Contents

Preface iii

Part 1: Scripts 1

Scripts for Two Actors 2

College Money by Megan Terry (two W) 3
Career Counseling by Madeleine Martin (two W) 9
(F-A-T) by Madeleine Martin (two W) 19
Elizabeth the Fourth by Madeleine Martin (two W) 28
Bind Them Continually by Adrienne Lamb (two W) 36
Fixin' It by Madeleine Martin (two M) 41
Half Truth by Michael Johnson-Chase (two M) 53
Don't Rent Furniture by Geoffrey Howard (two M) 64
The Laundromat by Eric Geyer (two M) 72
My Usual by Matthew Calhoun (two M) 81
Muse by William Borden (two M) 87
Mikey's Chair by Michael Moore (one W, one M) 93
Revelation by David MacGregor (one W, one M) 100
Hard to Be Happy by Julianne Homokay (one W, one M) 108
Philosophical Inquiry at the Edge of a Cliff
 by Matthew Calhoun (one W, one M) 114

Scripts for Three Actors 123

Interruptions by Robert Patrick (three W) 124
Clubs by Conrad Bishop and Elizabeth Fuller (two W, one M) .. 130
You've Never Left This Place by Denny Berthiaume
 (two W, one M or one W, two M) 138
One Evening in Prague by William Borden (one W, two M) .. 144
Give Me Your Tired, Your Poor by Norman A. Bert (three any) .. 151

Monologs 161

Does Anybody Want a Miss Cow Bayou?
 by Gary Garrison (one W) 162

Fallin' Together by Madeleine Martin (one W) 168

Pretenses by Louise Stinespring (one W) 172

Fear of Falling by Norman A. Bert (one M) 175

*Fathers and Sons: The Dust Chasin' Me Out, The Dark
House That Held You,* and *The Green Time*
by Geoffrey Howard (one M) 179

Part 2: Securing Rights for Your Production 183

Part 3: Rehearsing the Play 193

Scheduling the Rehearsals 195

Approaching Rehearsals 201

Rehearsing for Specific Objectives 203

Rehearsal Tools 218

Part 4: Book List 231

Rehearsal Helps 233

Other Scripts by Writers in This Anthology 235

About the Editors 241

Part 1
Scripts

Scripts for Two Actors

College Money
by Megan Terry

Megan Terry is Playwright-in-residence at the Omaha Magic Theater. She has won many major awards for playwriting, including an Obie Award for Best Play, several Rockefeller grants, and a Guggenheim. She is a performer, musician, and photographer with the Omaha Magic Theater Performing Troupe.

College Money has been workshopped at the Omaha Magic Theater, Omaha, Nebraska, and has been produced for invited audiences at various kitchens in private homes around town.

Playwright's Production Suggestions

College Money can be produced in a classroom with no props and all stage business mimed, or it would be fun to produce it in the home-economics room or any place on campus that has kitchen facilities or, as we did, in private homes.

Address all inquiries concerning performances, readings, or reprinting of this work *or any portion thereof* to Megan Terry, 2309 Hanscom Boulevard, Omaha, NE 68105. For details, see "Part II: Securing Rights for Your Production," pages 183 to 192.

1   The action takes place on a morning in the Midwest.
2   **CHARACTERS:** MOTHER — early 30s. A warm, excitable woman.
3   ALANA — a high school student, cool and confident.
4   **SETTING:** A sunny kitchen.
5
6   *(MOTHER is dishing up breakfast. The phone rings.)*
7   **MOTHER:** *(Into phone)* **Jordano residence.** *(Ultra smile)* **Why ...**
8   **hello, Mr. Griffiths. What? You said ... how much? Yes, we are**
9   **very proud of her. Thank you, thank you ... I'm ... very ...**
10   *(ALANA rushes in and tries to grab phone from MOTHER.)*
11   **MOTHER:** *(Putting hand over receiver)* **It's Loyola! Stop it! Yes,**
12   **Mr. Griffith ... That's very good ...** *(Between her teeth to*
13   *ALANA)* **I'm handling it.**
14   **ALANA: Let me hear, Mother!**
15   **MOTHER:** *(Into phone)* **I'm sure Alana will be as pleased as I am.**
16   **Thank you from the bottom of my heart. We'll be in touch.**
17   *(Hangs up phone, a smile of gratitude on her face. She turns to*
18   *her daughter and hugs her.)* **He added another ten thousand.**
19   **Ten thousand!**
20   **ALANA: Not enough.**
21   **MOTHER: I had to work my way through college.**
22   **ALANA: I'm not going to Chicago.**
23   **MOTHER: Are you insane? Free money. The whole four years!**
24   **ALANA: It's not New York.**
25   **MOTHER: I'd have to pay if it was New York.**
26   **ALANA: I'm worth it.**
27   **MOTHER: I agree you're worth it. I just don't have that kind of**
28   **money.**
29   **ALANA: Raise your rates.**
30   **MOTHER: Here's breakfast. Sit.**
31   **ALANA:** *(Pushing away food)* **Now who's insane?**
32   **MOTHER: You've got to keep your strength up. We've been**
33   **visiting colleges every weekend. I'm exhausted.**
34   **ALANA: I'm not.**
35   **MOTHER: I had energy like that once.**

1 ALANA: Why can't I go to school in New York?
2 MOTHER: They accepted you, but they aren't offering any
3   scholarship money.
4 ALANA: *(Flipping through a journal)* Let's try a different school.
5 MOTHER: You got accepted at Julliard, but they won't even let
6   you sing the first year. And I can't afford it.
7 ALANA: What about Grandma and Grandpa?
8 MOTHER: They're already paying for your singing lessons.
9 ALANA: If all these schools want me, why doesn't New York?
10 MOTHER: New York does want you but they don't want to pay
11   you.
12 ALANA: Who was on the phone?
13 MOTHER: If you eat your breakfast I'll tell you.
14 ALANA: I'm not eating all that grease. You can eat eggs and bacon
15   if you want to, but yukkkkk. Where's the juice? I have to get
16   to school early. We're having a meeting. We're gonna go down
17   to Lincoln to protest the death penalty. We might have to stay
18   up all night tonight and tomorrow to show our support.
19 MOTHER: Concentrate on one thing, please.
20 ALANA: I don't have any problem thinking about others besides
21   myself.
22 MOTHER: Your singing teacher said you had to eat three meals a
23   day.
24 ALANA: What's that got to do with the death penalty?
25 MOTHER: You'll find out if you don't eat. Look what happened to
26   Karen Carpenter.
27 ALANA: I'm not into pop, I sing opera.
28 MOTHER: You need meat on your bones to hit those notes.
29 ALANA: I don't.
30 MOTHER: Don't let that arrogance show when we go to the
31   college interview.
32 ALANA: I'm not worried.
33 MOTHER: Alana, please think about Chicago. They have a
34   campus. A real campus there.
35 ALANA: They don't have the Met.

1　MOTHER: The Lyric Opera's in Chicago.
2　ALANA: The school won't let me sing there. They're very
3　　　　restrictive.
4　MOTHER: That school is so generous. You must have knocked
5　　　　their socks off. They're offering you twenty-six thousand
6　　　　dollars. Dollars! Where's your flaky father? He never made
7　　　　that much money. They're offering you this because you have
8　　　　a gift. And you'll have support, a support group around you.
9　ALANA: Yeah, chaperons. You bet.
10　MOTHER: You got mugged when you tried out in New York.
11　　　　You're too naive to be in that big a city.
12　ALANA: The guy needed it more than I did.
13　MOTHER: Altruism can go too far. I paid three hundred and
14　　　　seventy-five dollars for your class ring!
15　ALANA: I can get another ring.
16　MOTHER: Here's your juice. At least put some protein powder in
17　　　　it. And if you drink it all down you'll find another ring at the
18　　　　bottom of the glass.
19　ALANA: Yeah, right.
20　MOTHER: Honey, you've got to face facts.
21　ALANA: It didn't get you very far.
22　MOTHER: That's not fair.
23　ALANA: I can't help it. I really feel most of the time that I'm your
24　　　　mother and you're my child. You're too emotional.
25　MOTHER: You'd be emotional too, if your only daughter wanted
26　　　　to go to that dirty city where people mug you the minute you
27　　　　walk out your door. You'd be emotional if you had a very
28　　　　gifted daughter and you knew that no matter how hard you
29　　　　worked you couldn't afford to give her what she wanted.
30　ALANA: Mother, you worry too much. Something good will
31　　　　happen. We haven't heard from all the schools yet.
32　MOTHER: I've heard enough to know that I make thirty-one
33　　　　thousand a year as a lawyer, and I have *three* degrees. After we
34　　　　pay for living expenses and all this flying around to visit
35　　　　colleges what do you think is left?

1 ALANA: I wish you believed in me as much as I did.
2 MOTHER: *(Standing with ALANA's plate and eating what she didn't)*
3   Look what you make me do. I've been going to Weight
4   Watchers six months, but every time I have a fight with you I
5   can't stop eating.
6 ALANA: I wasn't aware we were having a fight, Mother.
7 MOTHER: *(Talking with mouth full)* What about New Orleans?
8   They want you there. They offered thirty thousand plus living
9   expenses.
10 ALANA: Do you know how far New Orleans is from New York?
11 MOTHER: But they have the best food in the world there.
12 ALANA: I need plane fare to go to D.C. this weekend.
13 MOTHER: This weekend?
14 ALANA: It's a national march against the death penalty.
15 MOTHER: That won't work. It's up to the States.
16 ALANA: We have to raise awareness.
17 MOTHER: What am I going to tell Mr. Griffiths?
18 ALANA: Who's he?
19 MOTHER: Twenty-six thousand in Chicago.
20 ALANA: Oh that.
21 MOTHER: Listen, Ms. Casual. If you ever do become a famous
22   opera singer you better have a very good agent and a hard-
23   nosed business manager or you'll never save a penny.
24 ALANA: I don't care about saving. I was put on earth to give my
25   gifts away. And that's OK. Have some faith, Mother. Look
26   how much we've been offered so far and it's only March.
27 MOTHER: *(Gulping food)* You're my only child. How can you
28   think I can send you so far away when I can't be there to
29   watch over you?
30 ALANA: It'll be easier on you Mother, truly, when I'm away at
31   school. You'll only have to think about yourself. I know where
32   I'm going and I know I wouldn't have been given these gifts if
33   it wasn't going to work out for me to share them. In the
34   meantime, I've got to get to school. I'm running the meeting.
35 *(She downs o.j. and slings book bag over her shoulder.)*

1 **MOTHER: But what about Chicago?**
2 **ALANA: Think, New York.**
3 **MOTHER: Listen, if I get you the plane ticket to D.C., will you**
4   **take a cab over to Catholic University and check out their**
5   **music department?**
6 **ALANA: How will I have time for that?**
7 **MOTHER: Just do it. I heard they put on four operas a year and**
8   **freshmen are allowed to try out. And, they have a campus.**
9 **ALANA: Are you sure they put on four operas a year?**
10 **MOTHER: Cross my heart.**
11 **ALANA: Give me the cab fare.**
12 **MOTHER: You'll do it?**
13 **ALANA: I'm not promising anything. But I will check them out.**
14 **MOTHER: D.C. is the center of the political universe. Think of it.**
15   **If you went to school there you could march for something**
16   **every weekend.**
17 **ALANA: If I wasn't singing in *La Boheme*.**
18 **MOTHER: I'll arrange the travel stuff. I'm so proud of you.**
19 **ALANA: If I promise to check out that school will you promise me**
20   **to have more faith?**
21 **MOTHER:** *(Flinging her arms around her daughter)* **I promise.**
22 **ALANA: Don't get egg in my hair.**
23 **MOTHER: Go. I love you.** *(ALANA runs off to school. Humming,*
24   *MOTHER scrapes rest of breakfast food off plate and into*
25   *garbage.)*
26   ***The End***
27
28
29
30
31
32
33
34
35

Career Counseling
by Madeleine Martin

Madeleine Martin grew up in Montana. With the support of some teachers and in spite of others like Ms. Will in *Career Counseling*, she earned a college degree with high honors. Her plays have been produced in universities and off-off Broadway and have been published nationally and internationally.

Special thanks to Kirk Enstrom, Senior Editor of TheBostonChannel.com, winner of the 2002 Edward R. Murrow Award for excellence in electronic news broadcasting. The playwright also thanks Texas Tech University's playwriting class, spring 2002, for workshopping *Career Counseling*. The script has had no other publications or performances prior to publication in this anthology.

Address all inquiries concerning performances, readings, or reprinting of this work *or any portion thereof* to Madeleine Martin, PO Box 53521, Lubbock, TX 79453. For details, see "Part II: Securing Rights for Your Production," pages 183 to 192.

1   The action takes place in the present in a high school.

2   **CHARACTERS:** MS. WILL — a high school career guidance counselor.

3   WENDY — a high school senior.

4   **SETTING:** A high school counselor's office.

5

6   *(WENDY enters. Not looking up, MS. WILL shuffles officiously*

7   *through a stack of papers.)*

8   **WENDY: Hello?**

9   **MS. WILL: Yes, yes. Come in. Sit down. I'll be right with you.**

10   **Name?**

11   **WENDY: Wendy Cole.**

12   **MS. WILL: Purpose?**

13   **WENDY: My call slip says, "Career Counseling?"**

14   **MS. WILL: So, Wendy, what year are you?**

15   **WENDY: Senior.**

16   **MS. WILL: And have you given any thought whatsoever to what**

17   **you might wish to do with the rest of your life after you leave**

18   **this incubator?**

19   **WENDY: Incubator?**

20   **MS. WILL: Sit, Wendy!** *(WENDY sits, immediately.)* **High School,**

21   **Wendy. Are you in Special Ed? Try to keep up, OK?**

22   **WENDY: Excuse me?**

23   **MS. WILL:** *(Fiercely scribbling notes)* **… is a slow learner, possible**

24   **retardation.** *(To WENDY, speaking very slowly and clearly.)*

25   **What do you plan to do after you finish high school?**

26   **WENDY: I've been accepted at Brown University where I plan to**

27   **major in journalism.**

28   **MS. WILL: I see. So, you're floundering. No real plans. Just living**

29   **moment to moment, hoping that Mommy and Daddy will take**

30   **care of everything. But let me guess — your parents divorced**

31   **years ago — the typical alcohol/scummy-women scenario, and**

32   **now nothing is your fault, is it, Wendy! Blame it all on your**

33   **parents! Well Wendy, it's my job to make you sit up and take**

34   **notice that you're about to become an adult. A-D-U-L-T. It's**

35   **your job to plan for your future. Nobody is going to do it for**

1   you. But, I can help. What have you occupied yourself with
2   these last four years — besides drugs, I mean?
3 WENDY: Floundering?
4 MS. WILL: It's a simple question, Wendy. What have you done?
5   Extracurricular activities? How bad are the grades? Do we
6   need to cut any deals with your teachers?
7 WENDY: I've been on the forensics team for four years, and for
8   the last two years, my partner and I have taken state. I hold
9   the state track record in the mile. I'm editor of the school
10   paper for the second year. I've been on the honors track since
11   entering high school, and I have a 4.0 GPA. *(Pause)* And my
12   parents are not divorced!
13 MS. WILL: *(Scribbling like a maniac)* ... and also in serious denial
14   about disgusting home-life. So. Now. Wendy. It seems we have
15   got a lot of work to do to try to get you out of this raccoon pit
16   you've dug yourself into. Whom do you run around with!
17   What pack?
18 WENDY: *(Correcting MS. WILL)* With whom do I run around? I
19   have friends. I don't "run with a pack." Most of my friends
20   are athletes, other honor students, newspaper ...
21 MS. WILL: Boyfriend?
22 WENDY: I don't have one particular boyfriend. I like to keep my
23   options open. I'm not ready ...
24 MS. WILL: So, you're a tramp. You go with all the boys. Do you
25   like the fact that everyone in school sees you as a tramp, that
26   everyone is saying, "Oh, there goes Wendy-Cole-the-Tramp,
27   growing up just like her-mother-the-tramp?"
28 WENDY: I am not a tramp! And neither was my mother!
29 MS. WILL: Good Wendy, get angry — let it all out. If you keep it
30   in and let it fester, you'll be knocked-up by year's end and
31   then where will you be? You'll be shot-gun wed to one of those
32   baby-boys you fool around with — and you insist on calling
33   them "men!" You'll have a crying carpet-creature by this time
34   next year, all your friends will be in college, and you'll be
35   drowning your sorrows in Red Dog Wine and Little Debbie's

1   Cupcakes while your husband takes up with the latest skinny,
2   divorced, peroxide-blonde barmaid at the corner tavern. Not
3   a pretty picture, is it, Wendy?
4   **WENDY:** *(Speaking slowly and very, very clearly)* **Ms. Will, I am**
5   **going to attend Brown University. I am going to major in**
6   **journalism. I am not going to become pregnant because I do**
7   **not have sex. In order to become pregnant, one needs to have**
8   **sexual inter …**
9   **MS. WILL:** *(Writing ferociously)* ... **obsessing on sex. OK, Wendy.**
10   **So when did you become sexually active? At what age? Have**
11   **you been to Planned Parenthood?**
12   **WENDY:** *(Standing)* **I do not understand any of this. I am Wendy**
13   **Cole, Class Valedictorian, and if you'll excuse me, I have a**
14   **lead story due in two hours that I have yet to find a …**
15   **MS. WILL:** *(Interrupting, while tapping her pencil on her desk)* **You**
16   **can make this hard on yourself, or you can cooperate. I do**
17   **have the power to keep you back, Wendy. One stroke of the**
18   **pen, and you're here another year. I have that power.**
19   **WENDY: Hold me back? Fail me? Keep me here?**
20   **MS. WILL: Sit!** *(WENDY sits.)*
21   **MS. WILL: Look, I know this is hard. How? I have been in your**
22   **shoes. Hated by my peers, loved by** *all* **the boys. Oh yes — I**
23   **was pretty, like you. And I loved them. I wouldn't call myself**
24   **trampy, but I needed to be needed. Like you, my father**
25   **deserted me and my mother when I was small. Wanda, my**
26   **mother, she turned to heroin and later — the hard stuff. I was**
27   **forced to take care of the younger pups she whelped. Then**
28   **came the shoplifting charges, the jail time, the half-way**
29   **houses … Those were hard times for me. So I have been where**
30   **you are now, Wendy! I know! I can help you!**
31   **WENDY:** *(Thoughtfully sits.)* **It sounds like you've had a very rough**
32   **life, Ms. Will.**
33   **MS. WILL: Rough? Rough! You are still denying the core of the**
34   **problem. It was pure** *hell.* **To be a child, but not to be a child!**
35   **That was the problem! To live as a child prostitute! To suffer**

1   the scorn and ridicule! Oh, I saw the other kids on the
2   athletics teams with their expensive clothing; I wanted to be
3   them too! The cheerleaders ... now there's the tramps —
4   with their short skirts and matching panties, huh?
5   WENDY: *(Going along)* Oh, yeah. Trampy cheerleaders ... right.
6   Matching panties. Now there's a story.
7   MS. WILL: Oh, you know it. Can you believe the way they flirt
8   with their teachers?
9   WENDY: Unbelievable. Coach Barker too — I bet that's how they
10   pass history as well.
11   MS. WILL: I know. I see it everyday. *(Conspiratorial)* But see, this
12   is what I'm telling you, Wendy, if we need to cut a deal with
13   any of your teachers ... there are ways, you know? The
14   cheerleaders know how to do it, and they do it! Mark my
15   words. You can learn very well from them. Watch them
16   carefully. Learn!
17   WENDY: *(Glumly)* I'll be sure and take notes, Ms. Will. *(An idea*
18   *strikes!)* Notes! Of course. *(She takes out her reporter's*
19   *notebook.)* Do you mind if I write some of this down?
20   MS. WILL: Heidi Baskerville is the worst. I'm going to let her sink
21   her own petard. She'll be pregnant by the end of the year.
22   Mark my words. But you, Wendy, you remind me of me. So
23   tender, so fragile, so smart, but so neglected, so hurt, and
24   yet — a survivor. Let me help you, Wendy.
25   WENDY: By all means, Ms. Will. I can see that you are going to be
26   an immense help!
27   MS. WILL: Good girl! OK, then — first thing we need to do is get
28   those grades up and start improving your reputation around
29   here. Maybe, if we work real hard, maybe we can even get you
30   into a nice junior college next year.
31   WENDY: *(Jotting notes in her book)* A Ju-Co. There you go; that
32   would be fun.
33   MS. WILL: *(Slapping her desk)* You must stop thinking fun and
34   start thinking future, Wendy! Get serious!
35   WENDY: Serious! Of course! *(WENDY digs through her backpack.)*

1   Ms. Will? Speaking of serious, do you mind if I record this?

2   I ... I have trouble reading my writing sometimes — you

3   know. If you don't mind my asking, seriously, how did you go

4   about becoming a high school counselor? *(WENDY sets up the*

5   *recorder and punches the "record" button.)*

6   MS. WILL: By all means — record, Wendy! You must use every

7   available means of success at your disposal. Someday, you

8   know, someone will write about me. I'll show them all. They'll

9   see who I really am!

10   WENDY: Oh, I'm sure of it. No doubt about it. *(Pause)* Did you

11   earn your degree from a Ju-Co? A community college? A state

12   school?

13   MS. WILL: You learn fast, Wendy. I like that! I can see that you

14   look at me as something of a role model. I understand

15   completely. Well, my career's out of the picture for you, my

16   dear. I'm afraid you don't quite have what it takes to fill these

17   shoes. *(Pause)* See these? *(MS. WILL points to several gold-*

18   *framed diplomas hanging on the wall. WENDY nods.)*

19   Impressive, aren't they! U of M. Ever heard of it?

20   WENDY: University of Miami? *(MS. WILL shakes her head.)*

21   Michigan? Missouri? Montana? Massachusetts! *(MS. WILL*

22   *shakes her head.)*

23   MS. WILL: The University of Metaphysics! These babies cost me a

24   bundle. Twenty-five hundred bucks each! I have a Ph.D.

25   coming next week! That'll net me a nice little raise! But that's

26   what everyone who sees them thinks — U of Miami,

27   Michigan, Massachusetts, of course. People want to be fools,

28   Wendy. They want to be deceived. They have an innate desire

29   to fail. That's where people like me — and you — come in,

30   Wendy. We indulge them.

31   WENDY: *(Writing notes)* I think I'm getting the hang of it. An angle

32   on the story, you might say.

33   MS. WILL: Let's get to work then. First things first — drop the

34   boyfriend.

35   WENDY: Who? Oh — yes. Right away. Done. He's gone.

1   MS. WILL: All of them.
2   WENDY: All of them. Got it.
3   MS. WILL: It's not that easy, Wendy. Believe me, I know. I've been
4   there. When I tried to drop Bobby Hunt, well ... that's a
5   Lifetime movie in itself. You could read the court transcripts,
6   but they're sealed. And I was heavily sedated. But I don't care
7   what they say, I should not have been prevented from going to
8   his funeral! He was the love of my life! Besides restraining
9   orders aren't worth the paper they're written on, not if you
10   get yourself a good disguise and know their routines. Men are
11   such creatures of habit. *(MS. WILL acts as if she's aiming a*
12   *gun.)* Anyway, I dropped him like a cold potato.
13   WENDY: *(Writing madly)* Hot potato.
14   MS. WILL: Hm?
15   WENDY: *(Looking up from her notebook)* Ummm, I believe the
16   saying is that you "drop someone like a hot potato" because
17   when ... potatoes are hot, they're ... hot and they, um, burn ...
18   Oh my God! *(Speaking loudly into her recorder)* Are you saying
19   you killed your former boyfriend?
20   MS. WILL: Look, Wendy, you can ditz around pretending to be a
21   Pollyanna, or we can work on your problems. Are you ready
22   to get serious about your life, or not?
23   WENDY: *(Making more rapid notes in her notebook)* You use that
24   word "serious" a lot. What do you mean exactly when you say
25   "get serious about life?"
26   MS. WILL: I'm a serious person, Precious. Ah, you are so, so
27   innocent. But I am dead serious when I'm talking about
28   getting what I want out of life. So listen up! It's always best to
29   contact Women's Services just in case you need a safe place to
30   go — if you're serious about dumping the boys. Here's their
31   number. Your mom probably has it tacked-up on all the
32   cupboard doors anyway, hm? *(MS. WILL smiles, knowingly.)*
33   WENDY: Got it. Forewarned is forearmed.
34   MS. WILL: No! Don't go in armed. At least, not at first. I can
35   always get you a throw-away piece, if it should come to that.

1   **Now, how hard will it be to track down your father?**

2 **WENDY:** *(Getting into her role)* **Oh, gosh. Daddy comes and goes so**

3   **often ... Uh? Throw-away piece? What's a throw-away piece?**

4 **MS. WILL:** *(Stares at Wendy and then scribbles on her paper.)* **You're**

5   **not as street-wise as you should be. I'm surprised. A throw-**

6   **away piece — a non-traceable gun.** *(Whispering)* **I get them**

7   **from dirty cops. That way, you won't be tracked too easily**

8   **when you use it. Now, since your father's disappeared again,**

9   **it'll be a piece of fruitcake to get financial aid. They won't be**

10   **expecting the deadbeat to kick in. And if he does show up ...**

11   **well ... we can give him the old "hot potato" action too, huh?**

12   **I'd better pick up a piece immediately; I think you're going to**

13   **need one. Maybe two.** *(MS. WILL begins to sob softly.)*

14 **WENDY: Ms. Will? Are you alright?**

15 **MS. WILL: I'm fine, Wendy. All this talk about fathers**

16   **abandoning their family just reminds me of my own. It's just**

17   **something you never get over, do you?**

18 **WENDY:** *(Pen poised at her notebook)* **How old were you when your**

19   **father ... um ... left, Ms. Will?**

20 **MS. WILL: Oh, I hardly remember him, but Mother had his**

21   **pictures all over the house, so I felt like I knew him well. Most**

22   **of those photos showed him passed out on the couch. In one,**

23   **his friends had scrawled "loser" across his forehead with a**

24   **bright purple permanent marker.** *(She sobs loudly.)* **I think**

25   **that's my favorite because he looked so peaceful. Just like a**

26   **baby. Others showed him doing funny things like smashing**

27   **beer cans on his forehead, or crashing the ancient Plymouth**

28   **into the old oak tree in front of our house. He must've had a**

29   **great sense of humor. I consider him my number one role**

30   **model.** *(She sighs.)* **You know, Wendy, you've got so much**

31   **baggage here, I think I'm going to run a referral on you.**

32 **WENDY: Do you know where your father is now? What he's**

33   **doing? If he's ... alive?**

34 **MS. WILL: I know that sounds frightening, dear, but don't be**

35   **afraid. It just means that you'll be seen by a counselor here at**

1   school a couple of times a week to sort out all these issues.
2   WENDY: Oh, a referral. Good. Yes. And would that counselor who
3   I'm to visit with be you?
4   MS. WILL: If you want it to be! I am so thrilled that you want to
5   work with me. Since I have so much background in these
6   issues myself ...
7   WENDY: You already seem so busy with career counseling — do
8   you spend a lot of time with that?
9   MS. WILL: I'll check my schedule and see if I can fit you in.
10   WENDY: Are there any other counselors who work here — like,
11   men for example? Or are you the only one the district hires?
12   MS. WILL: You do have a tendency to come on to men, Wendy.
13   Like your teachers? You wouldn't want that to happen with a
14   counselor now, would you?
15   WENDY: Did you have to go through an extensive interview
16   process to get this position? *(Pause)*
17   MS. WILL: OK, then. The next thing we're going to do is get you
18   set up in the remedial program to get you caught up on a few
19   of the more basic skills. If you had not been so busy partying,
20   chasing boys, cleaning your guns, and writing threatening
21   letters, you would not be so far behind, you know.
22   WENDY: Do you read the records of the students you counsel?
23   And how many students would you say you have counseled
24   this semester?
25   MS. WILL: Ah, I see where you're going! Yes! I like to fly by my
26   own instincts, Wendy. Do you want to know why? I was a
27   victim like you. My teachers pegged me as a loser from day
28   one and never gave me the slightest chance. It didn't matter
29   what I did or didn't do, their perceptions of me were all that
30   mattered, so in the end, I was the one who lost out. I'm not
31   going to let that happen to you, Wendy. Here's what I think of
32   those teachers' perceptions of you, Wendy. *(She takes Wendy's*
33   *file and tosses it in the trash.)* And that's what you should think
34   of them too. No, I haven't read them, and I'm not going to. I
35   know instinctually when a girl walks through that door just

1   what her story is and what she needs from me. And the thing
2   is, nobody would ever believe I work the way I do, not in a
3   million years!
4   **WENDY:** *(Smiling)* **Yeah. You're probably right. Nobody is going to**
5   **believe this! To just stumble into something like this is like a**
6   **real dream come true for me.**
7   **MS. WILL: How flattering! But we'll have to save something for**
8   **our next session. We've gone over our time for today.**
9   **WENDY:** *(Disappointed)* **But I have several more questions! I**
10   **mean, there's so much to learn and so ... so little time.** *(She*
11   *checks her watch.)*
12   **MS. WILL:** *(Smiling knowingly)* **Nonsense. There's time. And you**
13   **have enough to sort through for one day. I am here anytime to**
14   **help you succeed, Wendy. And you will.**
15   **WENDY:** *(Scanning her notes quickly)* **You're probably correct.**
16   **With these and the tape to back it up, I probably have enough**
17   **material for a super stor — um, day. So thank you so much**
18   **for your time, Ms. Will.**
19   **MS. WILL: I'll see you next week then. Same day, same time.**
20   **WENDY: If not before!**
21   **MS. WILL: That's what I like! Commitment!** *(She winks at WENDY.)*
22   **WENDY: Yes, well ... that's what I'm hoping for, Ms. Will.**
23   **Commitment.** *(She winks back and flips her reporter's notebook*
24   *closed.)* **We can only hope, huh? Thanks again.** *(WENDY*
25   *collects her things, and she leaves, shutting the door behind*
26   *herself.)*
27   **MS. WILL: It's going to take more than "hope," Missy. Poor**
28   **misguided thing. You just gotta' love 'em!** *(MS. WILL sits at her*
29   *desk. She scribbles out a few notes. She sighs. Stretches. Smiles.*
30   *She looks intensely satisfied with herself. She presses the intercom*
31   *button.)* **Margaret? Will you please send in the next student**
32   **waiting for career counseling?**
33
34   ***The End***
35

(F-A-T)
by Madeleine Martin

Madeleine Martin's works have been published both nationally and internationally. An award-winning playwright, she has seen her plays produced in educational settings and off-off Broadway since 1993. She received her playwriting education as a private student of Dr. Norman A. Bert. Currently she is working on a children's book centered around a dog with silky white hair and placing the finishing touches on a full-length play about life after being a police officer.

The playwright thanks Texas Tech University's playwriting class, spring 2002, for workshopping *(F-A-T)*. The script has had no other publications or performances prior to publication in this anthology.

Address all inquiries concerning performances, readings, or reprinting of this work *or any portion thereof* to Madeleine Martin, PO Box 53521, Lubbock, TX 79453. For details, see "Part II: Securing Rights for Your Production," pages 183 to 192.

1   The action takes place in the present at a local mall at about 4:15
2   p.m. on Saturday.
3   **CHARACTERS:** KIM — a high school junior who happens to be very thin.
4   RACHAEL — Kim's friend, a high school junior. She also happens to
5   be quite tiny.
6   **SETTING:** A round table in the food court of a shopping mall.
7
8   *(KIM sits at the table counting her money. She rummages around*
9   *in one of the many bags beside her feet. Tissue flies everywhere.*
10   *Finally, pulling a piece of pink fabric towards her, she whispers*
11   *hot, negative words. She opens another bag and produces a stack*
12   *of magazines. Slamming them on the table, she feverishly begins*
13   *leafing through them. Suddenly she stops leafing, stares at*
14   *something she has found, and begins banging her head on the*
15   *stack of magazines.)*
16   **KIM: What have I done, what have I done, what have I done, what**
17   **have I done ...** *(RACHAEL enters with two bottles of Perrier*
18   *water.)*
19   **RACHAEL: They didn't have any "diet" so I had to get water.**
20   **What are you doing?**
21   **KIM:** *(Blinking vacantly at RACHAEL)* **No "diet?" I told you — I**
22   **need caffeine!**
23   **RACHAEL:** *(Handing a bottle to KIM)* **Look, I can go back and get**
24   **you a regular Dr. Pepper.** *(Speaking very slowly and plainly)*
25   **They don't have any "diet" anything, Kimmers. They have**
26   **regular. Sugared. Is that what you want, Kimberley Anne?**
27   *(Pause. KIM stares at the water before finally snatching it,*
28   *unscrewing the cap, and guzzling it. She stands, fists clenched,*
29   *facing the snack bar.)*
30   **KIM:** *(Screaming)* **Infidels! Cretins! Communists! No "diet?" You**
31   **call yourself "the" place to stop when you shop? I'm spreadin'**
32   **the word! They have no caffeine, people! No caff —**
33   **RACHAEL:** *(Grabbing KIM)* **Sit down! You're embarrassing me.**
34   **And I don't think you need any caffeine — I think you need a**
35   **nap. Let's just go home, OK? We're done!**

1   KIM: I'm taking it back.

2   RACHAEL : No way! You cannot be serious!

3   KIM: Rach, I have to take it back, I have to.

4   RACHAEL: Kim, if you take another dress back, I will have to kill

5   you. *(KIM crosses her arms and pouts.)* **Why! Why?** Why, why,

6   why! There's nothing wrong with it! Nothing! It's a beautiful

7   dress! It's taken us two months to find that dress. It's

8   wonderful. No. No, it's not wonderful — it's fantastic. It's the

9   best, most stunningest dress that anyone will be wearing at

10   this formal, and you, you — Kim — you, will not take it back!

11   KIM: It's pink.

12   RACHAEL: You just noticed that? After staring at it for three

13   hours in the stupid mirror to see if it was exactly right — you

14   just noticed it's pink?

15   KIM: It's pink-pink. *(Pause)* Pink is flesh tone, Rachael. Read this.

16   Read. This. *(As if the magazine were highly fragile [or maybe*

17   *explosive!], KIM hands it to RACHAEL who rips the magazine*

18   *out of KIM'S hands.)*

19   RACHAEL: Gimme' that. What! *(Scanning the page)* What!

20   Where! *(KIM pokes her finger at the page. RACHAEL reading)*

21   "Be most careful before choosing a pink gown, as under many

22   lights, pink has a way of appearing nearly nude, and you

23   would not want that faux pas on your special night! Also don't

24   forget that gorgeous pink-pink gown that Gwyneth Paltrow

25   wore for the 2001 Academy Awards. If you're not Paltrow

26   thin, don't even think about it. Never forget this general rule:

27   Wearing pink is the same as wearing nothing!" *(Pause)*

28   KIM: I am not "Paltrow thin," and I know it. I'm not. I certainly

29   cannot wear pink. I shouldn't even think about it. That's for

30   sure. We both know that!

31   RACHAEL: Oh, for God's sake. You know what you need? You

32   need a good shrink. *(Rummaging through her purse, RACHAEL*

33   *comes up with a card, which she hands to KIM.)* Here. Use mine.

34   KIM: I don't want a used shrink. She's yours. I have my own.

35   RACHAEL: She obviously hasn't done much in four years because

1   you still think you're fat.

2   KIM: Oh-my-God. You said it. I cannot believe you said it. Who's

3   behind me? Who? Is anybody around? Is anyone looking at me?

4   RACHAEL: There's nobody around here. Will you stop that?

5   Nobody heard me say that! And it doesn't matter. It's just a

6   word. Three letters. An "F," an "A," and a "T."

7   KIM: *(Eyes tearing)* You are so insensitive. Why don't you just

8   shoot me next time; it would hurt less. I thought you were my

9   best friend. Please stop. I can't take anymore today. Can't you

10   see I'm ready to snap? Don't spell it, don't say it.

11   RACHAEL: You loved the dress! It looked perfect on you.

12   KIM: But you read the magazine. "Be most careful." That means —

13   "Don't do it!" Wait until I get under those lights at the dance.

14   Then what will it look like? It'll look nude, that's what! And I

15   won't know until it happens — *at the dance*! In front of

16   everyone!

17   RACHAEL: Geez, Kim. *(Pause)* OK. Get this: I'm not going with you

18   to take that dress back. If you take it back, you're on your own.

19   KIM: You can't do that to me! You wouldn't!

20   RACHAEL: Yes, I would. And I will!

21   KIM: No you wouldn't! If I show up in a pink dress that makes me

22   look naked and … and … *(Whispering) fat* … then I will tell

23   everyone that Rachael Hart told me to buy it because it looked

24   "just fabulous."

25   RACHAEL: *(Gasping)* You would not!

26   KIM: *(Smiling)* Oh yes. I would. *(Pause)*

27   RACHAEL: You know what? I don't care. Tell the world. This is

28   your mental condition because you're not *fat* because you're

29   practically anorexic. You're thin, Kim. Thin. Very thin. Too

30   thin! Anorexic thin.

31   KIM: I am not anorexic! I have a high metabolism.

32   RACHAEL: And do you turn your metabolism to high gear with

33   the switch in your throat? Because that's where you stick your

34   finger after lunch!

35   KIM: *(Gasping)* How dare you! I do not eat lunch!

1 RACHAEL: Excuse me. I forgot. I know the rules by heart. Rule
2   Number One: Don't eat.
3 KIM: I eat! I eat all the time! Ask Chris! He takes me out to dinner
4   all the time!
5 RACHAEL: I know the dinner rules too — Rule Number Two:
6   Order the most expensive thing on the menu and then don't
7   eat it.
8 KIM: *(Smiling)* That is kind of fun, you have to admit. It separates
9   the wheat from the chaff.
10 RACHAEL: *(Smiling)* You're cruel, Kim.
11 KIM: So you'll take the dress back with me?
12 RACHAEL: *(Sighing)* What would you get instead? One of the
13   dresses we already looked at, I hope?
14 KIM: Black. Definitely black. Because black makes —
15 RACHAEL: *(Finishing KIM's line)* — makes you look thin.
16 KIM: Exactly! I don't know why I didn't do that before.
17 RACHAEL: I do. Because you have done it before! About a
18   gazillion times. If you were going to wear black you could
19   have just worn one of the gazillion black rags you have piled
20   in your closet.
21 KIM: Duh! I can't wear something that everyone has already seen,
22   stupid.
23 RACHAEL: *(Feigning a stupid voice)* Oh, stupid me. How can I be
24   so stupid! Duh, I dunno'!
25 KIM: I'm sorry, Rach. That was rude. I'm just a little tense, you
26   know. I feel so pressured.
27 RACHAEL: *(Showing a little anger for the first time)* You know, you
28   should feel pressured, Kim, since tonight is the dance. We've
29   been messing around with this stupid dress thing since the last
30   dance. It seems like we measure our lives from one formal to the
31   next, going from buying one dress to the next. Our weekends are
32   made up of malling for the perfect dress for you, and we never
33   find it — time just runs out, and you buy black ... And this
34   time, you have a stunning pink gown. It's extraordinary. It cost
35   a fortune — what more could you want?

1   KIM: I could want to look good in it. Is that too much to want?

2   RACHAEL: Do you really think that Chris would be taking you if

3   he didn't think you looked good?

4   KIM: Well ... yes. He just wants to go, and he has to go with

5   someone.

6   RACHAEL: Be honest, Kim. You're a cheerleader. You're popular.

7   You're pretty. I'm worried about you because you can't see

8   yourself as you really are. I care about you and Chris cares

9   about you and we want the best for you.

10 KIM: *(Teary eyed again)* I don't know why I'm crying. I think I

11   need my Zoloft adjusted! That is so cool what you said. You're

12   the best, Rach. The absolute best. Maybe I do have a bit of a

13   problem. My shrink says it has to do with self-esteem. Low

14   self-esteem.

15 RACHAEL: See, I don't get that at all. You have it all — everything.

16   Why would you, of all people, have low self-esteem?

17 KIM: I dunno'. Maybe because my dad has always called me his

18   little "babosa." *(She smiles.)* I always thought it was cute when

19   I was little, but then in fourth grade Bobby VanDale, the little

20   genius, told me what it meant, and then I was kinda' ... I

21   dunno', hurt — ya' know?

22 RACHAEL: I remember. "Babosa." Spanish for "drooling idiot."

23   That is just so mean!

24 KIM: But I can't blame my parents for everything. Everything is

25   not their fault. I'm responsible for my own problems. It's just

26   that when I look in the mirror and see globs and globs of faaa

27   ... you know. It's just hangin' there on me. *(Pause)* It's gross.

28   I hate it.

29 RACHAEL: I know, Kim. I understand that feeling. Maybe you do

30   need your meds adjusted. But it's too late to get another dress.

31   Can you just take my word for it that you look great? We have

32   known each other since we were in diapers, and I know

33   everything there is to know about you. We're like sisters, and

34   I would tell you if that dress looked bad. Here. Look at me.

35   Look at me, Kimmers. *(KIM looks at RACHAEL. RACHAEL*

1   *dabs at KIM'S eyes with a paper napkin.)* **You're gonna' knock**
2   **'em dead tonight. You're going to be the belle of the ball, the**
3   **star of the night!**
4   **KIM: The femme fatale?**
5   **RACHAEL: Um … sure. That too.**
6   **KIM: Better than Snow White?** *(Pause)*
7   **RACHAEL: Kimberley Ann — You are gonna' *be* Gwyneth Paltrow.**
8   **KIM: What? Me? *Be* Gwyneth Paltrow?**
9   **RACHAEL: Yes.**
10 **KIM: Yes … what?** *(Pause)* **Can you say that again, Rach?**
11   *(Hesitantly)* **The Gwyneth Paltrow … you know?**
12 **RACHAEL: Kim — you are *Gwyneth Paltrow thin!* *(Pause)***
13 **KIM: Oh my God. *Gwyneth Paltrow thin.* Me? Me! Me and**
14   **Gwyneth! You wouldn't lie to me. I know that.** *(Pause)* **I'm**
15   **wearin' that pink dress, Rach! I can do this! I can!** *(Pause)* **But**
16   **you have to promise me something.**
17 **RACHAEL: Sure. Anything.** *(Pause)* **Except to see your shrink.**
18 **KIM:** *(Smiling)* **Will you come over tonight so we can get ready**
19   **together, and then you can tell me again about Gwyneth**
20   **Paltrow and me, OK? Otherwise, I'll have to look in the**
21   **mirror. And then, see, I can do the same thing for you, OK?**
22   **It'll be fun!**
23 **RACHAEL: Sorry, Kim — *that*, I cannot do.**
24 **KIM: But you have to. I trust your judgment! You see things the**
25   **way they really are! I need you! I'm a sick woman! My shrink**
26   **said so!**
27 **RACHAEL: I can't. Kim, I … I mean … It's not that … See, I …**
28   **I …**
29 **KIM: Rach, what is it? You and Gregg didn't break up did you?**
30   **You didn't have another stupid fight? Did he make you watch**
31   **pro-wrestling again!**
32 **RACHAEL: No, no. It's nothing like that.**
33 **KIM: Then what?**
34 **RACHAEL: Kim, I'm not going to the dance.**
35 **KIM: Gregg didn't ask you?** *(She grabs her cell phone and starts*

1   *dialing.)* **I'm going to call that loser right now!**
2   **RACHAEL: No. Don't. He asked me.**
3   **KIM: What?**
4   **RACHAEL: He asked. I said "no."** Actually, I said "yes," then
5   **"no" — then "yes," then "no," then "maybe" and finally**
6   **today it became a definite "no," and we've decided to watch**
7   **movies at my place — no studly macho stuff though. Probably**
8   **a romance. Maybe a Meg Ryan ...**
9   **KIM: Why?**
10 **RACHAEL: I like romances. He wanted to rent *Fight Club*, but**
11   **I ...**
12 **KIM: Rachael! Why are you staying home instead of going to the**
13   **dance? We have been planning this night so meticulously that ...**
14   **Are you sick? Is something wrong? I deserve to know!**
15 **RACHAEL: Oh Kim — *you* have been planning this "so**
16   **meticulously."**
17 **KIM: Rach? What's wrong? Best friends? Come on. Out with it.**
18 **RACHAEL:** *(Tears welling in her eyes.)* **Because I knew I could**
19   **never find a dress to cover this body! At least one that would**
20   **look decent. So I never even bothered looking at dresses for**
21   **me. There! Are you happy? I'm not going because *I'm* F-A-T.**
22   **In the last few months, I have gained well over a pound.**
23   **Maybe even two! I can't go looking like this. And I needed to**
24   **lose at least twenty to look even halfway good.** *(Pause)*
25 **KIM: Uh. Huh. Yeah. OK. And *you* would tell *me* if *my* dress looked**
26   **bad on me. I should "just take your word for it" that I "look**
27   **great." "Stunning." "Fabulous."**
28 **RACHAEL: Oh Kim, don't start in on me. Please understand. I**
29   **can't do it. The lights, the other girls — all in their slinky little**
30   **strapless gowns looking so perfect with their tiny ballerina**
31   **arms and teeny waists. We've talked about this! You see it too!**
32   *(KIM pulls a bit of the cloth from the dress out of the bag and*
33   *looks at it as if seeing it for the first time. She strokes it. She*
34   *carefully tucks it back in the bag.)*
35 **KIM: It's pink. Pink-pink. Nude pink.**

1   **RACHAEL:** *(Sobbing)* **I know! It's pink! It is pink! Oh Kimmers, I**
2   **am so sorry!**
3   **KIM:** *(Taking a long, deep breath)* **OK, Rachael. It's OK.** *(She pats*
4   *RACHAEL's hand.)* **I understand. I really, really do.** *(Pause)*
5   **So ... what movie are we going to watch tonight — after we**
6   **return this dress?** *(RACHAEL takes KIM'S hand, gives it a sad*
7   *squeeze, and produces a weak smile. RACHAEL returns the*
8   *favor.)*
9
10   ***The End***
11
12
13
14
15
16
17
18
19
20
21
22
23
24
25
26
27
28
29
30
31
32
33
34
35

Elizabeth the Fourth
by Madeleine Martin

Madeleine Martin has two adult children — a journalist in Boston and a hospital administrator in Florida — and a granddaughter. She has owned championship dogs and cats. Currently she is working on a children's book about a dog with silky white hair and placing the finishing touches on a full-length play about life after being a police officer.

Elizabeth the Fourth was originally presented at the New Play Development Workshop of The Playwrights Program of the Association for Theatre in Higher Education in Atlanta in 1992 with Judith Royer as director, Michael J. Kane as dramaturge, and Dede Corvinus and Angela Latham-Jones in the roles of Betty and Liz, respectively. It was subsequently produced, in 1993, by Love Creek Productions under the artistic directorship of Le Wilhelm for Samuel French's 18th Annual Off-off Broadway Original Short Play Festival at New York City's Nat Horne Theatre. The production was directed by Sharon Fallon, artistic director for Love Creek Productions, with Joni Shumacher and Kristin Walsh in the roles of Betty and Liz, respectively.

Address all inquiries concerning performances, readings, or reprinting of this work *or any portion thereof* to Madeleine Martin, PO Box 53521, Lubbock, TX 79453. For details, see "Part II: Securing Rights for Your Production," pages 183 to 192.

1 The action takes place in the present in a middle to upper-middle-
2 class living room.
3 **CHARACTERS:** BETTY—in her late 30s.
4 LIZ—19 years old, BETTY's daughter.
5 **SETTING:** BETTY's living room. The front door is on the right. A
6 telephone rests Down Left on a small table. An entry to the other
7 rooms of the house is located on the left.
8
9 *(BETTY sits in her living room looking frantically through an old*
10 *photograph album. As she locates the pictures for which she has*
11 *been searching, LIZ enters from inside the house. LIZ hurries to*
12 *leave through the front door, and as she does so she notices the*
13 *photo album.)*
14 **LIZ:** Way to ruin your eyes on those old things! See ya' tomorrow.
15 **BETTY:** Lizzie? Do you have some time? Can we talk?
16 **LIZ:** No, Mom. Sorry. Gotta' go. Later.
17 **BETTY:** Please, Lizzie.
18 **LIZ:** I know I prob'ly did somethin' just horrible this time. What'd
19 I do — leave my socks on the floor in the bathroom? Squeeze
20 the toothpaste in the middle? *(LIZ smiles. BETTY does not.)*
21 **BETTY:** Can we have a serious talk without you trying to be cute?
22 This is important to me.
23 **LIZ:** And what isn't important to you? Gramma Ellie's waitin' and
24 I'm gonna' miss the bus! I gotta' go! *(LIZ kisses BETTY.)*
25 **BETTY:** Are you really going to Gramma Ellie's house?
26 **LIZ:** What! What do you mean "Are you really going to Gramma
27 Ellie's house!" Why don't you call her and ask her … if you
28 don't trust me!
29 **BETTY:** Don't speak to me that way, please. I'm worried about
30 you. Can I do that?
31 **LIZ:** Yes you sure can … You can do that better than anybody I
32 know. Only, it isn't necessary. *(Softening)* Look … Mom … I
33 know things have been rough for you lately, but you don't
34 have to go and make it worse for yourself by creatin' things to
35 worry about. You'll drive yourself nuts! I'm fine. My classes

1   are fine. My job's fine. Life's just peachy. I love life ...

2 BETTY: I was looking at some of your old baby pictures today. Do

3   you want to see them?

4 LIZ: No. Well, not right now, that is. Maybe later. Maybe

5   tomorrow night. Or Friday. Yeah, let's do it Friday when

6   Gram comes for dinner. That would at least give us somethin'

7   to do. Friday? OK?

8 BETTY: Why don't you want to look at them now?

9 LIZ: Because I gotta' go now! Mom, geez, ya' really need to get a

10   hold of yourself, ya know? I swear, the stress is gettin' to ya'.

11 BETTY: *(Paging through the album)* Look at this one. This is one of

12   my favorites. It was your first birthday ...

13 LIZ: *(Spoken under BETTY's words.)* Oh, no ...

14 BETTY: *(Continuing)* And Gramma Ellie had made a cake for you.

15   It was so cute. The big cake for everyone else was the skirt of

16   a Barbie Doll with the Barbie in the middle.

17 LIZ: *(Spoken in unison with BETTY's last words.)* "With the Barbie

18   in the middle." They're great, Mom. Really. Great. Friday.

19   OK? I'm outta' here.

20 BETTY: *(Quickly)* Lizzie, I know.

21 LIZ: *(Stopping)* You know—what?

22 BETTY: *(Producing a small piece of paper)* I found this telephone

23   number ...

24 LIZ: *(Grabbing the paper)* ... While you were snooping in my room

25   ... again.

26 BETTY: I ... called that number. I got ...

27 LIZ: Oh Jesus ...

28 BETTY: ... This lady ... rather pleasant sounding lady ... she said

29   "Valley Women's Clinic." That's an ... a ... an ... it's a ...

30 LIZ: It's a women's clinic, Mother.

31 BETTY: ... I only did it because I was worried ...

32 LIZ: Wrong. You only did it because you're a humongous snoop!

33   You always have been. Ya' always have to have your big nose

34   in other people's business. Well, this is none of your business.

35 BETTY: *You* are my business. *You* are my daughter.

1 LIZ: *Very* perceptive, *Mom*. I am your daughter ... but that doesn't
2   give you the right to snoop in my stuff. I thought we'd agreed
3   that you wouldn't do that anymore.
4 BETTY: Please. Don't. I'm sorry.
5 LIZ: Is that all? Can I go now?
6 BETTY: Please ... don't do it ...
7 LIZ: *Please don't do* what! Go to a doctor?
8 BETTY: *Stop it! Just stop it!* You are pregnant, aren't you?
9   *(Silence)*
10 LIZ: You disgust me.
11 BETTY: Lizzie, I've always wanted the very best for you, I've
12   always ...
13 LIZ: Oh please! Don't start ... *and it's Liz! Call me Liz!* I hate
14   Lizzie! Ya' know, you need to get a life ... to get out more ...
15 BETTY: We are talking about you here, Liz ...
16 LIZ: No, Mom. You are talking about me here. *(At the door)* I am
17   leaving.
18 BETTY: *Liz! Please don't kill your baby!*
19 LIZ: *(Stopping)* What ... *baby*? *(She spits out the word "baby.")*
20 BETTY: *Your* baby. Please don't have an ... a ...
21 LIZ: An abortion. It's called an "abortion," Mother. It's a simple
22   procedure and it has a name. An *"a-bor-tion."*
23 BETTY: *(Covering her ears)* Please ... don't ... please ... Liz ... it's
24   your baby.
25 LIZ: Oh, good. Here we go with the tears. If you couldn't handle it,
26   you shouldn't have snooped. *(Silence)* This isn't exactly easy
27   for me, ya' know. *(Silence)* OK, so ya' said ya' wanted to talk
28   and here I am doin' all the talkin' and you're not sayin'
29   anything. So I'll just leave and we'll both feel better.
30 BETTY: I'm sorry. You're right. I just need ...
31 LIZ: *You* need. *You* need. *You* need. Mom, what about what I need?
32   Or more to the point, what I don't need. I don't need a baby
33   right now.
34 BETTY: You should've thought of that before.
35 LIZ: Great ...

1   BETTY: I'm sorry. That wasn't fair. What's done, is done. Now we
2   have to figure out how we're going to deal with this.
3   LIZ: We? "We" are not gonna' deal with this. I'm gonna' deal with
4   this. I am dealing with this. I'm takin' responsibility for it …
5   BETTY: Responsibility? Killing your child is responsible?
6   LIZ: I don't need your guilt trip, Mom, so just lay off.
7   BETTY: You need my support more than you think. You live in my
8   house. As long as you live in my house, you will follow my rules.
9   LIZ: Your house. Your car. Your rules. God, I hate that. Is anything
10   mine around here?
11   BETTY: I am your mother and I …
12   LIZ: …Ya' know, Mom, it is my body and I will do with my body
13   what I damned well please … and right now I will have an
14   abortion because I am not going to be like you and spend the
15   next twenty years of my life lookin' after some brat that I
16   never wanted in the first place.
17   BETTY: You know that's not true! I always wanted you.
18   LIZ: Right ya' did! You weren't even married when I "happened
19   along."
20   BETTY: Granted, but your father and I …
21   LIZ: *(Finishing BETTY's sentence for her)* " … Did the right thing!"
22   Ya' got married and gave me a proper name and a proper
23   family. Ya' even did a proper wedding — all done up in white so
24   "no one would know." Tell me somethin', Mom, how does it feel
25   to always be doin' the right thing—for everyone else, that is?
26   BETTY: That's not fair.
27   LIZ: *(Continuing)* …Well, I don't wanta' do "the right thing,"
28   Mom. Guess I'm just not as good as you are.
29   BETTY: Have you even thought about what your daughter wants?
30   LIZ: Daughter? Daughter! Oh, I see you've already got its sex
31   picked out! Well, tell me Mom, would this "daughter" get to
32   be another Elizabeth? Is this one gonna' be Elizabeth the
33   fourth?
34   BETTY: What will people say? What will they think? Of you? Of me?
35   LIZ: Oh gracious yes, "What will people say?" Can't have them

1   thinking that Betty's kid is human now, can we?

2   BETTY: What will Gramma Ellie say when she finds out you're

3   going to have a baby?

4   LIZ: *I'm not going to have a baby!* I'm going to have an abortion.

5   So you can stop worrying about what people are going to say

6   or think because nobody's gonna know, unless of course, you

7   tell 'em.

8   BETTY: I will not allow you to have an abortion, Liz. I would *never*

9   give up any child of mine—not under *any* circumstances ...

10   LIZ: *(Spoken under BETTY's words.) Any* circumstances?

11   BETTY: *(Without pausing)* ... And I will not allow you to destroy

12   my grandchild.

13   LIZ: *You* don't have to "allow" anything. I am an adult. I don't

14   need your permission.

15   BETTY: You may not need my permission, but who's going to pay

16   for this ... this ...

17   LIZ: ... Abortion.

18   BETTY: ... Abortion. *(Pause)* Have you thought about that?

19   Where are you going to get the money, Miss "I-am-an-adult-

20   now!" I know you haven't saved a dime. You buy clothes and

21   make-up and more clothes ...

22   LIZ: Leave it alone, Mom ...

23   BETTY: ... And you go to the movies and buy Brian cards all the

24   time ...

25   LIZ: ... That's enough ...

26   BETTY: ... And then you expect me to give you money when you

27   run out. Well, no more, Liz! *No more money ... I will not pay*

28   *for murder ...*

29   LIZ: *I don't want your stupid money! I don't need your stupid*

30   *money! Gramma Ellie is giving me the money!*

31   BETTY: *(Silence)* What?

32   LIZ: *(Pause)* Gramma Ellie ... is giving me the money.

33   BETTY: Liar.

34   LIZ: No, Mom. I'm sorry I told ya' ... I promised Gramma Ellie

35   that I wouldn't ... but she offered to help out ... and I

1   couldn't ask you ...

2   BETTY: *(Stunned)* **My own mother?**

3   LIZ: ... And she said she knew how it felt to feel trapped, really

4   trapped, with nowhere to go ...

5   BETTY: What would she know about feeling trapped! You're

6   lying! You're always ...

7   LIZ: *No, I'm not!* She said that she might have done the same thing

8   at my age if she'd had the option ...

9   BETTY: Liar.

10   LIZ: Call her! Ask her! She said that you were a "surprise baby."

11   She and Gramps were just startin' their business and they

12   certainly didn't need ...

13   BETTY: Mother said she'd ... she would have ... could have ... .

14   *No!* I won't believe it. That would have been me! She would

15   have killed me?

16   LIZ: I'm not sayin' it to hurt you, Mom. I'm just tellin' ya' that

17   Gramma Ellie supports me. That she ...

18   BETTY: Well, it doesn't matter! It doesn't matter, that's all. It

19   doesn't. I couldn't kill my child ... and I know Mother

20   didn't mean it. I wouldn't give you up no matter how

21   "inconvenient" ...

22   LIZ: No. Instead you became a martyr. You gave up your life so

23   that I could have mine. That's pretty Christ-like isn't it, Mom!

24   Bet you'll go to heaven for that one. I've heard you tellin'

25   everyone, "I gave up everything for my daughter ... to do for

26   her ... to take care of her ... " But ya' know what Mom? You

27   make me pay for that choice of yours every day by lettin' me

28   know about everything you gave up for me. You're bitter and

29   you take it out on me. And it's not even my fault. I didn't ask

30   to be born ... and this ... this ... thing in me ...

31   BETTY: I know it's a sacrifice to ask you to give up so much for a

32   child, but it's your child ...

33   LIZ: Either way it's a sacrifice Mom. I don't see any way that it

34   isn't. Either I sacrifice my life for this—thing's—or I sacrifice

35   this thing's life for mine. You think I don't hurt when I think

1   about that? You think I haven't thought about that? Either
2   way, either sacrifice, it's something I have to live with for the
3   rest of my life. Not you. Me. Please ... don't make it any
4   harder. Can't ya' be more like Gramma Ellie?
5   BETTY: I don't want to hear about Gramma Ellie right now, and
6   I don't want to make life difficult for you, God knows, I have
7   done everything I know how to make your life ... *(Realizes*
8   *what she is saying)* ... well, you know. But, Liz, I have to say
9   this ... God forgive me, but I have to say this. Liz ... *(Steeling*
10   *herself)* Lizzie ... Liz ... If you ... if you have an ... Lizzie, I
11   love you. But ... if you go through with this abortion ... if you
12   go out that door and kill your child ... my grandchild ...
13   *(Suddenly rushing)* ... don't come back. *(Silence)*
14   LIZ: Is that your final word Mom?
15   BETTY: You heard me. *(Slowly)* Don't ... come ... back.
16   LIZ: *(Nods.)* I see. I get it. You would never give up a child of yours,
17   huh? Not under *any* circumstances? Well, what do you call this
18   "Don't-Come-Back" routine? I call it givin' up your child!
19   BETTY: There's a difference. I have no choice. You leave me no
20   choice.
21   LIZ: Yeah, right. You're trapped, Gram's trapped, and I'm
22   trapped ... either way. *(LIZ turns and exits out the door. BETTY*
23   *stands still. She looks toward the door and suddenly moves*
24   *quickly to the door and stops, her hand on the knob. She pauses,*
25   *turns, and looks at the telephone. Suddenly she moves*
26   *deliberately to the telephone, picks it up, and dials.)*
27   BETTY: Mother? Hi. Fine ... yes. Just fine ... um ... Do you have
28   some time? Can we talk?
29
30   *The End*
31
32
33
34
35

Bind Them Continually
by Adrienne Lamb

Adrienne Lamb is an independent artist living and working in Philadelphia. Since arriving in Philadelphia in 1998, she has collaborated as dramaturge and/or director on numerous creative projects in the area, many of which further the development of new work. She received an M.F.A. in Dramaturgy from SUNY Stony Brook.

Bind Them Continually was developed in the New Play Development Workshop during the 1997 ATHE Conference in Chicago. It was subsequently performed at SUNY Stony Brook and directed by the playwright at the Philadelphia Fringe Festival.

Address all inquiries concerning performances, readings, or reprinting of this work *or any portion thereof* to Adrienne Lamb, 217 Christian, Philadelphia, PA 19142. For details, see "Part II: Securing Rights for Your Production," pages 183 to 192.

1   The action takes place at various times in the relationship of a
2   mother and daughter.
3   *CHARACTER:* BLUE — a woman in her 50s. She wears a full-length,
4   navy blue slip, stockings, and jewelry.
5   IVORY — a young woman in her 20s or 30s. She wears an ivory
6   peignoir.
7   **SETTING:** A bare stage except for two ladder-backed chairs and
8   adjacent three-legged tables. One table — BLUE's — holds a
9   Scotch-on-the-rocks and a discarded corsage. The other table —
10   IVORY's — holds a flute of champagne and a garter.
11
12   *(BLUE is seated with a pin spot light focused on her face. IVORY*
13   *dances.)*
14   **BLUE: Certainly, she is good. She was beautiful. She will be happy.**
15   **I taught her. I've given her all. Taught her all: Life is painful,**
16   **humor is essential, beauty is ephemeral and often love follows.**
17   **She will be happy.** *(Beat)* **Here, into this room, I creep. Into the**
18   **stillness, silence unbearable. She is more. More me.**
19   **IVORY: More so.**
20   **BLUE: And you see, it hurts to touch her. But, without a touch, I**
21   **cannot know. I stare down upon her, watching, searching, to**
22   **see her unbreasted chest or her belly rise to meet her breath.**
23   **But she is so small and I cannot tell. Cannot see. So, I pinch**
24   **her. And she cries. Not a pierce, but a brand, that marks me,**
25   **makes her mine, and me her.**
26   **IVORY: Hers.**
27   **BLUE: Only then can I leave, knowing that she is alive.** *(Beat)*
28   **Here, near, as we watch together afternoon**
29   **IVORY: afterschool**
30   **BLUE: variations and distortions. She sits astride my back,**
31   **combing my hair, a meticulous ritual of lift and separate that**
32   **gently coaxes the ache from my head's center to the split ends**
33   **of my very worst hair. She struggles**
34   **IVORY: vainly**
35   **BLUE: to make Mommy pretty. She never thinks to ask why, on**

1   the television, that one man is kissing with, kissing on, all
2   those other straight struck women. How the same mouth can
3   always speak the same words, and yet always to a different
4   audience. When do we believe him? Why have we convinced
5   ourselves that there is a time when he is truthful?
6   I want not yet to tell her of the misdeeds and steps taken by
7   my husband. That will come later, in a darkened parking lot
8   of a restaurant
9   IVORY: as she and I huddle against the cold
10 BLUE: and my husband, her father, chooses one-more-for-the-road
11   over us. To her, here, he is still the perfect "Daddy's home,
12 IVORY: Daddy's home"
13 BLUE: father. *(Beat)* Here, she sits quietly. Her hair twisted into
14   braids and pulled gently from her face. In one hand, she holds
15   tightly a pencil, newly sharpened and ready for battle. I find
16   her amidst a field of encyclopedias, each one in order and
17   opened to its first page. A small unsure hand struggles with
18   each letter, learning to translate the dance from angles to
19   curves. As I peek around corners, she yells
20 IVORY: Don't look at me!
21 BLUE: and says to wait until she is done. A present, she says: she is
22   learning to write
23 IVORY: "I love you"
24 BLUE: a new way. *(Beat)* Here, she resists, hiding.
25   Her hand no longer fits so neatly into mine. I cannot
26   squeeze and lock to keep her near, a lock that opens
27 IVORY: with a twitch
28 BLUE: when the pressure becomes an ache. She knows better than
29   to cry out.
30   She has her father's hands
31 IVORY: short and thick knuckled
32 BLUE: made larger by the thin wrists inherited from me. She
33   never raises them to me; it is her words that bruise and scar
34   during our battles. My weapons are wooden spoons and
35   knowledge learned from my father when I foolishly thought I

1   could outrun him. She says it's abuse; I say it's relative. *(Beat)*

2   Here, near her teens. Now, bigger and stronger than me, she

3   allies herself with her father. She cannot see through her

4   anger and her acne that we

5   IVORY: she and I

6   BLUE: are more alike than they will ever be. She cannot see in my

7   face anything that resembles hers and, as she tosses aside dolls

8   for books, she hates me. Even after

9   IVORY: especially after

10   BLUE: the night I find her on her bedroom floor — the rug pushed

11   against the wall, the bed stripped of its linens — with a

12   washcloth and a cup of bleach. She sits, crying, sure that she

13   is punished, sure that she will be punished. Even as I explain,

14   she turns my tale into more fuel and hates me

15   IVORY: for fear of the body to come.

16   BLUE: As preteen becomes teen, she turns inward and away from

17   curves. She wants the geometric hard edges, ones impossible

18   to cuddle and soothe.

19   IVORY: Clean and crooked lines unmarked by tattle-tale stains

20   BLUE: Later, a high school biology class will confirm that it was

21   her father who made her a daughter. This knowledge brings

22   change, and she returns to me. Bigger.

23   IVORY: Stronger.

24   BLUE: But a stranger. *(Beat)* Here, she is gone. To Tahiti.

25   IVORY: To Greece.

26   BLUE: To Disney World.

27   IVORY: To Love and To Honor.

28   BLUE: Her loves were to be different and her options more. Not to

29   marry to escape, not necessary — she ran to college instead.

30   *Á l'université*, where she learned to climb higher and to lose

31   all perspective. Lost amid books and indulgence, her head

32   filled and her heart emptied. This clarity, she thinks, will reap

33   answers. And then she finds

34   BOTH: him.

35   BLUE: With a sweep and a sudden name change, she no longer is.

1   *(Beat)* **She will return. I wait. She will remember. As she ages,**
2   **I remind her. With her own daughter, she will remember how**
3   **well we walked together.** *(Beat)*
4   **IVORY: Certainly, she is good.**
5   **BLUE: Her father handed her to him.**
6   **IVORY: She was beautiful.**
7   **BLUE: My own place marked and kept.**
8   **IVORY: She will be happy.**
9   **BLUE: I never gave her away.**
10
11   *The End*
12
13
14
15
16
17
18
19
20
21
22
23
24
25
26
27
28
29
30
31
32
33
34
35

Fixin' It

by Madeleine Martin

Madeleine Martin received her playwriting education as a private student of Dr. Norman A. Bert. Her works have been published both nationally and internationally. Her plays have won awards and been produced in educational settings and off-off Broadway since 1993.

The playwright thanks Texas Tech University's playwriting class, spring 2002, for work-shopping *Fixin' It*. The script has had no other publications or performances prior to publication in this anthology.

Address all inquiries concerning performances, readings, or reprinting of this work *or any portion thereof* to Madeleine Martin, PO Box 53521, Lubbock, TX 79453. For details, see "Part II: Securing Rights for Your Production," pages 183 to 192.

1   The action takes place in the present in a west Texas high school.

2   **CHARACTERS:** DEAN WHITE — a high school dean of students.

3   JOE BILL — a high school senior and star football player.

4   **SETTING:** The dean's office of Levelridge High School, home of the

5   Fighting Bears, Class AA State Football Champions, five years

6   running.

7

8   **DEAN WHITE:** *(Sliding papers across desk towards JOE BILL)*

9   **Suppose let's just get on with this.**

10   **JOE BILL: Done purty good, huh?** *(He smiles his huge smile.)*

11   **DEAN WHITE: That's what it says there, Joe Bill. All "A's." What**

12   **you got to say 'bout that?**

13   **JOE BILL:** *(Smiling)* **Purty miraculous. I feel right blessed, I do.**

14   **DEAN WHITE: Cut the crap, Joe Bill. You know the drill.**

15   **JOE BILL: I know what you're thinkin', sir. You're used ta' callin'**

16   **me in here ta' talk 'bout the "F's" I'm getting before the final**

17   **state championship game of the season. This must be some**

18   **surprise ta' ya' …**

19   **DEAN WHITE: And to Ms. Kreiger too. She knows you aren't**

20   **up to this kind of work and so do I, so maybe you should just**

21   **tell me what happened so we can get this mess straightened**

22   **up. See, failin', I can understand; cheatin' — I got a problem**

23   **with that.**

24   **JOE BILL: Yes, sir. No, sir! I didn't cheat. I prayed.** *(Pause)*

25   **DEAN WHITE: You prayed.**

26   **JOE BILL: Yes, sir.** *(He smiles broadly.)* **I prayed.** *(Pause)*

27   **DEAN WHITE: You got yerself messed up with drugs, Joe Bill?**

28   **JOE BILL:** *(Smiling his winning smile)* **No, sir!**

29   **DEAN WHITE: And so what you're tellin' me is that God gave you**

30   **"A's" on these final English exams?**

31   **JOE BILL:** *(Laughing)* **Not exactly, sir. I mean, I took the exams, so**

32   **I earned the "A's," a course. But I'm thinking that God helped**

33   **me out a lot 'cuz I sure did need it!**

34   **DEAN WHITE: So you didn't have to study or nuthin', huh? You**

35   **just prayed and God let you "earn" these "A's."**

1   JOE BILL: It's weren't quite like that.

2   DEAN WHITE: I didn't think so. Why don't you tell me what it
3   was "quite like" then. Look, we can get this straightened out
4   easy, you know. Just like in the past. You tell me how you did
5   it, and we'll git it all fixed up, OK? All I want is the honest
6   truth.

7   JOE BILL: Well, see ... I been havin' a rough time after the
8   accident and all — you know that. *(DEAN WHITE nods.)* And
9   this one day I was havin' a really bad day, thinkin' about it
10   and all — it was just goin' round and round in my head real
11   bad. And I was sittin' down at the Dairy Queen drinkin' an
12   O.J. with Sprite because I got me a real bad hangover —
13   tequila, you know — and this guy's walkin' by me, and he
14   says to me just like this, he says, "Friend, if you don't look like
15   about the worst thang ever that the cat drug in!" I was 'bout
16   ready to hit 'im, but I didn't have the energy to even stand up
17   so he sat down ...

18   DEAN WHITE: *(Slams a book on his desk.)* I am not in the mood
19   for one of your long-winded and drawn-out stories, Joe Bill!
20   You have a way of makin' the most simple explanation take
21   longer than a cat beatin' up a dog, I will tell you! Make it
22   short, Joe Bill.

23   JOE BILL: Yes, sir. It turns out that this feller — his name's Charlie
24   — well, Charlie sits down, and we start talkin', ya' see ...

25   DEAN WHITE: Oh my God ...

26   JOE BILL: Exactly! We ended up talkin' 'bout God! At least —
27   some — but not a lot, and not at first. See, I wasn't fixin' to or
28   nuthin', but I wound up tellin' him 'bout nearly killin' Russell
29   and ... and how it was all my fault and all ...

30   DEAN WHITE: Hold on there! It was not your fault, boy! Now Joe
31   Bill, we all know what happened out there. Boys will be boys.
32   You boys was havin' some fun on those tractors and ya'all got
33   into some trouble you couldn't handle ... but heck! You saved
34   his life, Joe Bill. If it wasn't for you, he'd be dead and he
35   knows it! The whole town knows you're a hero for savin' him

1   like you did. He's lucky to have a friend like you and he

2   knows it. *(Pause)*

3   JOE BILL: *(Suddenly dead serious)* That's a lie and you know it.

4   DEAN WHITE: Excuse me? What did you say?

5   JOE BILL: That ain't true. What's true is if it wasn't for me,

6   Russell would not be sittin' out there in a wheelchair at every

7   football practice and game throwin' towels and water instead

8   of a football. That is my fault. Russ's "accident" was my fault

9   and the other ... the whole ... *(Pause)* Russ knows this, and I

10   know it, and the whole town knows it, but we all try ta' ignore

11   it by sayin' "boys will be boys," but because of me — Russ will

12   never walk again and ... and ... How would you like ta' live

13   with a lie like that every day, Dean White?

14   DEAN WHITE: I think it would be mighty hard, Joe Bill. But

15   you're a fine young man and everyone knows that. Your

16   daddy has forgiven you and everyone knows you meant no

17   harm. You didn't expect ...

18   JOE BILL: We expected to have fun. We took them girls out there

19   to watch the submarine races and maybe do some cow tippin.'

20   DEAN WHITE: I get the picture — you went out there to do some

21   neckin' — there's no crime in that.

22   JOE BILL: But then we saw them new tractors and decided to race

23   'em. We was all purty well lit.

24   DEAN WHITE: You gotta' move on, son.

25   JOE BILL: *(Suddenly enthusiastic)* And that's what I'm telling ya'

26   I'm doin'. Charlie talked to me 'bout movin' on but I didn't

27   know how to. See, I was stuck. I didn't care 'bout school or

28   girls. 'Specially girls. *(Pause)* I didn't care 'bout football.

29   Nuthin'. I was goin' through the motions.

30   DEAN WHITE: I'm glad you've finally seen this. We have all been

31   tryin' to tell you this since the accident, Joe Bill. You have a

32   future in football — a professional future — but only if you

33   get your head back together. It's time you started caring about

34   yer future.

35   JOE BILL: No, I think it's time I decided ta' care about what I'm

1 doin' that's right and what I'm doin' that's wrong. Charlie
2 taught me that.
3 DEAN WHITE: Well, that's OK too, but you gotta' think about the
4 professional scouts that're gonna' be out there watchin' you
5 play — if you play — and that means we need to get this
6 grade thing sorted out. Now look, it's not that big a deal. Mrs.
7 Kreiger says you're not capable of making these grades.
8 JOE BILL: But I did.
9 DEAN WHITE: OK. You say you did; she says you could not have.
10 So here's the deal: All you have to do is admit that you
11 cheated, sign the slip, and we'll let you retake the exams. If
12 you get the same score, then that proves she was wrong and
13 everyone's happy. And I can guarantee that you'll get a
14 passing score because you'll be taking it the same way you
15 retook all the other exams ... in the past.
16 JOE BILL: That, was cheatin'.
17 DEAN WHITE: *(Smiling)* I like to call it givin' you a nudge, a little
18 helpin' hand, when you need it. Your daddy is a big supporter
19 of the organization, and we like to see our boys go on to
20 excellent programs like Texas Tech, A&M, U.T. Or would you
21 rather end up at a Ju-Co somewhere around Abilene? That's
22 about as far middle-of-nowhere as you can get.
23 JOE BILL: I'm not thinkin' 'bout that right now. I'm thinkin'
24 'bout today and doin' what's right. I've been doin' my
25 studyin' and tryin' to live my life the way Jesus would want
26 me to.
27 DEAN WHITE: What is with this "Jesus" talk? You become a
28 Born-Again?
29 JOE BILL: No. I ain't even baptized as far as I know. Nobody put
30 any water on me or anything like that.
31 DEAN WHITE: Then what're you goin' on about?
32 JOE BILL: Charlotte in study hall said that you'd be all ears 'bout
33 this 'cuz you was a minister yerself one time.
34 DEAN WHITE: I went to seminary. That's very different from
35 being a minister.

1   **JOE BILL: Still you know about God and Jesus and puttin' yerself**
2   **in their hands because you just can't handle things for yerself**
3   **for the time bein'. That's what I'm doin'. And I pray. When I**
4   **get really down, I pray and ask God if he's listenin' and tell**
5   **Him that I need some help, and that's what I did before takin'**
6   **those exams.**
7   **DEAN WHITE: I understand about praying, and you better do**
8   **some of it right now because my patience is growing thin with**
9   **this, Joe Bill! I think you are puttin' me on.**
10   **JOE BILL: *(Smiles broadly.)* Yes, sir! *(He drops to his knees.)* Oh**
11   **Lord. This is Joe Bill again. I got me another problem. It's**
12   **Dean White again. *(Turning to DEAN WHITE)* I prayed 'bout**
13   **you before, sir, so he's real familiar with you already. *(Back to***
14   ***God)* See God, he's on my case 'bout cheatin' on those tests**
15   **you helped me with, and I think that your help is not cheatin'**
16   **so if you could just let him know that I did not cheat ...**
17   **DEAN WHITE: Joe Bill! Get up off that floor and sit down!**
18   **JOE BILL: *(Quietly)* Sir, I am talkin' ta' God! *(To God)* ... let him**
19   **know that I did not cheat on them English tests, I'd be**
20   **grateful. Thank you and have a good day. Amen. *(JOE BILL***
21   ***gets up, dusts off his knees, and sits in the chair.)***
22   **DEAN WHITE: That was quite a performance. So now, all I need is**
23   **a confession that you cheated, and we can get on with a re-take.**
24   **JOE BILL: No, sir.**
25   **DEAN WHITE: Excuse me? No?**
26   **JOE BILL: That's right. No.**
27   **DEAN WHITE: You can't just say, "No." It don't work like that,**
28   **son. If you do not sign the confession and retake, you're out of**
29   **the championship game, and you'll have to re-do fall semester**
30   **English, which means you won't graduate with your class,**
31   **which means you won't be eligible for the college drafts.**
32   **JOE BILL: Yes, sir. I understand.**
33   **DEAN WHITE: Then you better sign, son, and re-take those tests.**
34   **It's your best option.**
35   **JOE BILL: It's a lie, sir.**

1 DEAN WHITE: Look, it'll keep Ms. Krieger happy. We both know
2   she's a couple enchiladas short of a combo plate but let's just
3   play it by the rules and do it this way, boy. Sign the form and
4   everything's OK.
5 JOE BILL: That's what I did before. Just lie and everything's
6   OK — only it's not. Lyin' don't help nuthin'. It makes things
7   worse because I have to live with the lie.
8 DEAN WHITE: *(Laughing)* This is about term exams — not
9   exactly life and death, Joe Bill.
10 JOE BILL: No, but Rhonda Harper was about life and death,
11   Dean White, and funny how nobody wants to hear the truth
12   about that!
13 DEAN WHITE: We don't need to talk about that, Joe Bill.
14 JOE BILL: See? Nobody wants to hear the truth. Not you, not my
15   parents, not even the sheriff wanted to hear. "Dead is dead,"
16   is what they kept sayin', "Dead is dead. Doesn't matter how.
17   Ain't nobody comes back from dead." But Charlie, he says …
18 DEAN WHITE: *(Angry)* I do not want to hear another word about
19   this Charlie-feller! You got that! He sounds like some kinda'
20   nut! Just sign the confession for cheating, boy, and I'll set up
21   the re-takes.
22 JOE BILL: Well maybe you wanna' hear this then! That tractor
23   tipped over on her! She was never on 'em. Those girls were
24   never on the tractors with us! We lied! We all lied. We killed her.
25   But dead is dead and everyone wanted to hear the lie, except I
26   have to live with it. Me, and Russ, and Sallyanne — we all know
27   what happened. Nobody wants to accept the facts though.
28 DEAN WHITE: You can't remember clearly, Joe Bill. You were all
29   in shock when ya'all were helicoptered to the hospital over
30   there in Lubbock. But that's all past and you yerself said you
31   were movin' on. So do it. Let's just sign this confession, re-
32   take the tests, and get on with your life.
33 JOE BILL: You know, all my life I've been nuthin' but a jerk —
34   getting' in trouble, up to no good at all, but I could play ball
35   like a demon so everyone looked around all the no-good stuff

1	I did and said, "Joe Bill, now he's a good ole' boy." All ya'all
2	ever wanted was that trophy in the case. Ya'all don't care
3	nuthin' about Joe-Bill-the-person. And now you want me to
4	admit that I'm a cheater so that you can have your trophy
5	again this year. The way I see it is that I gotta' live with
6	myself — you don't. You're not signin' nuthin'. What I'm
7	tellin' ya' is the truth — God helped me with those tests and if
8	that's not good enough for you, then … then that's just tough.
9	I'll retake the semester. Hell, I'll retake the entire year, if I
10	gotta'. I won't graduate with my class. So what. But then, you
11	probably won't git your sixth-straight-year trophy either, and
12	that just seems to mean everything to you. How do you like
13	starin' truth in the eyes, Dean White? It ain't easy, is it?
14	DEAN WHITE: I can see you've been under a lot of pressure Joe
15	Bill. But you know as well as I do, as well as everybody does,
16	that you're slated to be the next Zack Thomas out of west
17	Texas. You got an eye for the ball, an eye for the quarterback.
18	Hell, you know what he's thinkin' even before he does. Are you
19	tellin' me you're willin' to throw that all away for some
20	misguided conception of the truth? We're talkin' millions of
21	bucks here, Joe Bill.
22	JOE BILL: Ya' know, Dean White, I would pay millions of bucks if
23	I never had to sleep with that dead girl's body in my head
24	again. I'd pay that much for one night's rest without
25	nightmares and cold sweats and screamin' myself awake.
26	DEAN WHITE: Maybe you need to talk to someone. I don't take a
27	lot of stock in them shrinks, but maybe you do need someone
28	professional. I dunno'. I think …
29	JOE BILL: I thought I was talkin' to someone professional right
30	now.
31	DEAN WHITE: You know what I mean.
32	JOE BILL: Yeah. I guess I do. Professionalism counts only when
33	you want it to. Morals count only when they mean winnin'.
34	It's got nuthin' ta' do with "how ya' play the game." I don't
35	think you know the first thing about ethics and respect for

1   other people. Or yerself. I think that's why ya' keep that bottle
2   in yer third drawer down.
3   DEAN WHITE: OK, Joe Bill. That's it. As far as I'm concerned,
4   we're finished here. I don't have to listen to this crap.
5   JOE BILL: No, you don't have to listen to the facts, but you gotta'
6   live with 'em, same as I do. See, here's the point. I ain't even
7   fer sure I want a football career anymore.
8   DEAN WHITE: You know that's not true.
9   JOE BILL: I know nuthin' of the sort. I'm thinkin' that football
10   ain't where my life's headed anymore. I used ta' think that
11   bein' a Cowboy'd be about the best thing since white-sliced
12   bread. They got themselves a life, they do — money, women,
13   parties. And jail and drug busts, ruined marriages and
14   screwed up careers. Maybe there's somethin' better out there
15   that needs me and that I need fer myself. Maybe I can't
16   handle bein' a football star any better'n some of them
17   professional boys can.
18   DEAN WHITE: What could be better than bein' famous and
19   makin' a livin' most people can only dream about? What
20   could be better than livin' each day doin' what you love?
21   What on God's green earth are you goin' ta' do if you don't
22   play ball, boy?
23   JOE BILL: Did I ever say I loved football? I don't 'member that.
24   I been thinkin' maybe workin' with screwed-up kids like
25   myself is what is I should do. Maybe bein' a social worker or
26   a counselor or somethin'. Like I said, I ain't fer sure 'bout
27   nothin' yet — just that I think maybe after high school it'd be
28   time fer me ta' hang up the helmet fer good.
29   DEAN WHITE: Have you talked to yer daddy about this, Joe Bill?
30   Have you thought about what he's gonna do 'bout this? You
31   think he's plannin' on payin' for a college education so you
32   can go work with a bunch of no-good, mixed-up kids and live
33   on poverty wages?
34   JOE BILL: My dad. *(JOE BILL laughs ironically.)* I figure he's goin'
35   to be 'bout as mad as a bull fixin' to be cut 'bout all this, and

1	I don't know if he'd be willin' to pay for my college schoolin'.
2	I can't worry 'bout that. If he don't see fit to pay, then maybe
3	I'll jest hafta work my way through waitin' tables like a lot
4	of them students do. See, I think football is his dream —
5	not mine.
6	DEAN WHITE: It's his dream for you, you idiot. He'd give
7	anything to see you make it big. He's worked hard for this
8	organization and contributed generously to our athletic funds.
9	JOE BILL: And you see that dryin' up, do you? Hell, I ain't stupid
10	Dean White. I know — and everybody else knows — that a
11	good amount of those contributions go straight into yer
12	retirement fund. You don't think that …
13	DEAN WHITE: You shut your mouth, boy! That is an evil lie! You
14	got no proof of that, and I am sick and tired of hearin' that
15	rumor! What I get in my retirement, I have worked for all my
16	life. You git that straight, you hear me?
17	JOE BILL: If that's true, why are ya'all so dead-set on what I do
18	with my life and why're ya'all so concerned 'bout me playin'
19	in this final game?
20	DEAN WHITE: It's my job to be concerned.
21	JOE BILL: I think all ya'all are concerned 'bout is yerself and yer
22	pocketbook. What you need to git straight is that I ain't gonna'
23	sign anything that says I cheated. I ain't gonna' say it. I ain't
24	makin' any deals — because I didn't cheat! See every day that I
25	can live with myself doin' what's right, I come that much closer
26	to bein' able to look at myself in that mirror in the morning and
27	not hate the reflection I see there. I think you know somethin'
28	about hatin' that reflection yerself, Dean White. *(Pause)*
29	DEAN WHITE: You're a punk — you know that? An' truth is, I
30	never have liked you much. But you gotta' know you're
31	ruinin' your life once again. Your only real choice is to sign this
32	and retake those tests so you can play.
33	JOE BILL: No, sir. I will not.
34	DEAN WHITE: Then kiss off your career, Joe Bill. You're here for
35	another year.

1   **JOE BILL:** If that's what it takes then that's what it takes. *(Pause)*
2   I guess I should go now? Are we done? *(Pause)*
3   **DEAN WHITE:** *(Completely flustered)* You think you can ...
4   *(Pause)* If you think ... Do you have any idea ...
5   **JOE BILL:** I know the rules of this game as well as you do. Maybe
6   better. *(Pause)*
7   **DEAN WHITE:** *(Looking over his papers)* I think there may have
8   been some failure to communicate here, Joe Bill. I wasn't
9   callin' you a cheater. Ms. Krieger was callin' you a cheater. I
10   think I can talk with that woman. She's got a few bones
11   buried around the yard that she'd just as soon stay
12   underground. I think I can might-maybe work something out.
13   **JOE BILL:** Oh, I'm sure you can, sir. Ya'all got a real knack for
14   that. I wouldn't exactly call it a gift, but you got a knack for
15   it, that's fer sure.
16   **DEAN WHITE:** Don't push your luck, kid. I'm just feelin' generous
17   today. *(Pause)* You have anything else on your mind — or do
18   you need to git to practice now?
19   **JOE BILL:** *(Thoughtfully)* Just one thing, sir. I think you helped me
20   a lot here today ta' make up my mind 'bout what I gotta' do.
21   I'm hangin' up my helmet today. You can make any ol' deal
22   you think ya' gotta' make with Ms. Krieger — I don't care.
23   I'm not playin' anymore. Way I see it, the only way I can cut
24   myself outta' this ugly game is ta' quit playin' it. Ms. Krieger's
25   a decent teacher — she's just tryin' ta do what she thinks is
26   the right thang, and I got no cause ...
27   **DEAN WHITE:** *(Interrupting and furious)* So you're a quitter now,
28   it that what you're tellin' me? That what you're gonna' tell
29   your team out there?
30   **JOE BILL:** I guess so, sir.
31   **DEAN WHITE:** Then, git out of my office! I have no use for quitters!
32   **JOE BILL:** *(Rising)* And I got no use for lyin' an' cheatin' an'
33   foolin' with other people's lives no more, sir. I ain't got the
34   stomach for it.
35   **DEAN WHITE:** Go. Get yer butt outta' my office.

1   **JOE BILL: Yes, sir.** *(JOE BILL walks to the office door and begins to*
2   *turn the doorknob. He stops. He turns around. He thinks of saying*
3   *something — but stops short of it. He turns and exits, shutting the*
4   *door softy behind him. DEAN WHITE sits, staring at the closed*
5   *door. After a few moments, he opens the third drawer down in his*
6   *desk and removes a bottle of Jack Daniels Whiskey and a glass.*
7   *He pours himself a drink and places the bottle back into the*
8   *drawer and closes the drawer. He raises the glass to his lips, but*
9   *stops just short of drinking. He looks at the glass of whiskey. He*
10   *swirls it. He sets the glass down softly on his desk. He places his*
11   *hands behind his head and rocks back slowly in his chair.)*
12
13   ***The End***
14
15
16
17
18
19
20
21
22
23
24
25
26
27
28
29
30
31
32
33
34
35

Half Truth
by Michael Johnson-Chase

Michael Johnson-Chase is the International Program Director at the Lark Theatre Company, where he also directs and dramaturges new plays. He has also served as Associate Professor of Theatre, Associate Chair and Director of the B.A. Program in Theatre for the Department of Theatre and Dance, and Associate Dean of Human Relations for The School of Arts at the University of Wisconsin — Milwaukee.

Half Truth is based on two imagined meetings between Nguyen Ngoc Loan and Eddie Adams after Mr. Adams took a photograph of Saigon Police Chief Nguyen assassinating a suspected Viet Cong guerrilla on the streets of Saigon in 1968. The photograph's stark image contributed to the peace movement in the United States.

Address all inquiries concerning performances, readings, or reprinting of this work *or any portion thereof* to Michael Johnson-Chase, 21 South End Avenue #522, New York, NY 10280. For details, see "Part II: Securing Rights for Your Production," pages 183 to 192.

1	The action of the first scene takes place in Walter Reed Hospital
2	in 1968. Scene Two takes place in the Library of Congress 25
3	years later.
4	**CHARACTERS:** EDDIE — a white American.
5	LOAN — a Vietnamese man. His name is pronounced "Low-ahn."
6	**SETTING:** Scene One requires an arm chair like those found in
7	hospitals. Scene Two calls for a library table.
8	
9	**Scene One**
10	
11	**EDDIE: Nurse ... nurse!** *(EDDIE clumsily places LOAN's leg back*
12	*on the chair. LOAN shifts in his sleep and his leg falls off again.*
13	*Once again EDDIE places LOAN's leg on the chair. LOAN*
14	*coughs. EDDIE hastily braces his leg against LOAN's to keep it*
15	*from sliding off.)* **Nurse!** *(LOAN opens his eyes and watches as*
16	*EDDIE takes off his jacket and wedges it under LOAN's knee. Still*
17	*bracing the leg, EDDIE grabs his camera for a shot.)*
18	**LOAN:** *(His speech is lightly slurred, as though the vowels and*
19	*consonants of English are a bit too much for his mouth.)* **Wone work.**
20	**EDDIE: What?**
21	**LOAN: Wone work.**
22	**EDDIE: The shot?**
23	**LOAN:** *(Bracing the leg)* **Has its own life. Obstine'.**
24	**EDDIE: No kidding.** *(EDDIE steps aside and LOAN's leg falls to the*
25	*floor. EDDIE aims his camera for a shot but LOAN grabs*
26	*EDDIE's jacket and covers his leg as one would cover a corpse.)*
27	**LOAN: They say it be only a stump, anyway.**
28	**EDDIE: I'm sorry.** *(Pause)* **You remember me?**
29	**LOAN: Of course.**
30	**EDDIE: Good, because —**
31	**LOAN: You know I am the *only* general in all of South Vietnam**
32	**injured in the Tet offensive?**
33	**EDDIE: I didn't know. That's —**
34	**LOAN: Bad luck. Bad luck like an earthquake. When there is one**
35	**there is another. Ky always tell me "you remain in power as**

1   long as I remain in power." Then he give up Premiership. For

2   South Vietnam, an earthquake. So, I get shot.

3   EDDIE: That's it? That's all of your bad luck?

4   LOAN: Is that not enough?

5   EDDIE: But ... I thought you'd feel ... what about the photograph?

6   LOAN: What photograph?

7   EDDIE: My photograph.

8   LOAN: You take lots of photographs.

9   EDDIE: The one ... when you executed that VC spy.

10   LOAN: Ah. *(Pause)* What about it?

11   EDDIE: Look, I brought you some beer. You want some?

12   LOAN: Of course.

13   EDDIE: I brought this because ... well, I wanted to say ... Toi ra't

14   la'y lam tie'c. *("I'm sorry.")*

15   LOAN: What?

16   EDDIE: Toi ra't la'y —

17   LOAN: Your Vietnamese awful. *(Pause)* You have cigarette?

18   EDDIE: Yea. *(Pulls out destroyed cigarette.)* Oh. Sorry ... I wrecked

19   it. Trying to quit.

20   LOAN: I take what I can get. *(EDDIE hands LOAN the remains.)*

21   EDDIE: Do you want me to get you some fresh? I can go get some ...

22   LOAN: You come to apologize?

23   EDDIE: No.

24   LOAN: Good.

25   EDDIE: Well ... it's just that ... I am sorry about what happened

26   to you, though ... because of it. The photo.

27   LOAN: Why?

28   EDDIE: I mean, I know why you had to come to Walter Reed.

29   LOAN: They tell me I get best medical care here.

30   EDDIE: That all they told you?

31   LOAN: Most of it.

32   EDDIE: You ... they didn't tell you why you had to leave

33   Australia? That the Australians ... they didn't want you.

34   There. In their country.

35   LOAN: I'm here for the leg. This best place —

1   **EDDIE:** Look, it's just as well. I mean, this is the best military
2   hospital in the world.
3   **LOAN:** I need ... what is English word? Pretend leg. Pro-fese ...
4   **EDDIE:** A prosthesis. You want to go back?
5   **LOAN:** If I go back they make me general.
6   **EDDIE:** Wow! That's great. A promotion.
7   **LOAN:** Maybe. But ... no ... I think I stay here. Start business.
8   **EDDIE:** Sure. Great idea. That is, if ... well, if they don't ... You
9   know, I think we're both moving up. They're giving me a
10   Pulitzer.
11   **LOAN:** What's that?
12   **EDDIE:** A photojournalism award. Big deal.
13   **LOAN:** Why?
14   **EDDIE:** For the photograph ... of you ... You don't think they should?
15   **LOAN:** What does it tell them, this photograph?
16   **EDDIE:** Well ... it tells them lots of things. Like how strange the
17   war is.
18   **LOAN:** All wars are strange.
19   **EDDIE:** Not like this one.
20   **LOAN:** New camera?
21   **EDDIE:** No. Just don't use it all that often.
22   **LOAN:** Small. Easy to get into hospital.
23   **EDDIE:** Yea ... my field camera would freak them out.
24   **LOAN:** Can I look?
25   **EDDIE:** At this?
26   **LOAN:** Yes.
27   **EDDIE:** OK. *(EDDIE tentatively hands over the camera. LOAN looks*
28   *through the viewfinder at EDDIE.)*
29   **LOAN:** Makes you small.
30   **EDDIE:** Not on the print. On the print you're normal size. *(LOAN*
31   *aims the camera around the room, checking out different*
32   *compositions.)* **Loan ... Loan!** I want to ask you something ...
33   there's something I don't get.
34   **LOAN:** What?
35   **EDDIE:** Why did you shoot that guy in front of us?

1 LOAN: He was a spy.

2 EDDIE: But ... you executed the guy in front of a photographer

3 and a camera crew. You didn't even ask his name. You

4 must've known how it was gonna look. Why didn't you take

5 my camera?

6 LOAN: I know his name. He Vietcong spy. He had a gun. He kill

7 policeman.

8 EDDIE: But you didn't try him. The VC at least hold a tribunal

9 when they capture a prisoner.

10 LOAN: And then they kill them. After they torture them. We know

11 this man Nguyen Tan Dat. He have alias, Han Son. If he was

12 in uniform I would not kill him. But he was war criminal.

13 EDDIE: How do you know?

14 LOAN: People do not know what we know in Vietnam ... Say I

15 don't shoot him? Then what? He goes to National Police

16 headquarters and he dies anyway. Dies after many days of

17 torture. In basement, like thousand others. You like that

18 better? *(LOAN abruptly tosses the camera to EDDIE, who barely*

19 *manages to catch it.)* I not coward like Australians say!

20 EDDIE: ... I gave my prize money to the Red Cross.

21 LOAN: All of it?

22 EDDIE: Yea.

23 LOAN: You are ashamed?

24 EDDIE: No! No ... I had to take the picture.

25 LOAN: You wish I take away your camera?

26 EDDIE: No! Well ... perhaps.

27 LOAN: Why you here? *(Pause)*

28 EDDIE: I came to apologize.

29 LOAN: Loan me money.

30 EDDIE: What?

31 LOAN: If you want help me —

32 EDDIE: Are you crazy?

33 LOAN: You think I crazy when I shoot VC?

34 EDDIE: Yes.

35 LOAN: So no difference now. Loan me money.

1   **EDDIE:** Jesus.

2   **LOAN:** Buddha put us together.

3   **EDDIE:** Well that's —

4   **LOAN:** I help *you*. Now you help *me*. Only loan. I pay you back. I

5   start business.

6   **EDDIE:** Here? In the States?

7   **LOAN:** Yes.

8   **EDDIE:** You can't do that ... they'll ... you're a villain here. To

9   Americans you're everything that's wrong with the war.

10 **LOAN:** Because of picture *you* take.

11 **EDDIE:** So?

12 **LOAN:** So help me.

13 **EDDIE:** I ... I'll think about it. OK?

14 **LOAN:** You have money now?

15 **EDDIE:** No! Of course not. I will have to make arrangements.

16   Maybe the CIA —

17 **LOAN:** I wait. They say four weeks more in hospital. *(LOAN*

18   *reaches for his crutches. EDDIE helps him up.)* I go find

19   cigarettes. You call me?

20 **EDDIE:** Sure. Yeah, I'll call you.

21 **LOAN:** Thank you, Eddie. Don't wait too long. I want stay in

22   America.

23 **EDDIE:** I don't ... well, it's your choice.

24 **LOAN:** Free country, right?

25 **EDDIE:** Yea.

26 **LOAN:** Bye, Eddie. You call me.

27 **EDDIE:** Bye, Loan. *(EDDIE exits as lights go to black, cross-fading*

28   *with Tomaso Albinoni's* Adagio in G Minor. *The music continues*

29   *through the scene shift.)*

30

31   **Scene Two — Apocalypse Now**

32

33   *(At rise, it is obvious many years have passed.*

34   *EDDIE is sprawled head down at a small table, asleep. Under*

35   *him lies an open book of photos. LOAN stands nearby, leaning on a*

1   *cane, a book tucked under his arm. He regards EDDIE thoughtfully.*
2   *The* Adagio *reaches its crescendo and there is silence. LOAN*
3   *lifts his cane and strikes the table just as there is the sudden*
4   *fusillade of an M60 machine gun. EDDIE sits bolt upright, takes*
5   *a moment, then reaches into his pocket for a pack of cigarettes.*
6   *He takes one out and places it in his mouth.)*
7   **LOAN:** *(His English is still rough, although it has noticeably*
8   *improved.)* **I don't think smoking allowed in here.**
9   **EDDIE: Huh?**
10   **LOAN: No smoking.**
11   **EDDIE: A cop on every corner.**
12   **LOAN: No any more. I not a cop. I'm businessman.**
13   **EDDIE: Wha ... Loan?**
14   **LOAN: Hi, Eddie.** *(LOAN reaches into his pocket, hands EDDIE a*
15   *small pill bottle.)* **Try one of these. Better than smoking.**
16   **EDDIE:** *You* **quit smoking? ... Valium? ... Haven't had one of**
17   **these in years.**
18   **LOAN: I take them all the time. I ... they call it ... bipolar.** *(EDDIE*
19   *pops a pill in his mouth.)*
20   **EDDIE: Bipolar? Fashionable disease. Very nineties. Like ADD.**
21   **My kid is ADD. And in case you hadn't noticed, I'm PTSD.**
22   **LOAN: What's that?**
23   **EDDIE: Post Traumatic Stress Disorder.**
24   **LOAN: You have that long time. Is it fashionable?**
25   **EDDIE: Not any more ... What're you doing here?**
26   **LOAN: Looking for you. But I do reconnaissance first.** *(He holds up*
27   *a book.)* ***Vietnam Reader.***
28   **EDDIE: O'Nan's new book. He's a jerk, you know ... How'd you**
29   **find me?**
30   **LOAN: I call your house ... talk to your son, I think.**
31   **EDDIE: That must've been entertaining.**
32   **LOAN: He doesn't know where you go. But your wife say Library**
33   **of Congress.**
34   **EDDIE: Well ... it's a big place. Glad you found me.**
35   **LOAN: Yes.**

1   EDDIE: Look, Loan, I don't know what you're doing with that

2   book, but ... you know, the war's over for me. Long time ago.

3   LOAN: Me too.

4   EDDIE: Good ... Well ... it's been a long time. Hasn't it?

5   LOAN: Twenty —

6   EDDIE: Twenty-five years ... See this? *Life in Sullivan County*. This

7   is about somebody else's past. A few of my better students did a

8   retrospective on Woodstock which made it into this book.

9   LOAN: Woodstock?

10   EDDIE: Yea. You wouldn't know about it. Anyway, I now live off

11   aging boomers who like to spend their time and money

12   cataloging the trivialities of their lost youth ... I teach

13   photography workshops at my barn in Jeffersonville.

14   LOAN: Teaching. Is it a good living?

15   EDDIE: No ... Hey, we all gotta take our lumps, my man. So what

16   the hell are you doing with that book?

17   LOAN: Looking for photograph.

18   EDDIE: The one of you? With Han Son?

19   LOAN: Yes.

20   EDDIE: Is it in there?

21   LOAN: Of course.

22   EDDIE: Well, you'd never know it. I have yet to receive a royalty

23   check.

24   LOAN: Eddie. I close my business. Things happened.

25   EDDIE: What? You were on a busy street, right?

26   LOAN: It wasn't about business. People found out about me.

27   EDDIE: Your identity?

28   LOAN: Yes.

29   EDDIE: How?

30   LOAN: I drink ... with my accountant ... he was American ...

31   Vietnam vet and he start complaining about war protesters. I

32   thought he would understand, so ... well, I tell him who I am.

33   But then he tell some friends at the Burke Register about me.

34   EDDIE: Oh, no ...

35   LOAN: They put me in newspaper. For a while no one care. But

1   then a lawyer in town —
2   EDDIE: A lawyer?
3   LOAN: Yes.
4   EDDIE: Rich?
5   LOAN: Yes.
6   EDDIE: Some liberal yuppie lawyer who got a deferment, no doubt ...
7   LOAN: He start a protest. In front of the store. And people stop
8   coming. I had to sell.
9   EDDIE: I'm sorry.
10 LOAN: *(Refers to book.)* That's why I look for this.
11 EDDIE: What the hell good will —
12 LOAN: Eddie ... Thank you for the loan.
13 EDDIE: What?
14 LOAN: You help me start the business, remember?
15 EDDIE: Will you forget that? That was a long time ago. Besides,
16   it's good when things are evened out between friends.
17 LOAN: Yes.
18 EDDIE: So what do you want with that picture?
19 LOAN: Eddie, I ... I want open a restaurant.
20 EDDIE: Loan, what do you want the damn photo for?
21 LOAN: Ti Tran will cook.
22 EDDIE: OK ... OK. We'll do this your way. What are you gonna
23   call the restaurant?
24 LOAN: "Les Trois Continents."
25 EDDIE: Nice title. And what are you gonna do if they find out again?
26 LOAN: I go other direction. *(Pause)* Create business connected to
27   my past. With photograph. Open restaurant near DC. Maybe
28   people like Ollie North come.
29 EDDIE: You are one whacked out dude! You just closed a business
30   because of who you are and now you think people will come
31   to your restaurant because of ... who you are?
32 LOAN: Don't people in America like to be around famous people?
33 EDDIE: Well yea, they do, but —
34 LOAN: That why I need the photo.
35 EDDIE: *What the hell for?*

1   LOAN: The foyer.

2   EDDIE: The *foyer.*

3   LOAN: Yes.

4   EDDIE: Of the restaurant?

5   LOAN: Yes.

6   EDDIE: You want to hang my photo in the *foyer* of a Vietnamese

7   restaurant? *Your* restaurant?

8   LOAN: Yes.

9   EDDIE: You are worse than whacked out. You are suicidal!

10 LOAN: I think people come because it unusual.

11 EDDIE: Unusual? You actually think upscale Washington

12   politicos will want ... what? ... spicy beef salad after seeing

13   a photograph —

14 LOAN: A famous photograph —

15 EDDIE: Of their friendly restaurant owner shooting some guy

16   point blank in the head? In the middle of a street in Saigon?

17 LOAN: It's unusual.

18 EDDIE: It's pathetic! Loan, Americans are not that depraved ...

19   They're not!

20 LOAN: I want to blow it up.

21 EDDIE: What?

22 LOAN: The photo. Make it really big. The wall about eight feet by

23   ten feet.

24 EDDIE: No. *No!* That photo has caused both of us enough pain

25   already. I will not allow it to be trivialized in that way!

26 LOAN: It won't be trivel, trivelee ...

27 EDDIE: Trivialized.

28 LOAN: ... What it did to me was not trivel!

29 EDDIE: That's not what I mean ... Of course it's affected your life.

30 LOAN: It destroy my life —

31 EDDIE: I printed what was there.

32 LOAN: It only a half-truth! You never tell anyone how I save Han

33   Son from torture —

34 EDDIE: Pictures don't lie!

35 LOAN: That one lies! It not whole story!

1   EDDIE: What's happened to you?
2   LOAN: I have no work!
3   EDDIE: That's no reason to —
4   LOAN: I have no money!
5   EDDIE: I'll give you mon —
6   LOAN: You have no money!
7   EDDIE: I have a little.
8   LOAN: A little! You had a lot! You give to Red Cross, you idiot!
9   You make money off me and you give it away! I never take
10   your money again.
11 EDDIE: Just get the hell outta here.
12 LOAN: Give me rights to photo.
13 EDDIE: You bastard.
14 LOAN: Give me rights and I go! *(LOAN strikes the table with his*
15   *cane.)*
16 EDDIE: Stop it, you slopehead!
17 LOAN: It my photograph too. I let you keep it.
18 EDDIE: You let me? You *let* me?! *(EDDIE swings at LOAN, who*
19   *intercepts the punch, knocks EDDIE to the floor and pins*
20   *EDDIE's neck with the cane.)*
21 LOAN: Give me rights.
22 EDDIE: … I'll never eat there.
23 LOAN: You not invited. *(LOAN increases the pressure.)*
24 EDDIE: All right … all right! I'll have my agent send you a copy.
25 LOAN: Use original negative.
26 EDDIE: Of course. I'm a pro. *(LOAN lets EDDIE up.)* You were
27   always crazy.
28 LOAN: Of course. I was head of Saigon National Police. But now I
29   just an American citizen making a living. *(LOAN reaches into*
30   *his pocket and pulls out his Valium bottle. He offers one to*
31   *EDDIE, who shakes his head no. LOAN pops one in his own*
32   *mouth and gathers his things.)* Bye, Eddie.
33 EDDIE: Bye, Loan. *(LOAN exits. Blackout.)*
34
35   *The End*

Don't Rent Furniture
by Geoffrey Howard

Geoffrey Howard has enjoyed a broad theatre experience as an actor, director, designer, and playwright. He received his M.F.A. in Directing/Acting from Texas Tech University.

Don't Rent Furniture has had no publications or performances prior to publication in this anthology.

Address all inquiries concerning performances, readings, or reprinting of this work *or any portion thereof* to Geoffrey Howard, 620 E. Escondido, Kingsville, TX 78363. For details, see "Part II: Securing Rights for Your Production," pages 183 to 192.

1   The action takes place now in MATT's new apartment.

2   ***CHARACTERS:*** MATT — a college-aged guy.

3   PHIL — another college-aged guy.

4   ***SETTING:*** MATT's new apartment — stark and bare, but roomy.

5

6   *(PHIL is helping MATT move into his new apartment. They enter*

7   *carrying boxes.)*

8   **MATT: So what do ya think? Beats that tiny dorm room, eh?**

9   **PHIL: I've seen worse.**

10   **MATT: I've seen your place.**

11   **PHIL: Like I said.**

12   **MATT: This place is going to be great. I can put the TV and stereo**

13   **over there. Set up a bar right here.**

14   **PHIL: With a keg cooler.**

15   **MATT: Yeah. Dress up the lighting a bit. Hang a few posters. That**

16   **rug from Cozumel will look great right here.**

17   **PHIL: That's a great rug.**

18   **MATT: My friend, you are standing in party central.**

19   **PHIL: Oh yeah, baby.**

20   **MATT: Oh. I can put the couch right over there.**

21   **PHIL: Whoa, Matt. You have a couch? I didn't see a couch in the**

22   **truck. I'm not moving a couch, man.**

23   **MATT: Don't worry. Some guys are bringing it by later.**

24   **PHIL: Some guys?**

25   **MATT: Yeah, some big sweaty guys with butt cleavage I guess.**

26   **PHIL: Who the hell do we know ...**

27   **MATT: I'm renting one from a place down the ...**

28   **PHIL: Oooooh. You don't want to do that.**

29   **MATT: It's a nice couch — a big one with all black leather and**

30   **gold trim.**

31   **PHIL: Don't rent furniture.**

32   **MATT: What's wrong with renting furniture?**

33   **PHIL: I mean it. Never rent furniture.**

34   **MATT: This is a nice place. It deserves a little class.**

35   **PHIL: The worse thing you could ever do.**

1   MATT: I'm just renting a couch, Phil. It isn't like I'm ...

2   PHIL: You can sit on the floor.

3   MATT: What if I have a girl over?

4   PHIL: You have a bed.

5   MATT: You are so crass.

6   PHIL: What else do you need?

7   MATT: What if I have friends over?

8   PHIL: They can sit on the floor.

9   MATT: I don't want them to see ...

10   PHIL: What? That you don't have a couch? So what?

11   MATT: So what?

12   PHIL: Throw down some pillows. Get a cheap futon.

13   MATT: I am not buying a cheap futon. You ever sat on one of
14   those?

15   PHIL: Oh, don't you start with ... you don't give a rip about your
16   friends being comfortable. You want to impress them with
17   your couch.

18   MATT: Impress them with my couch.

19   PHIL: You're selling out, Matt. Buying in to the great American lie.

20   MATT: I feel another one of your sermons coming on.

21   PHIL: We have made our homes into showcases of what we want
22   to be perceived as.

23   MATT: All I want is a freakin' couch.

24   PHIL: You want to impress people, little man.

25   MATT: With a couch.

26   PHIL: Exactly.

27   MATT: Must be one hell of a couch.

28   PHIL: It has to be. You're not going to rent a crappy couch.

29   MATT: Of course not.

30   PHIL: And I'll tell you why.

31   MATT: Of course you will.

32   PHIL: You are renting an image. You have no furniture, but you
33   want people to think you do. And not just ordinary furniture.
34   It has to be nice furniture. So, tell me, you walked into your
35   friendly neighborhood rental shop. What was the first couch

1   you saw?

2   MATT: I don't recall exactly …

3   PHIL: You saw a little one. Tan fabric with wood trim. A little ratty

4   but the kinda couch you can sit on and watch the game. The

5   kinda couch your friends can sleep on when they've had too

6   much to drink. You could eat pizza on that couch.

7   MATT: Yeah, they had something like that.

8   PHIL: But you didn't go for that one, did you?

9   MATT: Well, no, but there was this …

10   PHIL: A better couch right next to it — a big one with all …

11   MATT: Black leather and …

12   PHIL: Black leather and gold trim. It called to you. It sang to you.

13   It said, "What are you doing looking at that ratty tan when

14   you know you want me, Matt? You might be comfy on the

15   ratty tan. You could live with the ratty tan. You could own the

16   ratty tan in two months …

17   MATT: Is that how you got your crappy sofa?

18   PHIL: I've never rented furniture in my life.

19   MATT: Oh, I guess you found yours in an alley somewhere.

20   PHIL: That sofa came from my dad's basement.

21   MATT: There's a reason he was hiding it.

22   PHIL: Hey, I could live on that sofa.

23   MATT: You do live on that sofa.

24   PHIL: Don't change the subject. You gave in to the sirens on the

25   water. "Rent me, Matt. Take me, Matt. Take three years

26   paying for me. I'll make you look good."

27   MATT: Oh, come on. It was a better deal in the long run.

28   PHIL: A better deal?

29   MATT: Yeah. They threw in a coffee table …

30   PHIL: Oh, for …

31   MATT: A coffee table *and* a pair of black panther sculptures for

32   the wall.

33   PHIL: And this was a better deal?

34   MATT: Yeah. In the long run.

35   PHIL: There is no better deal! There is no long run! It is a system.

1 These people are insidious. They put crappy furniture in their
2 showrooms just to make you look at the more expensive stuff.
3 They feed off your insecurities. They know you are not coming
4 in to rent furniture.
5 MATT: Of course not. I came in for a manicure.
6 PHIL: They know you are coming in desperate for something that
7 will make you feel like a success.
8 MATT: We're talking about a couch where people sit.
9 PHIL: They know you want to put something in your house so that
10 when your friends come over they can enter your house and
11 say, "Oh my. What a beautiful couch. You must be rich. Can
12 we love you?" That is what is going on.
13 MATT: It's just my couch.
14 PHIL: It is not your couch, Matt. You don't own it. You miss that
15 weekly payment and see what happens. Those big sweaty guys
16 with butt cleavage come out and take it away. And you feel
17 what?
18 MATT: What?
19 PHIL: Violated.
20 MATT: Violated.
21 PHIL: You feel raped.
22 MATT: Oh brother.
23 PHIL: They had the gall to take away … to remove your value
24 from you. For what? What … what are you paying? Twenty-
25 five dollars a week?
26 MATT: Something like that.
27 PHIL: Your friends come back over. "Oh my, Frederick. He had his
28 couch taken away. It never was his. He must be … poor. Let's
29 leave before he makes us sit on a futon."
30 MATT: They're not going to take away my couch for missing one
31 payment.
32 PHIL: So you admit to the possibility.
33 MATT: Of what?
34 PHIL: That they can do this! Take away your couch!
35 MATT: I'll keep up with the payments!

1   PHIL: Makes you worry. Doesn't it, Matt? You know that your
2   image is only as good as that next payment. You are renting
3   who you want to be.
4   MATT: I'm renting a stupid couch, Phil.
5   PHIL: Just wait until you have the money in the bank and then go
6   buy a decent couch for a third of what you'd end up paying by
7   "renting to own" or whatever they say.
8   MATT: Well, I do have that option.
9   PHIL: Another sham, Einstein. They fool you into thinking you are
10   going to own that couch someday. But you know full well
11   you're not.
12 MATT: Why not?
13 PHIL: Because all rental furniture sucks. It's cheap imitation
14   leather with straw underneath and it never goes with anything
15   but other rental furniture. And by the time you get it "paid for"
16   it's time to rent new furniture because now it looks like crap or
17   you're tired of it. Don't do it, man. It leads to the dark side.
18   Before you know it, your entire life is rented. Bought on plan.
19   You find you are nothing but payments.
20 MATT: Nothing but payments?!
21 PHIL: Like I said.
22 MATT: I can afford this, Phil.
23 PHIL: Afford to buy your self-image on the installment plan?
24 MATT: You are so full of crap, Phil. You always do this.
25 PHIL: Do what?
26 MATT: Start going on with some self-righteous rant about how
27   shallow the American dream really is.
28 PHIL: It is shallow.
29 MATT: You're just …
30 PHIL: It *is* a shallow dream.
31 MATT: This is just your way …
32 PHIL: You're upset because you know I'm right.
33 MATT: I'm upset because you're a fraud, Phil.
34 PHIL: A fraud?
35 MATT: That's what I said.

1 PHIL: Where the hell do you get off ...
2 MATT: You live like a bum. You surround yourself with garbage. You
3   never clean your place. There is an ecosystem in your sink! And
4   rather than take a little pride ... or simple self-respect ... you
5   blanket yourself in these high morals so you can be lazy.
6 PHIL: I am my own man.
7 MATT: You talk about "society" as if it is this great evil.
8 PHIL: You're going to tell me it isn't?
9 MATT: This country is founded on the idea that every man can
10   better himself.
11 PHIL: How?
12 MATT: What?
13 PHIL: How? How does a man better himself?
14 MATT: Well ... open his own business. Be his own boss. Work his
15   way up. Have a nice home.
16 PHIL: In other words, "Through possessions." Look Matt. I'm the
17   philosophy student. You're the business major with daddy's
18   wallet. I understand the perversion of today's society. You
19   crunch numbers.
20 MATT: Well, at least you're being insulting.
21 PHIL: You remember the Puritan ethic?
22 MATT: I walked out on that lecture, Phil. It bored me then and I'm
23   sure it will bore me now.
24 PHIL: The Puritans came over with the idea of predestination.
25   There are those who are chosen by God and those who are not.
26 MATT: Oh, look at me. I'm bored.
27 PHIL: Puritan theology. The building block of our society. All these
28   Puritans are running around trying to figure out who is
29   chosen by God and who is not. What are we going to do? I
30   know. Surely God will bless those He has chosen.
31 MATT: You honestly think you're making sense, don't you?
32 PHIL: God will increase their wealth. Their properties. And so
33   began the mad rush to accumulate wealth. Or the appearance
34   of wealth.
35 MATT: Your leaps of logic are astounding.

1   **PHIL: Fine material possessions became the mark of the chosen.**
2   **Financial failure is taboo. A low bank account is shameful.**
3   **Poverty has become the ultimate disgrace.** And we will do
4   anything to surround ourselves with the appearance of wealth
5   and success so we won't be excommunicated from a society
6   that judges us by the quality of our furniture.
7   MATT: *It's just a couch, Phil!*
8   PHIL: That's how it starts, Matt. Before you know it, you are
9   living in a middle class cookie-cutter house alongside a bunch
10   of other houses that look just like yours with a sailboat sitting
11   outside on the weekends.
12   MATT: When did I get a sailboat?
13   PHIL: Working weekends.
14   MATT: I'm not going to work weekends.
15   PHIL: You have to work weekends.
16   MATT: Why do I have to work weekends?
17   PHIL: To pay for the boat you can't use on weekends because
18   you're working weekends to pay for the boat!
19   MATT: And to think all I wanted was a nice couch for twenty-five
20   dollars a week.
21   PHIL: You see how it all snowballs?
22   MATT: You know ... when I think about it ...
23   PHIL: You see my point.
24   MATT: My entire life ...
25   PHIL: Everything you've believed ...
26   MATT: All this time ...
27   PHIL: I know ...
28   MATT: I'd only suspected you were a pretentious, pseudo-intellectual
29   ass. But I believe this confirms what I've thought all along.
30   PHIL: *(Pause)* I'm going to unload this box and then I'm going to
31   leave.
32   MATT: Got somewhere to go?
33   PHIL: Yeah. I'm pledging a fraternity tonight.
34   MATT: *(Pause)* Do they come with a coffee table?
35   *The End*

The Laundromat
by Eric Geyer

Eric Geyer is a writer, teacher, and performing songwriter in San Antonio, Texas. He is the author of twenty plays and has enjoyed over thirty productions of his work in public theatres, colleges, and high schools across North America. His plays won Texas Educational Theatre Association Playfest awards in 1999 and 2001.

The Laundromat was first produced in New York City at Creative Place Theatre in 2000. Subsequent productions took place in Austin and San Antonio, Texas, and in Willow Springs, Missouri.

Address all inquiries concerning performances, readings, or reprinting of this work *or any portion thereof* to Eric Geyer, 327 West Ridgewood, San Antonio, TX 78212. For details, see "Part II: Securing Rights for Your Production," pages 183 to 192.

1   The action takes place in a laundromat.
2   **CHARACTERS:** MAN 1.
3   MAN 2 is haggard, and his hair is out of place. His clothes, once
4   respectable, appear worn and tattered.
5   **SETTING:** The portion of the laundromat that's visible is equipped
6   with a couple of washers and a few plastic chairs.
7
8   *(MAN 1 is putting the last few shirts into a washer unit. There is*
9   *a large basket to his left and a row of hangers laid neatly on*
10   *another washer to the side. MAN 2 enters with two heavy laundry*
11   *bags. Upon seeing the first MAN, he pauses and stares at him for*
12   *a moment. He surveys the room. MAN 1 sits down on the chair. He*
13   *pulls a sandwich out of a brown paper bag. MAN 2 sits down near*
14   *him. MAN 1 takes a bite out of his sandwich.)*
15   **MAN 2: Do you know how many laundromats there are in this**
16   **city?**
17   **MAN 1: Excuse me?**
18   **MAN 2: I say, I wonder if you know how many laundromats there**
19   **are in this fair city of ours?**
20   **MAN 1: There's a lot.**
21   **MAN 2: No. Please consider your answer, sir. I'm asking you this:**
22   **are you aware as to the number of laundromats which exist in**
23   **this, our fair city?**
24   **MAN 1: Well, I — you mean, the exact number?**
25   **MAN 2: Of course.**
26   **MAN 1: No, then, I guess not.**
27   **MAN 2: Seventy-nine.**
28   **MAN 1: Seventy-nine?**
29   **MAN 2: Seventy-nine. Exactly.**
30   **MAN 1: That's … uh … interesting.**
31   **MAN 2: Of course, that total pertains to the number of**
32   **laundromats which are open to the public. Therefore, any**
33   **private or otherwise clandestine laundromats would be**
34   **excluded from the total. Who knows how many laundromats**
35   **could be operating unbeknownst to us, yes?**

1   **MAN 1: Right.**
2   **MAN 2: So easy to be deceived, isn't it?**
3   **MAN 1: I —**
4   **MAN 2: You might turn your back for a moment, suddenly …** *(He*
5   *stares at the FIRST MAN.)* **Also, I presume that you are under**
6   **the assumption that I do not speak of "dry cleaning"**
7   **establishments or other such businesses which are similar, yet**
8   **not identical, to a laundromat such as the one we find**
9   **ourselves presently in.**
10   **MAN 1: Uh …**
11   **MAN 2: No. I speak exclusively of laundromats, where one sees to**
12   **the cleaning of one's laundry oneself.**
13   **MAN 1: Yes.**
14   **MAN 2: Quite pure, isn't it?**
15   **MAN 1: What?**
16   **MAN 2: To me, there is an inherent purity in the act of bringing one's**
17   **sullied garments to the altar of the laundromat. An opportunity**
18   **to cleanse one's apparel … perhaps, oneself. A moment of respite**
19   **in an otherwise filthy world, don't you think?**
20   **MAN 1: Um …**
21   **MAN 2: Look about you. It's a filthy world, sir, full of dirt and scum.**
22   **Everything stinks like … like something abundantly unpleasant.**
23   **MAN 1: Well, we're in a laundromat.** *(He chuckles. The SECOND*
24   *MAN stares at him.)*
25   **MAN 2: I'm speaking of the bleak situation outside this window.**
26   **The vast islands of garbage, the dilapidated structures, the**
27   **nameless, faceless, shameless creatures cast out into the street.**
28   **I ran into one such individual as I approached this very**
29   **establishment. He asked if I would donate a quarter to his**
30   **tenacious pursuit of a cheeseburger.** *(He stares at the FIRST*
31   *MAN, expecting a response. The FIRST MAN is at a loss.)*
32   **MAN 1: Uh-huh.**
33   **MAN 2: Did you hear me, sir? A cheeseburger.**
34   **MAN 1: Um … yeah.**
35   **MAN 2: A cheeseburger. Have you ever heard of anything so**

1	preposterous? *(Pause)*
2	MAN 1: I like cheeseburgers.
3	MAN 2: As if I were so naive as to accept that premise. As if I were
4	so naive as to assume he would not spend it on the nearest
5	quart of beer or vial of cocaine. You can't trust anyone's word
6	anymore. Can you, sir? *(The SECOND MAN walks over to the*
7	*window. The FIRST MAN searches for something to say.)*
8	MAN 1: I —
9	MAN 2: People don't tell the truth anymore. And why should they?
10	In a world where all that concerns people is themselves, what
11	is the benefit to being honest, to tipping one's hand to the
12	enemy? Our species is too evolved, too intelligent to be good
13	anymore. People do exactly what they want, no matter the
14	consequences to others around them. They lie, they cheat ...
15	and they steal. It's all falling apart, my friend. Nothing works
16	anymore. What's the point? Things that are built to be
17	airtight, simply leak. Things that are supposed to run, simply
18	stop. This entire laundromat, the washing units, the drying
19	machines, the ceiling tiles, the network of pipes surrounding
20	the perimeter of these premises, it could all fall to pieces
21	before your load is completed. Because no one cares. It's all an
22	elaborate hoax. *(The SECOND MAN begins to thumb through*
23	*the hangers.)* Isn't it amazing, sir, the relative ease with which
24	people initiate the most elaborate of deceptions?
25	MAN 1: Well —
26	MAN 2: Our entire system is collapsing. The social structure, the
27	moral and ethical foundation of our very existence is turning
28	to dust before our eyes, leaving us cold, crying children,
29	wandering in the street with the rest of them. *(Pause. He stares*
30	*at the FIRST MAN. Uncomfortable, the FIRST MAN begins to eat*
31	*his sandwich again.)* Do you remember how many
32	laundromats there are in this city of ours?
33	MAN 1: *(Mouth full of food)* Um ... seventy-nine?
34	MAN 2: Correct. Do you care to fashion a guess as to why I might
35	be privy to such otherwise useless knowledge?

1   **MAN 1: No.**

2   **MAN 2: In the last twenty-six days, I have visited each one. I have**

3   **visited all seventy-nine laundromats in the metropolitan area.**

4   *(Pause)*

5   **MAN 1: Why?**

6   **MAN 2: I am searching for something I've lost. I have quit my job,**

7   **I have abandoned the last of my family and friends. I am ever-**

8   **vigilant in the quest to find the rogue who robbed me of**

9   **something very precious.**

10   **MAN 1: What is it?**

11   **MAN 2: How bold of you to pretend not to know.**

12   **MAN 1: Do what?** *(Pause. The SECOND MAN surveys the FIRST*

13   *MAN's belongings.)*

14   **MAN 2: So many factors …**

15   **MAN 1: Wh —**

16   **MAN 2: So many factors can delay one's wash.** *(Pause. The FIRST*

17   *MAN is now quite engaged.)* **Do you not agree?**

18   **MAN 1: Uh …**

19   **MAN 2: So many elements. One piece falls away, all is lost, isn't it?**

20   **An otherwise perfect wash can be ruined. You may bring all**

21   **your towels, your shirts, your muddy socks. But you have**

22   **absentmindedly forgotten detergent. What good is cleaning**

23   **without cleanser, yes?**

24   **MAN 1: Uh-huh.**

25   **MAN 2: Perhaps you left your fabric softener at home.**

26   **MAN 1: Yes.**

27   **MAN 2: Have you?**

28   **MAN 1: What? Oh … no. I was just agreeing. I mean, no, I didn't.**

29   **MAN 2: Of course not. You are nobody's fool.**

30   **MAN 1:** *(Chuckling nervously)* **Right.**

31   **MAN 2:** *(Not chuckling)* **Do I humor you, sir?**

32   **MAN 1: No, I was just —**

33   **MAN 2: Many factors. Perhaps you did not manage to retrieve the**

34   **quarters from your kitchen table before you left and now you**

35   **find yourself helpless to activate the washing machines.**

1   Perhaps the laundromat is closed while the attendant
2   eliminates the lint from the filters. Perhaps in the middle of
3   the drying cycle, your hangers grow legs and disappear. Yes?
4   MAN 1: Yes, ha, that happens to me a lot.
5   MAN 2: Does it?
6   MAN 1: Well, yeah. *(Chuckling)* Happens to everyone.
7   MAN 2: Does it happen to you, sir, so often that you might be
8   tempted to take matters into your own hands once and for all,
9   lashing out rebelliously with your own makeshift brand of
10   justice?
11   MAN 1: Why do you say that? *(The SECOND MAN stands up and*
12   *points dramatically.)*
13   MAN 2: Because, sir, *those are my hangers!*
14   MAN 1: Do what?
15   MAN 2: Those hangers belong to *me*! Do you deny it, you villain?!
16   MAN 1: But they're mine.
17   MAN 2: How dare you?! How dare you, you despot?! You cheat!
18   You charlatan!
19   MAN 1: Hey, I didn't steal your hangers.
20   MAN 2: Oh, didn't you?! Didn't you?!! *(Composing himself)* Please,
21   the game is up. We have come this far, do not attempt to crawl
22   out from under your deed.
23   MAN 1: I don't know what you're talking about.
24   MAN 2: You amaze me, sir. I am in awe. I thought that I
25   understood the depths of the insincerity of man but no, here
26   is yet another rung. Another plane altogether. You are a
27   miracle, sir. You cannot even summon the self-respect to own
28   up to the bald theft of my hangers.
29   MAN 1: I've never stolen a thing in my life.
30   MAN 2: Haven't you?!! Haven't you, knave?! Twenty-seven days
31   ago, March seventeenth, a Thursday, I patronized this very
32   establishment, a load of laundry in each hand. Those very
33   hangers were on my person. I walked next door, for only a
34   moment, to purchase a scone. Meanwhile, *you*, sir, thieved the
35   hangers and sped away!

1   **MAN 1: And you went to seventy-nine laundromats looking for them?**

2   **MAN 2: I didn't think you'd have the gall to return to the scene of**

3   **the crime. I admit, a bit of poor psychology as well as poor**

4   **planning on my part. My hat is off to you for your bravery,**

5   **you petty scoundrel.**

6   **MAN 1: But I —**

7   **MAN 2: Enough, fabricator! You force me to embarrass you with**

8   **the evidence.** *(He turns to one side, shielding his view of the*

9   *hangers.)* **Is one of them made of plastic?**

10   **MAN 1: Yes.**

11   **MAN 2: Is one of them made of wire?**

12   **MAN 1: Yes.**

13   **MAN 2: Are some of them beige?**

14   **MAN 1: Yes.**

15   **MAN 2: Well, there you have it. Hand them over before I phone the**

16   **authorities.**

17   **MAN 1: That description could be anybody's hangers.**

18   **MAN 2: They're mine, I tell you.** *(He runs over to the hangers and*

19   *begins talking to them.)* **Timmy, Sara, Dennis! Come home,**

20   **please! He's got you under his spell, don't you see? He's a**

21   **deceiver! He's brainwashed you into believing you belong**

22   **to him!**

23   **MAN 1: Hey, leave those hangers alone!**

24   **MAN 2: You baseless brute! I'm taking them home, where they**

25   **belong!** *(He gathers them up and attempts to force his way out.*

26   *The FIRST MAN challenges. They struggle, clumsily. The hangers*

27   *are ripped out of the SECOND MAN's grasp and slip onto the*

28   *floor in front of them. The SECOND MAN trips and falls to the*

29   *floor, flailing helplessly. The FIRST MAN stands above him, filled*

30   *with adrenaline.)*

31   **MAN 1: Look, I'm telling you! These are my hangers! I didn't steal**

32   **them from you. It's just a coincidence. I mean c'mon! They all**

33   **look alike. Maybe someone thought they were theirs and**

34   **accidentally, accidentally took them. Maybe you just lost**

35   **them. You're working yourself up over nothing.** *(The FIRST*

1   *MAN sits down, exhausted. The SECOND MAN places a hand on*
2   *his forehead.)*
3   **MAN 2: My God. I'm all mixed up.**
4   **MAN 1: Look, just calm down for a second.** *(The FIRST MAN helps*
5   *the SECOND MAN to his seat.)*
6   **MAN 2: You're absolutely right. I have no sufficient proof**
7   **concerning the identifying traits of my hangers. I've gone on**
8   **a wild goose chase. I have made a colossal fool of myself.**
9   **MAN 1: Look, forget it.**
10   **MAN 2: You must understand. My hangers are important to me.**
11   **MAN 1: I can see that.**
12   **MAN 2: Why did they take them from me, sir? How could they do**
13   **such a thing and not care? How can they sleep at night? And**
14   **what's left for us? If a man can't rest assured that he can**
15   **complete a simple load of laundry without having to come**
16   **face-to-face with the ugliest side of the nature of the species,**
17   **what can he count on, sir?**
18   **MAN 1: You can't look at things like that. You're blowing it all out**
19   **of proportion. You can't sit around convincing yourself that**
20   **everyone's just out for themselves.**
21   **MAN 2: Perhaps. I must apologize. I'm quite ashamed.**
22   **MAN 1: Don't worry about it.**
23   **MAN 2: As I said, the structures of this species' ethical and moral**
24   **codes are collapsing right in front of us. Or were they ever**
25   **there? Did I just dream them? Perhaps it is simply my**
26   **ignorance that slowly melts away, awakening me to the**
27   **nightmare of reality. Perhaps that is all we are. Animals.**
28   **Animals who do what they want, without any regard for right**
29   **or wrong.**
30   **MAN 1: I ...** *(The SECOND MAN gets up from the chair and collects*
31   *himself.)*
32   **MAN 2: I've ruined your evening. I'm sorry.**
33   **MAN 1: It's no bother. Really. Please take care of yourself.**
34   **MAN 2: You are too kind. I'll leave you to your wash, sir. Good**
35   **evening.** *(The man slowly exits the laundromat and wanders into*

1   *the night. The FIRST MAN watches him leave. Eventually, he*
2   *walks to the door and peers out the window for any sign of the*
3   *SECOND MAN. Finding none, he walks over to the hangers. He*
4   *sits on the ground and gathers them up. He sits on the floor. He*
5   *embraces the hangers.)*
6   **MAN 1: He's gone now. Do you hear me? He's gone now and**
7   **there's nothing to be afraid of anymore. I knew he'd come**
8   **back. But you know I would never let him take you from me.**
9   **You know that. Did you hear those silly names he used?**
10   **Dennis? Fool. How could you live with someone like that for**
11   **all those years? That simpleton? That beast? You're so lucky.**
12   **Do you realize how lucky you are that I found you?**
13
14   ***The End***
15
16
17
18
19
20
21
22
23
24
25
26
27
28
29
30
31
32
33
34
35

My Usual
by Matthew Calhoun

Matthew Calhoun's produced plays include *Living in Sin, Kitchen Therapy,* and *Tortured People* (Chicago) and *Help! Sex-Tet, Career Counseling, Attractions, Conditions, Skits-Ophrenia, Restraint,* and *Worm Day* (New York). His short comedies, *Money, Audition!* and *The Breakfast Special,* appear in anthologies. *Audition!* has twice been presented during the Miss America Pageant.

My Usual was presented by the American Playwrights Theatre at the Miranda Theatre in Manhattan in 1998, and it was presented by the Queens Playwright Festival at the LaGuardia Performing Arts Center and at TSI in Manhattan in 1998. It was a finalist for the Actors Theatre of Louisville Heideman Award.

Address all inquiries concerning performances, readings, or reprinting of this work *or any portion thereof* to Matthew Calhoun, 23-51 19th Street, Astoria, NY 11105. For details, see "Part II: Securing Rights for Your Production," pages 183 to 192.

1   The action takes place in a city bagel shop at 8:45 a.m. on any
2   weekday in the present.
3   **CHARACTERS:** COUNTER PERSON—a man.
4   CUSTOMER—on his way to work. Both men are around the
5   same age and perhaps look somewhat alike.
6   **SETTING:** The counter of the bagel shop.
7
8   *(The COUNTER PERSON stands at his station, minding the shop*
9   *and whistling to pass the time. A CUSTOMER enters and nods to*
10   *him in a friendly way.)*
11   **COUNTER PERSON: Yes?**
12   **CUSTOMER: My usual.**
13   **COUNTER PERSON: Your usual?**
14   **CUSTOMER: Yes.**
15   **COUNTER PERSON: I don't know what your usual is.**
16   **CUSTOMER: I've been coming here for eight years.**
17   **COUNTER PERSON: I've never seen you before.**
18   **CUSTOMER: You've been giving my usual for four of those years.**
19   **COUNTER PERSON: I've been working here three years.**
20   **CUSTOMER: Four.**
21   **COUNTER PERSON: Three. And I don't remember seeing you in**
22   **here.**
23   **CUSTOMER: Amnesia?**
24   **COUNTER PERSON: What?**
25   **CUSTOMER: Do you have amnesia? Blow on the head?**
26   **Dementia? Something like that?**
27   **COUNTER PERSON: I'm fine.**
28   **CUSTOMER: I don't think so. You don't remember me.**
29   **COUNTER PERSON: I can't remember everyone who comes here.**
30   **CUSTOMER: You gave me my usual yesterday.**
31   **COUNTER PERSON: Remind me.**
32   **CUSTOMER: It was 8:45 a.m. I came in here, we nodded, you gave**
33   **it to me. No words were spoken. You just knew.**
34   **COUNTER PERSON: Are you sure it was *this* place?**
35   **CUSTOMER: It was absolutely this place!**

1   COUNTER PERSON: Well I'm not going to argue with you. But
2   I've never seen you before.
3   CUSTOMER: You've seen me. You've seen me.
4   COUNTER PERSON: Last month? A year ago? Possibly. But
5   every day for the past three years?
6   CUSTOMER: Four years!
7   COUNTER PERSON: I don't think so. *(There is a pause.)*
8   CUSTOMER and COUNTER PERSON: *(Simultaneously)* Is this
9   an April Fools joke?
10   CUSTOMER: It's not April Fools Day.
11   COUNTER PERSON: I know that.
12   CUSTOMER: Look, the last four years haven't been the easiest for
13   me. My dog died.
14   COUNTER PERSON: I'm sorry.
15   CUSTOMER: Trixie was my best friend.
16   COUNTER PERSON: I know how dogs are.
17   CUSTOMER: Got me through my separation and divorce.
18   COUNTER PERSON: I don't think I would have survived mine
19   without *my* dog.
20   CUSTOMER: Then the cleaner loses my suit ...
21   COUNTER PERSON: *(In sympathy)* **Cleaners.**
22   CUSTOMER: I lost most of my money in the stock market.
23   COUNTER PERSON: Yeah, everyone else is getting rich, my
24   damn broker has me invest in ...
25   CUSTOMER: *(Disgustedly)* **Ferguson Chemicals.**
26   COUNTER PERSON: We must have the same broker.
27   CUSTOMER: My ex-wife starts seeing my best friend.
28   COUNTER PERSON: It's a *killer*, isn't it?
29   CUSTOMER: We have a fist fight in a bar.
30   COUNTER PERSON: Hey, he started it!
31   CUSTOMER: How do you know?
32   COUNTER PERSON: Oh. I mean the fight I had with *my* best
33   friend.
34   CUSTOMER: Benny?
35   COUNTER PERSON: Yeah, Benny.

1   CUSTOMER: You have a friend named Benny?

2   COUNTER PERSON: Not any more.

3   CUSTOMER: He starts telling me all about how good sex is with ...

4   COUNTER PERSON: Rhonda.

5   CUSTOMER: You had a wife named Rhonda?

6   COUNTER PERSON: Blonde hair? Blue eyes?

7   CUSTOMER: Five-foot-four.

8   COUNTER PERSON: Four-and-a-half, as I recall.

9   CUSTOMER: I miss her.

10   COUNTER PERSON: I get mugged waiting for a subway.

11   CUSTOMER: Just been to the bank, cashed my *entire* paycheck ...

12   COUNTER PERSON: And it's the one time in my life I get

13   mugged!

14   CUSTOMER: *(Off-handedly)* Oh yeah, and my mother dies.

15   COUNTER PERSON: *(Disgustedly)* And I gotta go all the way to

16   Frisco and my *brother's* there.

17   CUSTOMER: Parading his money around.

18   COUNTER PERSON: I thought that suit was a *little* gaudy for a

19   wake.

20   CUSTOMER: A *little*? Please.

21   COUNTER PERSON: I even slip in the bathtub.

22   CUSTOMER: I *knew* that bar of soap was around there somewhere!

23   COUNTER PERSON: Right under my left foot.

24   CUSTOMER: Right foot.

25   COUNTER PERSON: Right?

26   CUSTOMER: Uh huh.

27   COUNTER PERSON: I think it was the left.

28   CUSTOMER: And then my *hat* blows into the East River!

29   COUNTER PERSON: And that girl laughs!

30   CUSTOMER: And the same wind that blows it off my head blows

31   a speck in my eye.

32   COUNTER PERSON: And it seemed to stay in there a week.

33   CUSTOMER: A couple days.

34   COUNTER PERSON: Three, maybe.

35   CUSTOMER: And the only stable thing in this *entire* time, the only

1   thing that gets me *through* all these hideous happenings, is I
2   come in here every morning at 8:45 a.m., and you know me
3   here! And you give me my usual!
4   COUNTER PERSON: No, I don't recall seeing you in here.
5   CUSTOMER: *(Looking at his watch)* And now I'm going to be late
6   to work! *(He starts to storm out.)*
7   COUNTER PERSON: Sir?
8   CUSTOMER: *(Stopping)* Yes? *(He turns.)*
9   COUNTER PERSON: Doesn't it seem strange to you?
10   CUSTOMER: That you don't remember me after all this time?
11   COUNTER PERSON: No, that we've been through all these
12   common occurrences.
13   CUSTOMER: What are you talking about?
14   COUNTER PERSON: We both get divorced ...
15   CUSTOMER: Lots of people get divorced.
16   COUNTER PERSON: We both lose our suit at the cleaners ...
17   CUSTOMER: *(Disparagingly)* **Cleaners.**
18   COUNTER PERSON: Both lose our money investing heavily in
19   Ferguson Chemicals.
20   CUSTOMER: So we have the same inept broker.
21   COUNTER PERSON: We both have a blonde wife named
22   Rhonda?
23   CUSTOMER: Yeah but mine was five foot four. Yours was four-
24   and-a-half.
25   COUNTER PERSON: My hat flew into the Hudson River.
26   CUSTOMER: See? Totally different experiences.
27   COUNTER PERSON: What's your name?
28   CUSTOMER: Sam Dopple.
29   COUNTER PERSON: I'm Sam Ganger.
30   CUSTOMER: See? Totally different names. *(He looks at his watch*
31   *again.)* My boss is totally going to chew me out.
32   COUNTER PERSON: Where do you work?
33   CUSTOMER: Bagel shop.
34   COUNTER PERSON: Harry's Bagel Shop?
35   CUSTOMER: Yeah, that's the one.

1   **COUNTER PERSON:** Yeah, they used to know me there.

2   **CUSTOMER:** Yeah?

3   **COUNTER PERSON:** I went in there all the time. Sometimes too

4   depressed to speak. I wouldn't have to. They knew what I

5   wanted.

6   **CUSTOMER:** Cream cheese and tomato on a whole wheat bagel.

7   **COUNTER PERSON:** Toasted.

8   **CUSTOMER:** It kinda gets you through the day, doesn't it?

9   **COUNTER PERSON:** And then one day the guy stares right at me

10   like he doesn't know me. I say, "My usual, please," and he

11   says, "What's your usual?" I couldn't believe it. I turned

12   around and never went back.

13   **CUSTOMER:** Who was this guy?

14   **COUNTER PERSON:** *(Looking at him, remembering)* **You.** *(Lights*

15   *fade.)*

16

17   ***The End***

18

19

20

21

22

23

24

25

26

27

28

29

30

31

32

33

34

35

Muse

by William Borden

William Borden's plays have won twenty-one national playwriting competitions and have had over two hundred productions. The film version of his play, *The Last Prostitute*, was shown on Lifetime Television and in Europe and is on video. His novel, *Superstoe*, was republished by Orloff Press. A Core Alumnus Playwright at The Playwrights' Center in Minneapolis, he is playwright with Listening Winds.

Muse was produced at the Festival of Ten, State University of New York, Brockport, in 2001; by Drama West in Los Angeles in 2000; by Expanded Arts, New York, NY, in 1997; and by Heartlande Theatre Birmingham, MI, in 1997.

Address all inquiries concerning performances, readings, or reprinting of this work *or any portion thereof* to William Borden, 7996 S. FM 548, Royse City, TX 75189. For details, see "Part II: Securing Rights for Your Production," pages 183 to 192.

1   The action takes place in a writer's workroom in the present.

2   **CHARACTERS:** CAL — a frustrated writer. RON — a muse.

3   **SETTING:** The classic scene: CAL sits at a typewriter, all around him,

4   a sea of wadded-up sheets of paper.

5

6   *(CAL types; he reads; he jerks the paper out of the typewriter; he*

7   *wads it up.)*

8   **CAL: I need a muse. Where's my muse? Homer had a muse,**

9   **Shakespeare, Dante ... Reams of paper ... editor's forgotten**

10   **me, my agent's lost my phone number ... If I had a muse ...**

11   *(RON enters, swishy, but not too swishy.)*

12   **RON: Hi, Cal.**

13   **CAL: Who the heck are you?**

14   **RON: You called.**

15   **CAL:** *(Beat)* **No, no.**

16   **RON: Ron.**

17   **CAL: No.**

18   **RON: I can leave.** *(He starts to leave.)*

19   **CAL: Wait! Just a brief moment, for clarification.**

20   **RON: Anything.**

21   **CAL: See, you cannot be —**

22   **RON: Your muse?**

23   **CAL: Correct. Because all through literary history, when a guy**

24   **calls for his muse, it's always a girl.**

25   **RON: Really?**

26   **CAL: See, there were nine muses. They were the daughters of Zeus.**

27   **There was Calliope — she was the muse of heroic poetry. There**

28   **was Clio, history; Terpsichore, dance; there was ... let's see ...**

29   **RON: Euterpe, music; Thalia, comic and lyric poetry; Erato, love**

30   **poetry; Polyhymnia, sacred poetry; Melpomene, tragedy; and**

31   **Urania, astronomy.**

32   **CAL: Astronomy?**

33   **RON: They didn't have telescopes back then. They had to make it up.**

34   **CAL: They must have some new ones now, you know, for the novel,**

35   **modern plays, abstract expressionism ...** *(RON smiles, preens.)*

1   I've seen paintings of the Muses! They're always women!
2   Voluptuous, long-haired —
3   RON: When Oscar Wilde called for a muse, who do you think they
4   sent?
5   CAL: Oscar Wilde, sure ...
6   RON: And Gide, and Proust, and Tennessee Williams —
7   CAL: Exactly. Exactly my point.
8   RON: I don't have time to argue, Cal. I'm run ragged as it is —
9   Albee, McNally, Kushner — when everybody was in the closet,
10   we could send anybody, who would complain? But now ...
11   CAL: Young, old, I don't care, but breasts, you know what I mean?
12   RON: Are you ... phobic?
13   CAL: No, no. It's not that. I'm sure you're a fine guy. I'm sure we
14   could be good friends. Some of my best friends —
15   RON: Please!
16   CAL: It's true!
17   RON: Please!
18   CAL: I just think a lady muse would ... understand me better.
19   RON: No doubt.
20   CAL: So.
21   RON: So?
22   CAL: Go. Send a broad.
23   RON: I'd love to. But. It's too late. Assignments cannot be changed.
24   CAL: I'm sure ...
25   RON: No.
26   CAL: If there's been a mistake ...
27   RON: There are no mistakes. So I've been told.
28   CAL: If you think that I'm ... If they think that I'm ...
29   *Somebody's made a mistake!*
30   RON: I'll leave. *(He starts to leave.)*
31   CAL: They'll send — if you go — that means you admit there's
32   been a mistake, and they'll send — breasts ...
33   RON: Do you think everybody gets a muse? Do you think any
34   schmuck hammering at a typewriter who whines, "Where's
35   my muse, I want a muse — "

1   CAL: I didn't whine!

2   RON: — gets one?

3   CAL: No?

4   RON: It is very rare.

5   CAL: How rare?

6   RON: Very.

7   CAL: Then why me?

8   RON: I have no idea.

9   CAL: Why you? To me?

10   RON: Big mystery.

11   CAL: So it's either you, or I'm on my own again.

12   RON: How perceptive of you.

13   CAL: Well, those guys were pretty good writers — Proust, Gide,
14   Wilde …

15   RON: Shakespeare.

16   CAL: No!

17   RON: One of the few who was blessed by two muses. Moi, and a
18   certain dark lady.

19   CAL: Well, he had to experience everything, is the way I see it.

20   RON: Could we get on with it?

21   CAL: *(Disturbed)* What?

22   RON: Your writing!

23   CAL: Right. I'm trying to get started on this novel, a boy's initiation
24   into adulthood, see, and his dad takes him hunting, and they
25   meet this woman deer hunter, and while the dad is off tracking
26   this twelve-point buck to drive him to the stand, up in the stand,
27   the kid, see, and the woman, she's a divorcee, a little older than
28   the kid, and she sees that the kid … What? What is it?

29   RON: What is it? It's like ten million other novels!

30   CAL: There are only twenty-two plots.

31   RON: This one's been used twenty-two million times!

32   CAL: Okay. They don't go deer hunting, they go duck hunting —
33   *(RON grimaces.)* Moose. Caribou. Bear — no, Faulkner did the
34   bear — lion! No, Hemingway. They hunt the yeti! Bigfoot! Only
35   Bigfoot is a female bigfoot. And she shows the kid … Okay, okay.

1	Forget coming of age, forget it. Here's a guy, mid-life crisis, has
2	an affair, wife leaves him — *(RON despairs.)* No, see, it's heavily
3	existential — *(RON is in agony. CAL tries again.)* **Man versus**
4	**nature.** An old man, he's lived through everything, he gets lost
5	in the woods, he's surrounded by wolves, it's a Jack London
6	situation in the style of Garcia Marquez, maybe he's an Indian,
7	a Shoshone, maybe, or he's an Eskimo, on the polar ice cap, and
8	he talks to the beluga whales and the polar bears —
9	RON: And he meets this Eskimo woman —
10	CAL: Yeah.
11	RON: And she pulls him into her igloo, and she's wise in the way
12	of the world, her husband was eaten by a polar bear —
13	CAL: Yeah, yeah!
14	RON: And they kiss, wrapped in her furs —
15	CAL: Yeah, that's it!
16	RON: And just as they ...
17	CAL: Let me get this down.
18	RON: — the ice, the polar ice cap, heaves —
19	CAL: *(Writing)* Heaves ...
20	RON: She turns into a polar bear —
21	CAL: Great! Magic realism, I got you! Oh, man, I'm so glad you
22	came ...
23	RON: ... because of global warming, pollution, hole in the ozone —
24	CAL: The ecology angle! Yes!
25	RON: And she gives birth to his child, who is Jesus —
26	CAL: I don't know ...
27	RON: Buddha —
28	CAL: Buddha!
29	RON: And then Satan —
30	CAL: No, no Satan.
31	RON: That's what Milton said at first.
32	CAL: Okay, Satan.
33	RON: Appears in the shape of a musk ox ...
34	CAL: Musk ox?
35	RON: It's the arctic.

1   CAL: *(Writing)* Musk ox ...

2   RON: — destroys the world —

3   CAL: It's got to have some hope at the end.

4   RON: — to bring forth a new world —

5   CAL: Okay, new world ...

6   RON: Where the polar bears lay down with the musk ox.

7   CAL: What do you mean?

8   RON: What I said.

9   CAL: The polar bears and the musk ox ...

10 RON: Leave it ambiguous.

11 CAL: Good idea. Where's Satan?

12 RON: Dead.

13 CAL: And the guy?

14 RON: What guy?

15 CAL: The hero. My protagonist.

16 RON: I forgot about him.

17 CAL: You can't forget about him, he's the hero.

18 RON: The title is, *No More Heroes.*

19 CAL: I get your point.

20 RON: Do you?

21 CAL: It's post-post-modern. It's the first post-post-modern novel.

22   You did it! *(RON stares at him.)* What? What, Ron?

23 RON: You fool.

24 CAL: What do you mean?

25 RON: It's a dumb story!

26 CAL: No.

27 RON: It's the worst story I've ever told.

28 CAL: It's a great story.

29 RON: You think so?

30 CAL: It's a novel for today. For tomorrow. For the twenty-first century.

31 RON: Here's the thing. I forgot this part.

32 CAL: *(Eagerly)* What?

33 RON: The polar bear and the musk ox are gay. *(CAL stares at him. Beat.)*

34 CAL: I can see that. I can definitely see that.

35   *The End*

Mikey's Chair
by Michael Moore

Michael Moore is a theatre teacher, actor, director, and playwright. He received his M.F.A. in playwriting from Texas Tech University.

Mikey's Chair has had no publications or performances prior to publication in this anthology.

Playwright's Production Suggestions

Notice that there are a number of issues going on between Joey and Louisa besides the matter of Mikey. Both characters are trying to deal with both internal and external struggles. Both are concerned about how they are being perceived by the opposite sex, and both are concerned with the issue of their own self worth. Joey is coming to grips with his feelings of guilt. His laughter is as much a mask as it is a real expression of delight. Acceptance is an especially big issue for both characters. Their sizes have made them targets before and they are both very afraid of being rejected based upon their looks. Their interactions are a series of give and take negotiations with signs often being subtle. Facial expressions and hand gestures can say a lot about these two characters. The eyes are all important in communicating what is going inside both of them.

Address all inquiries concerning performances, readings, or reprinting of this work *or any portion thereof* to Michael Moore, 2234 Patriot Commons Road, Abilene, TX 79601. For details, see "Part II: Securing Rights for Your Production," pages 183 to 192.

1 The action takes place in the present in a middle school in a small
2 Texas town.
3 **CHARACTERS:** JOEY — 13. A heavy Mexican-American boy.
4 LOUISA — 13. A heavy Mexican-American girl.
5 **SETTING:** A table in the corner of a middle school cafeteria. There are
6 two empty chairs at the table besides the one JOEY occupies.
7
8 *(JOEY sits alone at the table with his cafeteria tray and his school*
9 *food. LOUISA approaches carrying a tray of food.)*
10 **LOUISA: Ah … hi. Is this seat taken?**
11 **JOEY:** *(Without looking up)* **Yep.**
12 **LOUISA: How about this one?**
13 **JOEY: It's taken, too.** *(JOEY returns to eating. LOUISA looks at him*
14 *for a moment, then tries to eat her lunch while holding her tray.*
15 *After a moment:)*
16 **LOUISA: You sure these are taken?** *(JOEY hooks each chair with his*
17 *foot and pulls them tight against the table. He points as he speaks.)*
18 **JOEY: This is Freddy's, and this one's Mikey's.** *(Again JOEY*
19 *returns to eating. LOUISA tries to eat, but almost drops her tray.)*
20 **LOUISA:** *(Frustrated)* **Excuse me, but I don't see anybody coming.**
21 **JOEY: They'll be here. How come you're not sitting with the other**
22 **girls?**
23 **LOUISA: Because I don't know any of the other girls. This is my**
24 **first day. Besides, there aren't any chairs over there. Just**
25 **these, and you won't let me sit down.**
26 **JOEY:** *(Motioning off)* **There's Gina. Go ask her.**
27 **LOUISA: I don't know Gina.**
28 **JOEY: Just as well. She wouldn't like you, anyway.**
29 **LOUISA: What — ? Why do you say that?**
30 **JOEY: Cause she's a snob and you're not. At least, you don't act**
31 **like one.**
32 **LOUISA: Ah … thanks. And I'm not. Really.** *(A beat)* **Would you**
33 **really mind if I sat down? Please? This is really hard. I'll get**
34 **up when your friends get here. I promise.** *(JOEY considers her*
35 *for a moment.)*

1   JOEY: Okay. You can sit. *(She starts to sit in one of the chairs.)*
2   LOUISA : Thanks.
3   JOEY: No! That's Mikey's chair. Here. Sit in Freddy's. *(LOUISA*
4   *slides into the other chair.)*
5   LOUISA: You don't think he'll mind?
6   JOEY: Nah. He's not here anyway.
7   LOUISA: But you just said you were saving it for him.
8   JOEY: I know.
9   LOUISA: Why were you saving a seat for somebody who's not
10   even here? Did you just not want me to sit down? *(JOEY just*
11   *shrugs as he returns to his eating. LOUISA watches him for a*
12   *moment and then returns to her meal, too. A beat.)*
13   JOEY: So, you're new, huh?
14   LOUISA: Yeah.
15   JOEY: Where you from?
16   LOUISA: McAllen.
17   JOEY: Yeah? My grand-ma-ma lives in McAllen. On El Dorado
18   Street.
19   LOUISA: I know where that is.
20   JOEY: You do?
21   LOUISA: Yeah. You lived here long?
22   JOEY: Forever, I guess. So, how do you like it here?
23   LOUISA: Fine, I guess. I don't know anybody yet, but all the
24   teachers have been nice.
25   JOEY: Yeah. But stay away from Mrs. Damford, the librarian.
26   She's mean. You got lots of friends in McAllen?
27   LOUISA: Yeah. Some. My best friend, Maria. We promised to
28   e-mail each other every day.
29   JOEY: Have you?
30   LOUISA: No. We haven't got Internet yet. But we will. We tell
31   each other everything.
32   JOEY: That's me and Mikey — he's my brother — except we
33   don't really talk that much. We just laugh.
34   LOUISA : Yeah? What about?
35   JOEY: Everything. We get here at lunch and just start laughing.

1   We laugh and laugh. People think we're loco, but we're just
2   having fun. Sometimes guys get mad at us, and we have to
3   fight 'cause they think we're laughing at them, but we're not.
4   We're just laughing.
5   LOUISA: So, will he get here soon?
6   JOEY: In a little bit.
7   LOUISA: Are you both in the same grade?
8   JOEY: No. Mikey's a freshman — they get out in about five more
9   minutes. He's real good in sports. He plays everything.
10 Football, basketball, baseball, track. The last year, he won
11 three medals running the eight-eighty. He's the fastest boy in
12 school. Me, I'm the slowest.
13 LOUISA: Me, too. The slowest girl, I mean.
14 JOEY: *(Laughing)* You're funny. Mikey, he's good in school, too. He
15 makes the honor roll all the time. Not me. I make C's.
16 LOUISA: Me, too. I can't read. I've got ... dyslexia. I see things
17 funny. It's hard.
18 JOEY: I can read. I just can't do math.
19 LOUISA: Oh, I can. But it's mostly cause I can do it in my head.
20 JOEY: I hate math.
21 LOUISA: Well, sometime maybe, I can help you with your math,
22 and you can help me with my reading — I mean, if you want.
23 JOEY: Yeah. Okay. Maybe. *(A beat)* So, are you good at anything
24 else? Besides math?
25 LOUISA: I can play the piano.
26 JOEY: Yeah? What can you play?
27 LOUISA: Anything. I play by notes and ear. If you can sing it, I can
28 play it.
29 JOEY: No way! Geesh. I wish I could do something like that. People
30 find out you do that, you'll have lots of friends. Misty — I'll
31 show you her — she's okay — she thinks she's Jennifer Lopez
32 or something. All the time singing. She finds out you play like
33 that, she gonna stick to you like Superglue. Hey, next period,
34 you got Ms. Dickey?
35 LOUISA: I think so.

1   JOEY: Me, too. Misty's in there. I'll tell her your mi amiga, to treat
2   you right.
3   LOUISA: Okay. Thanks. That's very nice of you.
4   JOEY: Not a problem. Everybody oughta have friends. *(JOEY eats*
5   *some more.)*
6   LOUISA: So, what are you good at?
7   JOEY: Me? *(Holding up his plate, laughing)* This! Daddy says I'm
8   eatin' us out of house and home. Momma says, when I was born,
9   she had me in the kitchen, and the doctor dropped me into a pie,
10   and I ate it all up! Been eatin' ever since. *(They both laugh.)*
11 LOUISA: You're the one who's funny. You should be a comedian —
12   like Paul Rodriguez.
13 JOEY: *(Mimicking Rodriguez)* Jal-a-pen-os on a stick! *(LOUISA*
14   *laughs at his imitation.)*
15 LOUISA: So, is your brother a big eater, too?
16 JOEY: *(Suddenly losing his humor)* Nah. Mikey don't eat.
17 LOUISA: Excuse me?
18 JOEY: Mikey eats through a tube.
19 LOUISA: "Through a tube"?
20 JOEY: Yeah, my Momma and Daddy, they hook up this bag with
21   liquid food in it, and it runs down this tube through this hole
22   he's got in his side, and it goes into his stomach.
23 LOUISA: Oh.
24 JOEY: Mikey had an accident. Last May. He got hit by a car. Hurt
25   his head real bad.
26 LOUISA: Oh. I'm sorry.
27 JOEY: Yeah, Momma's had to quit her job to stay home with him
28   cause he's just like a little baby now. Can't do nothing. Can't
29   eat, can't talk. Can't even move. I have to help Momma turn
30   him over at least four times a day or he'll just stare up at the
31   ceiling all day. Gettin' real skinny, too. And sometimes, I'm
32   not — I'm not sure he even knows who I am anymore.
33 LOUISA: Oh, I bet he does. You're his brother.
34 JOEY: That's what Father Rios said. *(Brighter)* But, hey! He's
35   getting better. Everyday! I'm helping him. When I get home,

1   I lay down next to him and tell him everything that happened
2   at school. What we ate. What we did. What people said. Shop
3   class. I make him things all the time. His room's full of stuff
4   I've made him. That makes him happy. Better.
5   LOUISA: *(Indicating Mikey's chair)* So, you were just holding it,
6   right? He's not coming back to school.
7   JOEY: *(Adamantly)* He is, too! Don't say that. He is coming back! He's
8   getting better and better everyday. Tomorrow, he's gonna wake
9   up, and look at me and say "Hey, que paso, hermano, get me a
10   taco!" — like he does all the time ... like he does. And then —
11   then — he's gonna get up and come up here and kick
12   everybody's butt in basketball and baseball and — and he's
13   gonna win a bunch more medals. And he's gonna sit in that
14   chair — and we're gonna laugh and laugh — me and him —
15   everyday! And if you don't believe me, you can go sit with those
16   other silly muchachas. They're loco. Not me. *(A long beat)*
17   LOUISA: What about Freddy, tomorrow? Will he be here? *(JOEY*
18   *looks at Freddy's chair for a long moment, then turns back to his*
19   *food.)*
20   JOEY: Nah. You can have his chair. He's gone. He moved to Belton.
21   To live with his dad.
22   LOUISA: So, you were saving both these chairs for nobody?
23   JOEY: No! For somebodys! Freddy's mi mejor amigo! Okay, maybe
24   I oughtn't save his chair anymore, but I gotta save Mikey's. He's
25   my brother! I don't care what Mamma or Daddy or Father Rio
26   or anybody says. He's coming back! I know he is! *(LOUISA looks*
27   *down at her plate. JOEY gazes at LOUISA desperately.)*
28   JOEY: You believe me, right? *(After a moment, she nods "yes.")* No,
29   you don't. Nobody else does. Doctor, nobody. Why should you?
30   LOUISA: *(Gently)* Because you do. *(A beat as JOEY's emotions rush*
31   *over him. He can't look at her.)*
32   JOEY: We were playing catch.
33   LOUISA: What?
34   JOEY: When it happened. The ball. It went ... bad. *(Rising in*
35   *volume)* Man! Right over his head. He was chasing it. If it

1   hadn't — Man — he wouldn't have run out in the street.
2   *(Angry)* I didn't mean to. I really didn't mean to. *(A beat)* But,
3   it's all my fault.
4 LOUISA: No, it's not.
5 JOEY: *(Loudly)* Yes, it is! You weren't there. You don't know. I
6   threw it! I'm the one who threw it!
7 LOUISA: So? *(A beat)* You didn't force him to run out in the street.
8   You didn't tell him not look, did you?
9 JOEY: No, but he always looked. Always! *(A beat)* Why didn't he
10   look this time?
11 LOUISA: Maybe he forgot. Maybe he was thinking about
12   something else. Maybe he didn't want to look. I don't know.
13   He made a mistake. People do that sometimes. We all do.
14 JOEY: But not Mikey! *(JOEY wipes his eyes and his nose with a*
15   *sleeve.)* Geesh. Guess everybody's looking, huh? *(LOUISA*
16   *simply shrugs.)* Nobody likes a cry baby.
17 LOUISA: You're not a cry baby.
18 JOEY: Yes, I am. I cry all the time and I can't stop. They're
19   making me go see that stupid Counselor, Mrs. Arzola.
20   Everybody knows. That's why nobody sits with me.
21 LOUISA: I'm sitting with you.
22 JOEY: *(Motioning off)* Cause you had to. Tomorrow, you'll sit with
23   them.
24 LOUISA: No, I won't. Not if you save me a seat.
25 JOEY: Why you want to sit with me?
26 LOUISA: Because — like you said — everybody needs a friend. *(A*
27   *beat)*
28 JOEY: Yeah? Well, what if you get here first?
29 LOUISA: Then, I'll save you a chair … and one for Mikey. *(A beat)*
30 JOEY: Thanks. That'd be nice. *(A beat)* That'd be real nice. *(They*
31   *exchange shy, brave smiles, and turn back to their trays and pick*
32   *at their food.)*
33
34   ***The End***
35

Revelation

by David MacGregor

David MacGregor teaches film and English classes at Wayne State University in Detroit. In addition to his script work, he has published a variety of short fiction, literary, theatre and film reviews, and encyclopedia articles. He resides in livable Livonia, Michigan, with his wife Louise and their two children, Torin and Kelsey.

Revelation was performed at Heartlande Theatre's One-Act Marathon and at the Livonia-Redford Theatre Guild's One-Actstravaganza.

Address all inquiries concerning performances, readings, or reprinting of this work *or any portion thereof* to David MacGregor, 31100 Westfield, Livonia, MI 48150. For details, see "Part II: Securing Rights for Your Production," pages 183 to 192.

1   The action takes place in a suburban home in the present.

2   ***CHARACTER:*** KIM — in her 20s or 30s.

3   GREG — in his 20s or 30s. Husband of Kim.

4   ***SETTING:*** A typical suburban living room.

5

6   *(KIM applies lipstick as she looks in a mirror. GREG enters,*

7   *adjusting his tie.)*

8   **KIM: Honey, did you pick up that Beaujolais Nouveau like I asked?**

9   **GREG: Yeah, you bet! It's right on the side table there.**

10   **KIM: Are you about ready? Diane said dinner would be around**

11   **seven.**

12   **GREG: Which means eight.** *(KIM moves from the mirror and GREG*

13   *takes her place, checking his tie and hair.)*

14   **KIM: Well, we should try to be there on time, just in case.**

15   **GREG: I'll tell you, I am really looking forward to this evening. I**

16   **feel like I've been running around like an idiot all week. It's**

17   **going to be nice to sit down with you and some friends, have a**

18   **few drinks, a good dinner, and just relax.**

19   **KIM: I think Marty and Colleen are going to be there. They said**

20   **they want to hear about our trip to the Caymans. I guess**

21   **they're thinking about going.**

22   **GREG: Do you want to bring our pictures?**

23   **KIM: Are you kidding? I don't think we want to inflict the sight of**

24   **us in bathing suits on anyone.**

25   **GREG: Good point ... you know, I hate to say it, but I think I'm**

26   **starting to thin out a little up top.**

27   **KIM: Don't be silly.**

28   **GREG: No, I definitely am. I can see ...**

29   **KIM: And even if you are, so what?**

30   **GREG: Hon, could you come here a second?**

31   **KIM: What is it?**

32   **GREG: There's something ... it looks like there's something**

33   **written on my scalp.**

34   **KIM: What?**

35   **GREG: Can you see? I can't make it out.** *(GREG bends over as KIM*

1 *examines him.)*
2 KIM: I can't believe that — oh, there it is! You're right! There is
3 something! Why, they're little numbers! Six-six-six!
4 GREG: Are you sure? You're sure it's not nine-nine-nine?
5 KIM: No, it's six-six-six all right. The numbers have those little
6 lines under them and everything. Oh my gosh, Hon! You know
7 what that means, don't you? You're the Antichrist!
8 GREG: Well, that's just great. That's terrific. This morning my car
9 starts making that weird clunking sound, and now this.
10 KIM: Talk about a surprise.
11 GREG: You're telling me.
12 KIM: Well. Do you think we should pick up a cheesecake from
13 Beaubien's for the party?
14 GREG: What?
15 KIM: I'm not sure what Diane has planned for dessert, but it
16 couldn't hurt to have a little back-up.
17 GREG: Honey, I just found out that I'm the Antichrist! Don't you
18 think that changes our dinner plans slightly?
19 KIM: Oh, I see what you mean. You want to be late.
20 GREG: No, I don't want to be late! I just ... don't you think ... ?
21 KIM: What?
22 GREG: Well, shouldn't I be doing something?
23 KIM: Like what?
24 GREG: I don't know! Something ... evil, I guess. I mean, think about
25 it. When you think Antichrist, do you think dinner party?
26 KIM: Are we including in-laws?
27 GREG: Maybe, maybe this is some kind of mistake. It has to be!
28 We've known each other for what, nearly seven years now?
29 Do I seem like the Antichrist to you?
30 KIM: Well, you can be a little moody.
31 GREG: I am not moody!
32 KIM: Don't you think you're being a little moody right now?
33 GREG: I just found out I'm the Antichrist! I think I'm entitled to
34 be a little bit upset!
35 KIM: You don't have to raise your voice.

1   GREG: I'm sorry. It's just ... this Antichrist business has me a
2   little wound up, that's all.
3   KIM: Now that I think about it, I seem to recall something about
4   the Antichrist from Sunday school.
5   GREG: What?
6   KIM: Well, I could be wrong, but I think you're supposed to arrive
7   on Earth riding a white horse.
8   GREG: I am?
9   KIM: I'm pretty sure.
10   GREG: Well, then it's not me! I've never ridden a horse! I don't
11   even like horses! Boy, that's a relief!
12   KIM: Are you sure you've never ridden a horse?
13   GREG: I'm positive!
14   KIM: Then maybe ... oh! Oh, I just remembered something!
15   GREG: What?
16   KIM: You're not going to like it.
17   GREG: What? Tell me!
18   KIM: What was the very first car that you owned?
19   GREG: Well, you know that, Hon. It was my Mustang.
20   KIM: Your *white* Mustang.
21   GREG: Huh? Oh, come on!
22   KIM: A white horse! It's a prophecy!
23   GREG: No, it isn't!
24   KIM: It is too!
25   GREG: Listen, God is all-knowing, right? Well then, why didn't He
26   just say in the Bible that the Antichrist will arrive on Earth
27   driving a Mustang GT350 with dual exhaust and mag wheels?
28   KIM: It's symbolic! The Bible can't come right out and say
29   something that specific!
30   GREG: Why not?
31   KIM: Because ... well, look at it this way. Don't you think the
32   peasants in the Middle Ages would have been just a little
33   confused by references to mag wheels?
34   GREG: Yeah, I suppose you're right. I just wish I had some kind
35   of direction or guidance, or something.

1   KIM: Oh, I know! Why don't we look it up in the Bible right now?

2   GREG: That's a great idea! Let's do that! *(KIM moves to a bookcase*

3   *and pulls out a Bible.)*

4   KIM: You'd think your mother would have noticed those numbers

5   on your head when you were a baby. Didn't she ever mention

6   it to you? *(KIM sits on the sofa and leafs through the Bible.)*

7   GREG: No! How could she have known? I was born with a full

8   head of hair!

9   KIM: Oh, that's right! I remember seeing those pictures! You were

10   so cute! Such a little mop top!

11   GREG: Yes, yes, I was a little mop top. Now could we please —

12   KIM: Oh, right! Okay, here we are! Oh, you know what? I was

13   wrong. It's God who arrives on the white horse, not you.

14   GREG: Well, I guess that makes sense. He is the good guy, right?

15   But what does it say about me?

16   KIM: I'm looking! All right, apparently, you are referred to as the

17   "Beast." Well, I can attest to that.

18   GREG: What do you mean you can attest to that?

19   KIM: Honey, do you remember our wedding day?

20   GREG: Of course!

21   KIM: Well, do you think most newlyweds consummate their

22   marriage in the alley behind the church?

23   GREG: But, I was just so … happy!

24   KIM: And I love it when you're "happy!" I do! But you have to

25   admit that —

26   GREG: Okay, fine! Fine! You made your point! What else does it say?

27   KIM: Well, after you arrive here, your primary goal is to "deceive

28   those who dwell on Earth."

29   GREG: Now, come on! What is that supposed to mean? Does that

30   sound like me?

31   KIM: You are in advertising, Honey.

32   GREG: Oh, right. Damn!

33   KIM: This is very impressive so far.

34   GREG: But wait! I was thinking of a career change! You know,

35   maybe trying to write for a sit-com, or something. Does it say

1   anything about that?

2   KIM: Mmm ... no.

3   GREG: Okay, okay. So I'm the beast and I deceive people. What

4   next?

5   KIM: Well, it doesn't go into a lot of detail. But apparently at some

6   point you will be opposed by 144,000 people and a lamb.

7   GREG: A lamb?

8   KIM: I'm guessing that's symbolic.

9   GREG: Right.

10   KIM: And then, an angel is going to pour a bowl of wrath on your

11   throne.

12   GREG: Ooh, I've got a throne? Really?

13   KIM: That's what it says.

14   GREG: Huh! Well, that's not too shabby. Do I get to keep it?

15   KIM: I don't think so.

16   GREG: Why not?

17   KIM: Because then you make war on God and His army of

18   believers with your army of deceived people.

19   GREG: And? What happens?

20   KIM: Let's see ... oh, here it is. You lose.

21   GREG: I lose?

22   KIM: Yep. Oh jeez, sorry, Hon.

23   GREG: Ah, that's okay. I guess somebody's got to lose, right? I

24   kind of expected it, to tell you the truth. So what happens

25   after that? I learn my lesson and get redeemed or something?

26   KIM: No. Actually, you're thrown alive into the lake of fire that

27   burns with brimstone.

28   GREG: You're kidding.

29   KIM: Nope.

30   GREG: I'm not redeemed?

31   KIM: Not according to this.

32   GREG: There's no ... happy ending?

33   KIM: Not for you. Although everyone else seems to make out

34   pretty good.

35   GREG: Well, that doesn't sound very merciful.

1   KIM: Actually, if you read through the Bible, God has His merciful
2   days and His not so merciful days.
3   GREG: Well, in that case, I just don't get it. I don't get the whole
4   deal.
5   KIM: What?
6   GREG: Think about it, Honey! Think about what you just told me.
7   If I'm the Antichrist, what's my motivation?
8   KIM: To do what?
9   GREG: To do anything! If I know I'm going to lose, and I know
10   I'm going to get thrown into a lake of brimstone, what's my
11   motivation?
12   KIM: Um ... oh! You're evil incarnate!
13   GREG: Okay, so I'm evil incarnate! But I'm literate, right? I can
14   read a book! If I want to, after a hard day deceiving people, I
15   can sit down and look through the Bible, can't I?
16   KIM: I'm not sure I see what you're getting at.
17   GREG: What I'm getting at is this — why should I play along? I know
18   how the story ends, and between you and me, I don't particularly
19   like that ending! Oh, it's all a bed of roses for everyone else, but
20   it's fire and brimstone for me! You see what I mean?
21   KIM: You know, you might have a point there.
22   GREG: What kind of idiot do they think I am?
23   KIM: Honey, the Bible never said you were an idiot.
24   GREG: You're damned right I'm not an idiot! Well, I'll tell you
25   what I'm going to do. I'm going to fix them. I'm going to fix
26   them good.
27   KIM: Fix who?
28   GREG: Everybody! God, angels, even that lamb if he's mixed up in
29   this.
30   KIM: What are you going to do?
31   GREG: Picture it, Honey! Right now, they're up there ... up there
32   waiting. They've got the white horse, the bowls of wrath, the
33   whole kit and caboodle all ready to go. And what are they
34   waiting for? Me. They are waiting for me to make my move.
35   KIM: That's what it seems like, all right.

1   GREG: Well now, suppose I don't make that move? Suppose I
2   don't assemble an army of deceived people. Suppose ...
3   suppose I just go out to a dinner party with my brilliant and
4   breathtakingly beautiful wife?
5   KIM: Oh! Oh, that is evil.
6   GREG: Isn't it? They can just cool their heels for awhile! I'm the
7   guy who decides when there's going to be an Apocalypse, and
8   you know what I'm deciding? There ain't going to be one! Not
9   as long as I'm Antichrist! Shall we? *(GREG offers KIM his arm*
10   *and they walk to the door.)*
11   KIM: Do you think we should tell anyone about this?
12   GREG: Nah. It might put kind of a damper on the dinner
13   conversation.
14   KIM: Well, if you don't talk about something, you know that we're
15   going to have to listen to Jerry's golf stories all night.
16   GREG: I'll tell you what, if he gets on your nerves, just let me
17   know and I'll turn him into a pillar of salt.
18   KIM: Hon, I think it's God that turns people into pillars of salt.
19   GREG: Oh yeah? Well, I'll turn him into a pillar of something.
20   KIM: You'd do that for me?
21   GREG: Of course. Anything for you, babe. *(They kiss, and GREG*
22   *takes the opportunity to pinch KIM'S behind, making her squeal*
23   *a little.)*
24   KIM: You are a beast!
25   GREG: Hey, just wait until you see me after a couple of glasses of
26   Beaujolais. Sodom and Gomorrah, here we come!
27   KIM: No, we don't.
28   GREG: Say, what actually happened in Gomorrah, anyway? *(KIM*
29   *rearranges GREG'S hair slightly.)*
30   KIM: Honey, there are some things you just shouldn't think about.
31   GREG: Ain't that the truth? *(They both exit on this last line.)*
32
33   ***The End***
34
35

Hard to Be Happy
by Julianne Homokay

Julianne Homokay, a 2001 graduate of the Playwriting Program at the University of Nevada Las Vegas, has had over thirty productions and staged readings. Her awards include the 1997 Rod Parker Playwriting Fellowship, semi-finalist in the Chesterfield Film Workshop Competition and Jackpot and Professional Grants from the Nevada Arts Council.

Hard to be Happy was first presented in UNLV's festival of ten-minute plays, Choice Cuts, in 2000 and was included in UNLV Department of Theatre's Velvet Vipers presented at the Edinburgh Festival Fringe in August the same year. The play was further developed in the New Play Development Workshop of the Playwright's Program of the Association for Theatre in Higher Education in Chicago in 2001.

Address all inquiries concerning performances, readings, or reprinting of this work *or any portion thereof* to Julianne Homokay, c/o The Fulton Opera House, PO Box 1865, Lancaster, PA 17608. For details, see "Part II: Securing Rights for Your Production," pages 183 to 192.

1   The action takes place in PATRICK's apartment, two days before

2   LANI's wedding.

3   ***CHARACTERS:*** PATRICK — 22.

4   LANI — 34.

5   ***SETTING:*** Apartment furnishings.

6

7   *(LANI and PATRICK sit opposite each other, cross-legged on the*

8   *floor.)*

9   **PATRICK: You're amazing.**

10   **LANI: You're stupendous.**

11   **PATRICK: You're inspiring.**

12   **LANI: You're admirable.**

13   **PATRICK: You're the best wifey in the world.**

14   **LANI: To the best hubby in the universe.**

15   **PATRICK: I love you.**

16   **LANI: I love you more.**

17   **PATRICK: I love you up.**

18   **LANI: I love you down.**

19   **PATRICK: I love you all around.**

20   **LANI: What shall we do tonight?**

21   **PATRICK: Contemplate our perfect love.**

22   **LANI: And take in a movie?**

23   **PATRICK: Naturally.**

24   **LANI: Following dinner?**

25   **PATRICK: One would assume.**

26   **LANI: Where shall we dine?**

27   **PATRICK: Our Italian restaurant.**

28   **LANI: Bottle o' red?**

29   **PATRICK: Bottle o' white?**

30   **LANI/PATRICK: It all depends upon your appetite.**

31   *(Singing)* **Meet you any time you want**

32   **In our Italian restaurant.**

33   **LANI:** *(Laughing)* **That was a good one. We've never gone there**

34   **before.**

35   **PATRICK: Let's play some more.**

1   LANI: No, let's get dinner. Billy Joel's got me in the mood for some
2   Eggplant Parmesan and Valpolicella.
3   PATRICK: I didn't even drink wine before I met you, you owe me.
4   Let's go. You're amazing.
5   LANI: Patrick, c'mon.
6   PATRICK: This might be our last chance to play.
7   LANI: How do you figure that?
8   PATRICK: Richard's gonna let his wife go running around with a
9   twenty-two-year-old convicted felon?
10   LANI: My friends will still be my friends after I'm married. Even
11   if they are gorgeous blond bad boys. Richard'll get over it.
12   PATRICK: What if he doesn't?
13   LANI: Then I'll divorce him and come live with you. What are you
14   hungry for?
15   PATRICK: I didn't let you go, you know. Just for the record.
16   LANI: I know. I'm totally psyched we're still friends.
17   PATRICK: No. I mean, last summer. I didn't answer your pages
18   because I was afraid of what you'd say.
19   LANI: It's OK, you don't have to explain.
20   PATRICK: I know you thought I moved on. I know why you
21   thought I moved on 'cause Trini told me what you said in the
22   bar, but I never cared about the age difference. I didn't call
23   because I was afraid of what you'd say.
24   LANI: Maybe we shouldn't talk about this. Let's play. You're
25   amazing.
26   PATRICK: I just wanted you to know. For the record.
27   LANI: Now I know. C'mon, go, it's your turn.
28   PATRICK: Now you know. *(Long pause)* What do we do?
29   LANI: We get dinner.
30   PATRICK: What shall we eat?
31   LANI: Northern Italian.
32   PATRICK: French Continental.
33   LANI: Spanish Continental.
34   PATRICK: Portuguese Nouveau.
35   LANI: California Nouveau.

1   PATRICK: Tex-Mex.
2   LANI: Mex-mex.
3   PATRICK: Continental Mex-Nouveau.
4   LANI: I like bread and butter.
5   PATRICK: She likes toast and jam.
6   LANI/PATRICK: *(Singing)* I found my baby eatin' with another man.
7   LANI: Wait a minute, what do you mean what do we do?
8   PATRICK: You settled it. We're going to dinner. Except now I'm
9   more in the mood for IHOP.
10   LANI: Why are you assuming there's something to be done?
11   PATRICK: Are we still playing?
12   LANI: Like I'm going to walk out on my fiancé two days before the
13   wedding.
14   PATRICK: To my knowledge, I didn't ask you to walk out on your
15   fiancé two days before the wedding.
16   LANI: He's perfect. He's my age, he's got a marketing job, my
17   family loves him, he's the nicest person on the face of the earth.
18   PATRICK: Well, there you go.
19   LANI: So what would there be to do? Everything's ordered.
20   Everyone's in town.
21   PATRICK: Who are you trying to convince?
22   LANI: I care about him very, very much.
23   PATRICK: So you're doing the right thing.
24   LANI: I'm doing the right thing.
25   PATRICK: Can we play? *(PATRICK holds a chair for LANI.)* You
26   are amazing, madam.
27   LANI: Why thank you, sir.
28   PATRICK: You look exquisite.
29   LANI: You look divine.
30   PATRICK: Your hair is lustrous.
31   LANI: Your suit is fashionable.
32   PATRICK: Your earrings are unique.
33   LANI: Your cologne is exciting.
34   PATRICK: You are absolutely the most beautiful thing I have ever
35   seen in my whole stupid life.

1   LANI: You, uh … um …
2   PATRICK: I don't want to play at this anymore. I don't want the
3   game.
4   LANI: Maybe I should go.
5   PATRICK: Why does everyone always say that? What does that
6   mean?
7   LANI: It means exactly what it says.
8   PATRICK: What's wrong, Lani? Why do you want to leave?
9   Afraid you might have to admit you still love me?
10 LANI: That's not the issue.
11 PATRICK: So you do still love me.
12 LANI: You're over the line.
13 PATRICK: Why? What line? Who drew that line? I don't think
14   you're doing the right thing. You're doing the easy thing. The
15   hard thing would be to go against your family and your
16   friends and your rules and all that stupid perfection and call
17   it off and be with the one everyone tells you is the wrong
18   choice. It's easy to be safe. It's hard to be happy.
19 LANI: You're assuming an awful lot, baby boy.
20 PATRICK: I miss you calling me that.
21 LANI: This can't — you've got to stop.
22 PATRICK: All right. You look me in the eye, girl. Tell me you don't
23   love me anymore. Then I'll stop. *(A Pinteresque pause)*
24 LANI: You should have had faith in me. Last summer. I wouldn't
25   have cared what trouble you were in. Why didn't you have
26   faith in me? *(Another pause. PATRICK sits back down.)*
27 PATRICK: The dinner was delicious. *(LANI sits back down.)*
28 LANI: Scrumptious.
29 PATRICK: Delectable.
30 LANI: Savory.
31 PATRICK: The waiter deserves a sizeable tip.
32 LANI: The bus boy deserves a promotion.
33 PATRICK: The chef deserves an award.
34 LANI: The maitre d' deserves his own restaurant.
35 PATRICK: It was the best dinner of my life. *(Pause)* Your turn.

1   **LANI: It was the best time of my life, Patrick. You really were.** *(He*
2   *holds her hand. She stands up. He stands up.)*
3   **PATRICK: Stay.**
4   **LANI: I want to.** *(She leaves. He stays. Lights down.)*
5
6   ***The End***
7
8
9
10
11
12
13
14
15
16
17
18
19
20
21
22
23
24
25
26
27
28
29
30
31
32
33
34
35

Philosophical Inquiry at the Edge of a Cliff
by Matthew Calhoun

Matthew Calhoun's produced plays include, *Living in Sin, Kitchen Therapy,* and *Tortured People* (Chicago) and *Help! Sex-Tet, Career Counseling, Attractions, Conditions, Skits-Ophrenia, Restraint,* and *Worm Day* (New York). His short comedies, *Money, Audition!* and *The Breakfast Special,* appear in anthologies. *Audition!* has twice been presented during the Miss America Pageant.

Philosophical Inquiry at the Edge of a Cliff was developed in readings at the New Directions Theatre in New York City and produced at The Neighborhood Playhouse in New York in April of 1999.

Address all inquiries concerning performances, readings, or reprinting of this work *or any portion thereof* to Matthew Calhoun, 23-51 19th Street, Astoria, NY 11105. For details, see "Part II: Securing Rights for Your Production," pages 183 to 192.

1   The action takes place on the edge of a cliff just as a woman is
2   about to jump off.
3   **CHARACTERS:** NANCY — a woman on the edge of suicide.
4   The MAN — a person who once felt he had no value.
5   **SETTING:** The edge of a cliff. A stage would be nice.
6
7   *(NANCY is staring off the edge of the cliff. A MAN wearing a*
8   *knapsack comes up behind her.)*
9   **MAN: Are you going to jump?**
10   **NANCY: How did you know?**
11   **MAN: I didn't know.**
12   **NANCY: How did you know to ask?**
13   **MAN: I was just wondering.**
14   **NANCY: Wondering if I was going to jump off a cliff?**
15   **MAN: I was just wondering why.**
16   **NANCY: Why am I going to jump off this cliff? Well, jumping off**
17   **a chair wouldn't be nearly as effective, would it?**
18   **MAN:** *(Peering over the cliff)* **Effective in accomplishing what?**
19   **NANCY: Obliterating myself.**
20   **MAN: A worthy goal, certainly, but I don't see how jumping off the**
21   **cliff will accomplish that.**
22   **NANCY: It'll smash me to pieces.**
23   **MAN: It'll smash your body to pieces. It won't smash you to pieces.**
24   **NANCY: If you believe in a soul.**
25   **MAN: Do you?**
26   **NANCY: I think it's a romantic notion, but that's all it is. A**
27   **comforting wish.**
28   **MAN: A wish, eh?**
29   **NANCY: A wish.**
30   **MAN: You believe the soul is a wish. Why?**
31   **NANCY: You can't touch it, see it, taste it, smell it, hear it.**
32   **MAN: So it's a wish.**
33   **NANCY: Yes.**
34   **MAN: You believe that there's such things as wishes?**
35   **NANCY: What do you mean?**

1   MAN: Just what I said. Do you believe that there's such things as
2   wishes?
3   NANCY: I don't know.
4   MAN: Then how do you know that a soul is a wish, if you don't
5   even know if wishes exist?
6   NANCY: I don't know.
7   MAN: When in doubt, do nothing, they say.
8   NANCY: Screw you.
9   MAN: Would you like an orange? *(He takes his knapsack off, takes*
10   *out an orange, sets the knapsack on the ground.)*
11 NANCY: I'm about to jump.
12 MAN: No you're not.
13 NANCY: Why not?
14 MAN: Because before you thought you knew that you had no soul,
15   but now, upon the merest passing examination, you're not so
16   sure.
17 NANCY: I'm sure.
18 MAN: Are you certain you're sure?
19 NANCY: Yes.
20 MAN: Do you believe in certainty?
21 NANCY: Yes.
22 MAN: Can you touch it, taste it, see it, smell it, hear it? *(She shakes*
23   *her head no.)* Then it can't be real, can it?
24 NANCY: Screw you.
25 MAN: It's an organic orange. *(He holds it up to her nose.)*
26 NANCY: Yes, I'm really worried about the long-term effects of
27   pesticides right before I jump off a cliff.
28 MAN: I don't think you're ready to jump yet.
29 NANCY: I was.
30 MAN: You're beginning to realize that it's not so easy to dispose of
31   your soul. Not that one shouldn't try to — I've done it myself —
32   but the mere act of jumping off a cliff proves to be most feeble.
33 NANCY: Then it suits me.
34 MAN: What if you change your mind on the way down?
35 NANCY: Then it'll be too late.

1   MAN: What if you step off and then you see it?

2   NANCY: See what?

3   MAN: See that it's not going to do any good. See that perhaps

4   eating an orange would have been preferable.

5   NANCY: I don't like oranges.

6   MAN: You'll like this one.

7   NANCY: How do you know?

8   MAN: Because I'll show you how to eat it.

9   NANCY: How?

10 MAN: Like this. *(He carefully peels it; then, with great gusto, he*

11   *smashes it on the ground, jumps on it, begins to dance on it,*

12   *giving a couple of joyous whoops.)* Now *that's* the way to eat an

13   orange.

14 NANCY: *(Dryly)* And luckily, it was organic.

15 MAN: It wouldn't have been nearly as satisfying if it wasn't organic.

16 NANCY: What you've done to that orange, I'm going to do to me.

17 MAN: You're already like this orange. *(Using his foot, he shovels the*

18   *pieces off the cliff.)* Do you think that when they land they're

19   going to be significantly different than they are now?

20 NANCY: So if it doesn't make anything different, why not just

21   do it?

22 MAN: Hm. *(Pause)* You've got me on that one.

23 NANCY: I do?

24 MAN: You may have stumped me. *(Pause. Some enjoyment comes*

25   *over her features.)* If you don't want to eat an orange, you may

26   as well throw it over a cliff. And if there's nothing in life you

27   want, you might as well throw your*self* over a cliff.

28 NANCY: Right.

29 MAN: And there's nothing you want.

30 NANCY: Nothing.

31 MAN: You don't want an orange.

32 NANCY: No.

33 MAN: Lifesaver? *(He takes out a pack from his pocket.)*

34 NANCY: No. I like Lifesavers even less than oranges.

35 MAN: How about an orange Lifesaver?

1　NANCY:　I don't like Lifesavers!
2　MAN:　Very good. A orange that's been stamped on doesn't want
3　　　　anything, does it?
4　NANCY:　No.
5　MAN:　And you want nothing.
6　NANCY:　Nothing.
7　MAN:　Of course, a stamped on orange can't want to throw itself
8　　　　over a cliff. And if you're no different from that orange ... *(He*
9　　　　*puts on knapsack, exits Stage Right.)*
10　NANCY:　*(To herself)* Jerk. Stupid jerk. *(She steels herself to jump.)*
11　　　　One, two ... *(Pause)* I was all ready to do it: three! *(She doesn't*
12　　　　*jump.)* Come on, Nancy. How hard can this be? You can jump.
13　　　　*(She gives a little jump in the air. Gesturing over the cliff.)* You
14　　　　have a cliff. *(Pause)* Jump! *(Pause)* One, two ... three! *(Pause)*
15　　　　Come on, legs, jump! *(Pause)* OK, do it. Don't count. Do it.
16　　　　*(Pause. She sits, dangling her feet off the cliff, her hands in*
17　　　　*position to push off.)* Push! *(She doesn't. She gets up, backs up.*
18　　　　*Runs to the edge of the cliff. Stops.)* Wimp. *(She backs up. Turns.*
19　　　　*Walks backwards towards the cliff. Stops, just in time,*
20　　　　*automatically.)* Step! *(She doesn't. She turns, looks over cliff, then*
21　　　　*turns and yells after the man:)* You screwed it up for me! *(Turns*
22　　　　*face forward, disgustedly.)* Stupid jerk. *(He enters from the Stage*
23　　　　*Left wings. She turns, quite startled.)* How'd you get there?
24　MAN:　Huh?
25　NANCY:　*(Pointing Stage Right)* I saw you go off in that direction.
26　MAN:　Me?
27　NANCY:　Yes. You walked off over there and kept walking.
28　MAN:　Over there?
29　NANCY:　Yes! You disappeared behind that clump of trees just as I
30　　　　yelled at you. There's no physical way you could have come
31　　　　from that direction. *(Indicating Stage Left)*
32　MAN:　Ah, well. Maybe I'll try the other way, then. *(He exits Stage*
33　　　　*Left.)*
34　NANCY:　*(Watching him)* You walked away, just like that. I wasn't
35　　　　watching the whole time, but I kind of saw you out of the

1   corner of my eyes. I shut my eyes at one point, but then I
2   turned and yelled at you. I saw your knapsack quite clearly,
3   and then you disappeared behind some trees. Just like now.
4   They blocked my view, but only for a second, and then ... *(He*
5   *enters from stage right. She whirls, startled.)* **Would you stop**
6   **doing that!!!** *(He peers at her as if he has never seen her before.)*
7   **I'm about to jump off this cliff!**
8   MAN: I did that once.
9   NANCY: Huh?
10   MAN: Problems over a woman, you know. But my last thought
11   before jumping wasn't about her. It was about myself. I
12   thought, "I have no value," and I jumped.
13   NANCY: Huh?
14   MAN: But on the way down, a series of startling thoughts went
15   rapidly through my head, refuting me entirely, and I thought,
16   "Yikes, I've made a mistake." But it was rather late to turn
17   back, so I kept falling. I believe I yelled: "You damn fool!"
18   but that may have been my imagination.
19   NANCY: You're a ghost?
20   MAN: I was a ghost when I was alive. Now, I'm simply haunted.
21   NANCY: By what?
22   MAN: This knapsack. Would you help me off with it? *(He turns*
23   *with his back to her.)*
24   NANCY: I don't know. You're creepy.
25   MAN: Yes, there is something creepy about suicide.
26   NANCY: You're not real.
27   MAN: I'm perfectly real. *(She touches him quickly.)*
28   NANCY: You're real.
29   MAN: As real as life and death. *(She lifts off the knapsack. He*
30   *stretches.)* Ahhhh! Thank you most earnestly. *(She takes an*
31   *orange out of the knapsack.)* That knapsack has held many
32   valuable items, but never a parachute. When it comes to
33   jumping off cliffs, it's utterly worthless. I've been carrying
34   around that feeling of worthlessness for so long ... it feels
35   good to get it off my back.

1   NANCY: So what happened when you jumped off the cliff?

2   MAN: Must we go through that?

3   NANCY: Please?

4   MAN: When I stepped off the cliff, I immediately thought, "Oh no,

5   the oranges may get smashed. They're organic. Some farmer

6   worked hard to grow these oranges. Now they're going to get

7   smashed up in a suicide's foolish jump." That unnerved me —

8   that phrase, "foolish jump." I had to ask myself, "Why

9   foolish?" Because of the oranges, I thought, trying to comfort

10   myself. That's the only thing foolish about this jump. I have no

11   value — so it wasn't foolish of *me* to jump, but these lovely

12   organic oranges that represent a better way of life, full of health

13   and respect — I shouldn't have dragged them along with me.

14   NANCY: You thought all this?

15   MAN: Thought travels very fast when it's falling off a cliff.

16   NANCY: You seem like a nice person.

17   MAN: I was very nice.

18   NANCY: To think about the oranges so much.

19   MAN: Of course I didn't think much of myself.

20   NANCY: No.

21   MAN: But I was soon forced to. You see, it's quite an unsettling

22   thing to be falling towards certain death realizing that you

23   value two organic oranges. You see the point, of course.

24   NANCY: No.

25   MAN: The point is that you believe that you have no value, or you

26   wouldn't be jumping in the first place.

27   NANCY: Me?

28   MAN: Yes. You believe that you have no value, correct?

29   NANCY: No, I don't believe I do.

30   MAN: Less than that orange you're holding.

31   NANCY: Yes.

32   MAN: None at all.

33   NANCY: None.

34   MAN: You have no value as anything?

35   NANCY: No value as anything.

1   MAN: How 'bout as a judge?

2   NANCY: No.

3   MAN: So you wouldn't be fit to judge the worth of that orange.

4   NANCY: No.

5   MAN: Or the tree it grew on?

6   NANCY: No.

7   MAN: Or the hand that holds it? *(Pause)*

8   NANCY: No.

9   MAN: What about yourself? Would you have any value as a judge

10   of yourself? *(Pause)*

11   NANCY: None.

12   MAN: That's the point, of course, because if you wouldn't, then who

13   are you to say whether you should live or die? Who are you to

14   stand in judgment of your life? Why should you trust your

15   opinion on the matter? *(Pause)* It was that conversation that

16   went through my head. Probably it means little to you, now, but

17   you'll see it all when you jump. *(Taking the knapsack from her;*

18   *leaving her with the orange)* I leave you with this: it is good to

19   keep in mind the difference between worthless and priceless.

20   *(He gives her a little bow of respect; exits. She watches him go,*

21   *whirls around to see if he will come back from the other side. He*

22   *doesn't. She looks at the orange; a devilish look of satisfaction,*

23   *maybe some pleasure, comes over her face. She hurls the orange to*

24   *the ground, smashing it. She steps on it. She stamps on it, then*

25   *shovels it over the cliff with the side of her foot. Turns, exits.)*

26

27   ***The End***

28

29

30

31

32

33

34

35

Scripts for Three Actors

Interruptions
by Robert Patrick

Robert Patrick was born in Kilgore, Texas, in 1937. He is the author of sixty published plays including *Kennedy's Children* and is the winner of the International Thespian Society's 1980 Founders Award for Services to Theatre and Youth.

Interruptions premiered at Merced Community College as a half-time entertainment at a basketball game in 1992.

Address all inquiries concerning performances, readings, or reprinting of this work *or any portion thereof* to Robert Patrick, 1837 N. Alexandria Avenue #211, Los Angeles, CA 90027. For details, see "Part II: Securing Rights for Your Production," pages 183 to 192.

1   The action takes place in the present outside a church in a
2   southern town.
3   **CHARACTERS:** BRENDA — a school girl, dressed in black.
4   ELSIE — a school girl.
5   MARGE — a school girl.
6   **SETTING:** A bare stage.
7
8   *(BRENDA is On-stage alone.)*
9   **ELSIE:** *(Off-stage)* **Brenda!**
10 **MARGE:** *(Off-stage)* **Brenda!**
11 **ELSIE:** *(Off-stage)* *I'll* **yell for her!** *(She and MARGE enter. They are in*
12 *appropriate funeral wear, preferably not black.)* **Brenda! Honey!**
13 **BRENDA:** *(Warily)* **Hello, Marge.**
14 **MARGE: Brenda, Elsie and I know …**
15 **BRENDA:** *(Sharply)* **You know what?**
16 **ELSIE: … We know you have to get out to the cemetery …**
17 **MARGE: … Out to the cemetery for the service …**
18 **ELSIE: … For the service and to help protect your mama …**
19 **BRENDA: What?**
20 **ELSIE: … Support your mama, of course …**
21 **MARGE: … But while she's still thankin' all the people at the**
22 **church door …**
23 **ELSIE: … With that remarkable aplomb of hers …**
24 **MARGE: … We had to tell you, of course, we know …**
25 **BRENDA:** *(Sharply)* **You know *what*?**
26 **MARGE: … Brenda, how you *feel* …**
27 **ELSIE: … How you *must* feel …**
28 **MARGE: … How you *all* must feel …**
29 **ELSIE: … But we had to stop you because we don't know …**
30 **BRENDA: Don't know what?**
31 **ELSIE: … Don't know your mama well enough …**
32 **MARGE: … Well enough to talk about a thing …**
33 **ELSIE: … A thing like that …**
34 **MARGE: … So we just had to stop you and ask you …**
35 **ELSIE: … *Tell* you …**

1   MARGE: ... And *tell* you how sorry we are about your papa ...
2   ELSIE: ... Who seemed so nice ...
3   MARGE: ... And who all the town knows was the apple of your
4   eye ...
5   ELSIE: ... And you of his, of course ...
6   MARGE: ... About your papa passin' so suddenly ...
7   ELSIE: ... So suddenly, it just took us all by surprise ...
8   MARGE: ... And surely must have taken you ...
9   ELSIE: ... Who loved him so special much ...
10 MARGE: ... By surprise that a strong, fine, healthy man ...
11 ELSIE: ... A strong, fine healthy man like that could pass ...
12 MARGE: ... Could pass so suddenly without any warnin' ...
13 ELSIE: ... Without any warnin', just fine one day, and then ...
14 MARGE: ... And then just like a light be lost forever ...
15 ELSIE: ... Be lost forever. My mama was wonderin' aloud ...
16 MARGE: ... Wonderin' aloud, mine, too, how could the Lord ...
17 ELSIE: ... *Exactly* how could the Lord take one so fine and
18   strong ...
19 MARGE: ... So fine and strong so that just days after he fell ill ...
20 ELSIE: ... Fell ill with no warnin' or even a diagnosis ...
21 MARGE: ... A public diagnosis of why he did die ...
22 ELSIE: ... Did die so suddenly ...
23 MARGE: ... Suddenly and unexpectedly ...
24 ELSIE: ... And hadn't even been seein' a doctor ...
25 MARGE: ... At least not locally ...
26 ELSIE: ... It seems such a mystery ...
27 MARGE: ... Does seem a mystery ...
28 ELSIE: ... Isn't it ... ?
29 MARGE: ... Doesn't it ... ?
30 ELSIE: ... Was it ... ?
31 MARGE: ... *Was* it ... ?
32 ELSIE: ... *Is* it ... ?
33 BRENDA: *(Shocked, begging for relief)* **Please!**
34 ELSIE: ... Not that we'd interrupt ...
35 MARGE: ... Interrupt your poor family ...

1   ELSIE: ... Your poor family ...

2   MARGE: ... That must be so upset ...

3   ELSIE: ... Upset to be interrupted ...

4   MARGE: ... To be interrupted in your life ...

5   ELSIE: ... To lose a papa and a husband ...

6   MARGE: ... And to lose him that way ... !

7   BRENDA: *What* way?

8   MARGE: What?

9   BRENDA: What way?

10 MARGE: *(To ELSIE)* What way?

11 ELSIE: *(To MARGE)* Suddenly and unexpectedly.

12 MARGE: Right! Without a diagnosis.

13 ELSIE: A public diagnosis.

14 MARGE: Well, *is* it?

15 BRENDA: Is it *what*?

16 ELSIE: She means "was it?"

17 BRENDA: Was it what?

18 ELSIE: She means was it upsettin', was it hard?

19 MARGE: That's all I mean.

20 BRENDA: I don't know what y'all are talkin' about. Oh, unless

21   you could be referrin' to that horrible rumor ...

22 MARGE: Yes?

23 ELSIE: Not that we are.

24 MARGE: Not that we are reactin' to a horrible rumor.

25 ELSIE: If there had been any.

26 MARGE: We don't know what you're talkin' about.

27 ELSIE: But don't let us interrupt you.

28 BRENDA: There have been rumors, we know it ...

29 MARGE: ... Well, you would ...

30 ELSIE: ... We haven't heard it ...

31 MARGE: ...Them ...

32 ELSIE: ... Anything.

33 BRENDA: ... Because Papa traveled ...

34 ELSIE: *(To MARGE)* You see, it *was* a doctor out of town!

35 BRENDA: ... and because he passed so suddenly ...

1 MARGE: … My folks said they'd never heard …
2 ELSIE: … Such a thing. *(To BRENDA)* Go on.
3 MARGE: *(Thinking she is being told, "Go on")* That's all.
4 ELSIE: Not *you*!
5 BRENDA: … That he had somethin' terrible …
6 MARGE: I can't think what!
7 BRENDA: … Besides just heart failure …
8 MARGE: My daddy says *everyone* dies of heart failure.
9 BRENDA: … but he had never had a blood transfusion …
10 MARGE: We keep our own in the blood bank now!
11 ELSIE: Hush *up*!
12 BRENDA: … So there is no ground to the rumors …
13 MARGE: … We know there wasn't …
14 ELSIE: … We never heard them …
15 BRENDA: … And you will observe from the speed of his demise …
16 MARGE: … Which caused all the talk …
17 ELSIE: … Of which there was none …
18 BRENDA: … That he cannot have had anything so shockin',
19   because obviously he was not treated for it …
20 ELSIE: Well, we know there was nothin' in it …
21 MARGE: … because y'all certainly loved him and would have
22   treated him …
23 BRENDA: … Yes …
24 MARGE: … And so that proves right there there's nothin' to it.
25 ELSIE: *(Looking off, to BRENDA)* Your mama is beckonin' you.
26 MARGE: … So if there was any talk …
27 ELSIE: … Which there wasn't …
28 MARGE: … As far as we know …
29 ELSIE: … Because we wouldn't …
30 MARGE: … And which we never believed …
31 ELSIE: … if we had heard any …
32 MARGE: … Which we would have stopped if we'd heard …
33 ELSIE: … Except we wouldn't have listened …
34 MARGE: … And we won't say a word …
35 ELSIE: … Which we haven't got to say …

1   MARGE: ... because if there had been any signs of it ...

2   ELSIE: ... your mama ...

3   MARGE: ... Who surely must have loved your papa ...

4   ELSIE: ... Oh, surely, why wouldn't she ... ?

5   MARGE: ... Would certainly have insisted on treatment for it ...

6   ELSIE: ... If there was anything ...

7   MARGE: ... To have been treated ...

8   ELSIE: We have to go.

9   MARGE: I was gonna say that.

10   ELSIE: Good bye, Brenda.

11   MARGE: Good bye, Brenda.

12   ELSIE: Our best to your mama.

13   MARGE: Mine too. I mean that.

14   ELSIE: I said "ours." Come on.

15   MARGE: Yes.

16   ELSIE: *(To BRENDA)* Sorry to interrupt.

17   MARGE: ... Yes, sorry to interrupt ...

18   ELSIE: *(To MARGE)* Then don't interrupt *me*, then.

19   MARGE: *(To ELSIE)* I'm sorry. *(To BRENDA)* I'm sorry. *(Runs off,*

20   *crying.)* I'm sorry.

21   ELSIE: ... Sorry, as I was sayin' before I was so rudely

22   interrupted, to interrupt your sorrow at this ... interruption

23   ... of y'all's lives. *(She exits. BRENDA is left alone. After a*

24   *moment she continues.)*

25   BRENDA: ... And of course, they do say none of those treatments

26   work ... *(She interrupts herself and calls to someone Off-stage.)*

27   Yes, Mama, I'm comin'. I know you need me. *(To herself,*

28   *again, after a pause)* ... Anyway. *(She exits.)*

29

30   ***The End***

31

32

33

34

35

Clubs
by Conrad Bishop and Elizabeth Fuller

Conrad Bishop and Elizabeth Fuller are directors of The Independent Eye, a national touring ensemble. Their sixty plus plays have been staged by the Eye and by Actors Theatre of Louisville, Circle Rep, Mark Taper Forum, and many others. They are recipients of fellowships from the National Endowment for the Arts and produce the NPR program "Hitchhiking Off the Map" which can be accessed at www.independenteye.org

Clubs was produced by The Independent Eye in the 1979 revue, *Who's There*, created with students at University of Delaware. It was revised for a 1994 production of *Dividing Lines* at University of the Arts in Philadelphia. It is published in *Seismic Stages: Five Plays for Teens* (Word Workers Press).

Address all inquiries concerning performances, readings, or reprinting of this work *or any portion thereof* to Conrad Bishop, 502 Pleasant Hill Road, Sebastopol, CA 95472. For details, see "Part II: Securing Rights for Your Production," pages 183 to 192.

1   The action takes place at three different times and places in the
2   characters' lives: during their childhood in a sandbox, in their
3   high school years in a classroom, and in their 30s in a Manhattan
4   coffee shop.
5   ***CHARACTERS:*** BEV, DAN, and HONEY—childhood friends.
6   ***SETTING:*** Throughout the play, the setting represents first a sandbox
7   then a classroom and finally a coffee shop.
8
9   *(Two children, BEV and HONEY, play in a sandbox. DAN*
10   *approaches them.)*
11   **BEV: OK, you make the castle and I'll make the wall. Pack it real**
12   **hard.**
13   **DAN: Can I play?**
14   **BEV: No, this is for girls.**
15   **DAN: I can play too.**
16   **BEV: This is a club for girls. You gotta be in the club.**
17   **DAN: What club?**
18   **BEV: The Girls' Sandbox Club.**
19   **DAN: Wanta play dinosaurs?**
20   **BEV: Dinosaurs are all dead.**
21   **DAN: I can draw.**
22   **HONEY: No you can't.**
23   **DAN: I can draw a horse. In the sand.** *(Drawing)* **I can draw good.**
24   **HONEY: Horses are dumb.**
25   **DAN: I wanta be in the club.**
26   **BEV: You like to play dolls?**
27   **DAN: No.**
28   **BEV: We're gonna play dolls.**
29   **DAN: OK, I'll play.**
30   **HONEY:** *(Calling out)* **Danny plays dolls! Danny's a sissy!**
31   **BEV: His sister said he pees in his bed.**
32   **DAN: There's a horse.**
33   **BEV and HONEY: Peepee, peepee! Sissy pissy, sissy pissy!**
34   **DAN: I spilled some water!**
35   **BEV: His sister saw his tinky.**

1 HONEY: Let's play guns. And shoot Danny!
2 BEV: Shoot off his tinky! *(They swarm around him, shooting.)* You're
3 dead! You have to die! *(He stands motionless, trying not to cry.)*
4 BEV: Danny's gonna cry! Danny's gonna cry!
5 HONEY: End of recess. *(BEV stomps all over the drawing.)*
6 BEV: *(Going out)* He messed up the game. You get shot you die.
7 Dummy! *(They go out, leaving him in misery. Freeze. Each is
8 given a different costume element. They animate, now as
9 teenagers.)*
10 HONEY: We're doing this new one. *(She demonstrates a
11 cheerleading routine. BEV comes in, is ignored.)*
12 DAN: Cool. Only do more stuff for the linemen. Jeez, I'm gonna
13 make All-State. I should get a cheer whenever I knock
14 somebody on his ass.
15 HONEY: It sounds funny to yell, "Wibberly, Wibberly!"
16 DAN: No, come on! "Dan the Man, Dan the Man!"
17 BEV: Excuse me. Is this where the yearbook committee is?
18 HONEY: Yes.
19 BEV: Mr. Miller said I was supposed to be the editor or something?
20 DAN: Hi.
21 BEV: I'm Beverly Shoemaker.
22 HONEY: I'm Honey.
23 DAN: Dan Wibberly.
24 BEV: Oh, I know who both of you are. I'm very glad to —
25 HONEY: Let's get started.
26 BEV: Where's the other people on the …
27 HONEY: You're s'posed to know that. You're s'posed to be the
28 editor.
29 BEV: Joellen was, but she quit. So, well, gee, I have sort of an
30 agenda …
31 DAN: A what?
32 HONEY: Well we were going to break into committees, and Dan
33 and I are the photo committee. So why don't you talk to the
34 other people and do something with them, and Dan and I will
35 go through these candids and write captions.

132

1 BEV: OK, well, they're not here, so maybe I could help out ... I
2   wrote a list of things from previous years, maybe we could put
3   on different ones ...
4 HONEY: Uh-huh ...
5 DAN: *(Reading from her list)* "A good sport."
6 HONEY: "Preparing for the future." That's very nice.
7 DAN: You got that one of Mary?
8 HONEY: Coming out of the locker room, with the towel? She'll
9   die!
10 DAN: Here it is!
11 BEV: She's so pretty.
12 DAN: Huh?
13 BEV: Mary Turner is so pretty.
14 DAN: She's a cow. OK, we gotta find a good caption.
15 BEV: How about ... "Spring Morning?"
16 DAN: I got it: "Oh, was this supposed to be formal?"
17 HONEY: She'll die! *(He writes.)* There's Mark.
18 DAN: What's that?
19 HONEY: That's Karen's party. God, everybody's in that. I don't
20   mean everybody, I mean everybody that's ...
21 DAN: *(Looking at photo)* What's that?
22 HONEY: That's the class play.
23 DAN: "Faggots on Parade." *(HONEY laughs.)* No. *(Lisping)* "My
24   goodnesth me! Mr. Miller is such a sthweetie!"
25 BEV: Oh, that's me. I just had a little part. I always look funny
26   when I take off my glasses.
27 DAN: OK, so you can write a caption.
28 BEV: I couldn't write for my own picture.
29 HONEY: Tell you what. Why don't you get the other pictures, in
30   Mr. Miller's room, and look for stuff that might fit one of
31   these ...
32 BEV: Oh. OK. *(She goes out. Dan takes the photo.)*
33 DAN: Lemme see that. "I didn't know I left my boobs at home."
34   *(Prints it on the list.)*
35 HONEY: Come on, she is a jerk but that's a bit —

1   **DAN: I wanta puke. "I'm s'posed to be the editor or something."**
2   **How'd we get stuck with Miss Hemorrhoids?**
3   **HONEY: Mr. Miller.**
4   **DAN: Fags.**
5   **HONEY: We could just take off.**
6   **DAN: Look, after practice I'll get Cindy and Matt, and we'll come**
7   **over to your place and do this.**
8   **HONEY: We can have some beer. My folks don't care.**
9   **DAN: All right! 'Bout eight?**
10   **HONEY: Bye.** *(BEV comes in, having heard them. She sees the list.*
11   *Starts to erase it violently. Freeze. Each is given a different*
12   *costume element. They animate, now in coffee shop. HONEY is*
13   *waitress. BEV sits at a table.)*
14   **BEV: Hi, could I have a —**
15   **HONEY:** *(As waitress)* **Hold on.** *(DAN enters, with shoulderbag,*
16   *mildly gay mannerisms. Looks around for a seat.)*
17   **DAN: 'Scuse me, is anybody sitting here? You mind?** *(BEV gestures*
18   *assent.)* **Coffee and a plain doughnut, please.**
19   **HONEY: In a minute.**
20   **DAN: La-dee-dah.**
21   **BEV: Good luck.**
22   **DAN: God, I can spot 'em. Thirty years old, professional actress,**
23   **"studied with Uta Hagan," never been cast. In this city, they**
24   **are mass-produced.**
25   **BEV: Really.**
26   **HONEY: Can I get you something?**
27   **DAN: Coffee and a plain doughnut.**
28   **BEV: Maybe a menu?**
29   **HONEY: Sorry.**
30   **BEV:** *(To DAN)* **Is my watch right?**
31   **DAN: Quarter of three.**
32   **BEV: I'm on a tight schedule. It's a little nervewracking.**
33   **DAN: Same here.** *(HONEY brings menus.)*
34   **BEV: Tell you, could I just have a plain salad, oil and vinegar,**
35   **whole wheat toast, Diet Coke.**

1   HONEY: **Yeh.** *(To DAN)* Sorry, did you want one slice or two?

2   DAN: **You slice your doughnuts?**

3   HONEY: **Oh.** Sorry. *(To BEV)* You look familiar.

4   DAN: You *act* familiar. *(HONEY starts to say something, goes out.)*

5   BEV: **Ouch.**

6   DAN: **I know. I'm sorry. I just get very ... tacky sometimes with**

7   **people who want to be part of the club. Actually, you do look**

8   **familiar.**

9   BEV: **"If it's soft enough for baby's tender skin ... "**

10   DAN: **Yes! The Charmin Girl! Omigod, a celebrity! Is it really that**

11   **soft?**

12   BEV: **Well try it!** *(They laugh.)*

13   DAN: **But that's fabulous. That's very good money.**

14   BEV: **Really. Although I don't want to spend my whole career in**

15   **toilet paper.**

16   HONEY: **Did you say coffee?**

17   DAN: **Yes, and could I have real milk instead of the artificial?**

18   HONEY: **If you want to order milk.**

19   DAN: **Love you too, honey.** *(She stops. Tired rage:)*

20   HONEY: **In fact, my name is Honey, thank you.** *(Goes out.)*

21   DAN: *(Indicating HONEY)* **Well! Let's buy brains for our Barbie!**

22   *(They laugh. He picks up a napkin, starts sketching on it.)*

23   BEV: **Are you an artist?**

24   DAN: **Designer.**

25   BEV: **Of what?**

26   DAN: **Oh, this and that. Couple of bands, new club, some very**

27   **upscale interiors ... I've had some nice write-ups — I'm**

28   **doing a fabulous new restaurant up on East 53rd.** *(Holds up*

29   *napkin. Caricature of the waitress. BEV laughs.)*

30   BEV: **Oh, that is so cruel! God, now she looks familiar.**

31   DAN: **In this city, everybody looks familiar. It's because we all feel**

32   **we've escaped from our old home town, and the posse is**

33   **tracking us down.**

34   BEV: **Did you ever think, if you ran into somebody from high**

35   **school —**

You've Never Left This Place
by Denny Berthiaume

Denny Berthiaume is a San Francisco Bay area playwright and pianist/composer. He has ten recordings including a solo piano project, *Sentimental Journey*, for Sugo Records (he has performed as a sideman with Ed Thigpen, Bobby McFerrin, Diane Schuur, Bob Hope, and Red Skelton) and has conducted for Bob Newhart, Johnnie Ray, and Tony Martin. He is a full professor of literature and music at Foothill College in Los Altos, California.

You've Never Left This Place began as an alternative ending to a full-length play, *Playtime*. It was published in *The Forum: Journal of the Academic Senate for California Community Colleges* (1998). In August 2001, it was part of the Twelfth Annual New Play Development Workshop during the Association for Theatre in Higher Education Conference in Chicago. Professor Gary Garrison, "dean of the ten minute play" and professor of playwriting at NYU, praised the work as "one of the best ten minute plays I have ever seen."

Playwright's Production Suggestions

The action of the play is a fantasy only if dreams may be said to be less real than waking reality. The role of Ho Chi Minh is perhaps best played by a woman. The Vietnamese Peasant may be played by either a man or a woman.

Address all inquiries concerning performances, readings, or reprinting of this work *or any portion thereof* to Denny Berthiaume, 12345 El Monte Avenue, Los Altos, CA 94022. For details, see "Part II: Securing Rights for Your Production," pages 183 to 192.

1   The action takes place in a late afternoon in the 1960s in a peasant
2   hut in Vietnam.
3   **CHARACTERS:** DAVE SINGLEMAN — early 40s. Single parent.
4   Former U.S. Marine. Current director of a theatre company.
5   HO CHI MINH — late 60s. Leader of the Viet Minh, later the
6   Viet Cong; the "Father" of modern Vietnam.
7   VIETNAMESE PEASANT (non-speaking part) — Soldier with
8   gun, wearing village garb. He or she kills and is killed.
9   **SETTING:** The hut is furnished with little more than the mat upon
10   which HO CHI MINH sits. The GIs at whom the PEASANT fires
11   may be represented as cardboard targets.
12
13   *(Bombs. Explosions. The battle subsides. HO CHI MINH sits on a*
14   *mat. A PEASANT pours tea for "Uncle Ho." The PEASANT then*
15   *patrols the firing line. Armed with a rifle, the PEASANT fires at*
16   *American GIs throughout the scene. The PEASANT will die from*
17   *returned American firepower and then rise again. SINGLEMAN*
18   *backs into the hut. He is dressed in Marine Corps battle fatigues.*
19   *His pistol rests in his hand. He is ready to fire at any moment.)*
20   **HO: Please sit down, Mr. Singleman.** *(Indicates a mat on the ground.)*
21   **SINGLEMAN:** *(Pointing a pistol)* **Mom? What are you doing in … ?**
22   **Where are the doctors?** *(Notices his own clothes.)* **Why are we**
23   **dressed like this?**
24   **HO: Please sit down, David.** *(DAVID sits on mat and places pistol*
25   *next to his leg.)* **There is no visit, no conversation, that begins**
26   **without tea and ceremony. How is your health?**
27   **SINGLEMAN: My health?**
28   **HO: Yes. How are you feeling?**
29   **SINGLEMAN: I'm … feeling … Forget about how I'm feeling.**
30   **HO: And your daughter, Christine — excuse me — Tine? How is she?**
31   **SINGLEMAN: Well, last time I saw her she was with friends**
32   **and … She was talking to some guy so I couldn't … I wanted**
33   **to tell her …**
34   **HO: Tine is almost in her last year of adolescence, isn't she?**
35   **SINGLEMAN: Her what? No, she's only eighteen. She just**

1   graduated from …

2 HO: And to what does she aspire? What are her interests?

3 SINGLEMAN: Well, we have a life together in the theatre. When I

4   direct plays she …

5 HO: Yes, of course. And without you she does … *what?*

6 SINGLEMAN: She … she sometimes goes out with …

7 HO: What does Christine want to do when she grows up?

8 SINGLEMAN: Grows up? Christine?

9 HO: Yes, what is her great task? In Vietnam we have a saying:

10   Give up your personal concerns

11   In favor of the great task.

12   We are a country that believes — truly believes — in the

13   power of the people. The term "individual" is dangerous and

14   associated with cannibals.

15 SINGLEMAN: Dinkydao! Dinkydao! *(Grabs his pistol and shoots the*

16   *Vietnamese PEASANT twice. The PEASANT falls. SINGLEMAN*

17   *reloads. Stiff and wooden, the peasant rises and resumes patrol.)*

18 HO: To what do Tine's abilities reach?

19 SINGLEMAN: I don't know. I never asked her.

20 HO: Children are our preciousness. Our ancestors taught:

21   Antiquity Modernity Moon Sun

22   A person's talents must reach beyond the mundane, the

23   mediocre, and the routine. We are a practical people always with

24   an eye on the mythic and the prosaic. Will you have some "ca"?

25 SINGLEMAN: Some —

26 HO: "Ca" … You remember, David. Eggplant. *(Offers it and*

27   *indicates.)* Yes, use salt. "Whoever eats 'ca' with salt is —

28 SINGLEMAN: Blessed." Thanks. *(He eats.)* What's the difference

29   between the Marine Corps and the Boy Scouts?

30 HO: The Boy Scouts have adult leadership. *(They laugh.)*

31 SINGLEMAN: Yessir. Marine Corps is the finest instrument ever

32   devised for killing young American men. *(He fires three times*

33   *and kills a Vietnamese PEASANT. The PEASANT falls and then*

34   *rises woodenly after HO's next line.)*

35 HO: Boys.

1   SINGLEMAN: What?
2   HO: Killing young boys. Men do not allow themselves to be
3   killed ... unnecessarily.
4   SINGLEMAN: Bull! We went on liberty in China Beach. Da-*nang*!
5   Kilo Company! R 'n' R! The White Mice! *(Fires a few rounds*
6   *from his pistol. A PEASANT is wounded. After falling, the*
7   *PEASANT slowly and with effort rises.)*
8   HO: In 1952, eighty-five percent of weapons, war materials —
9   even canned food — captured from the French by the Viet
10   Minh were labeled "made in the U.S.A." My country ...
11   where the Trail of Tears was headed all along.
12 SINGLEMAN: Bao Bang. Dak To. Plei Mei. Feeling you were dry-
13   sniped every time a short timer looked at you.
14 HO: Khe Sinh. Con Thien. Kontum. Dang Ha —
15 SINGLEMAN: Bo Doi: that was *your* own personal division.
16 HO: "No lie, GI" *(They laugh.)*
17 SINGLEMAN: Nguyen Tat Tanh.
18 HO: Here.
19 SINGLEMAN: Nguyen Ai Quoc.
20 HO: Present.
21 SINGLEMAN: You were also Nguyen O Phap, Line, Tran, Ban,
22   "Orwald" —
23 HO: Never!
24 SINGLEMAN: Nguyen Sinh Cung.
25 HO: A third son.
26 SINGLEMAN: Ho Quong.
27 HO: Only to the Chinese!
28 SINGLEMAN: Thau Chin, Tong Van So —
29 HO: Yes, yes. And Ly Thay, Lee Suei, Vuong Son Nhi ... and "Bac
30   Ho."
31 SINGLEMAN: Yes. "Uncle." Uncle Ho! *(They laugh.)*
32 HO: An old man likes to have a little air of mystery about himself.
33   I like to hold on to my little mysteries. Some more tea? *(HO*
34   *pours.)* But you are still a young man. You needn't hold onto
35   your secrets.

1   SINGLEMAN: What are you talking about?

2   HO: Christine's mother.

3   SINGLEMAN: She's dead ... the "rags of time."

4   HO: You learned much from her about our culture.

5   SINGLEMAN: I don't want to talk about her.

6   HO: She opened to you like a flower and you fell on her like a stone.

7   SINGLEMAN: You don't know!

8   HO: I know!

9   SINGLEMAN: Abysmal moments. Glorious hours.

10 HO: You left her behind!

11 SINGLEMAN: She was VC! *(Fires at a PEASANT and misses.)*

12 HO: Misfortune is a test of man's fidelity.

13 SINGLEMAN: She was responsible for the murders of my family.

14   I mean my friends. *(Gunshots. Several GI cardboard targets fall*

15   *as Vietnamese PEASANT fires.)*

16 HO: She was your wife! The care of society is the family!

17 SINGLEMAN: You don't understand. You never married.

18 HO: You do not know that! I would never have abandoned my

19   family.

20 SINGLEMAN: What?

21 HO: Your wife ... and son. You abandoned your family.

22 SINGLEMAN: I did not!

23 HO: Say it! "I abandoned my family!"

24 SINGLEMAN: The "chopper" was lifting off. The Military police

25   made me choose. There was only room for one child.

26 HO: That is a lie! Say, "I abandoned my family!"

27 SINGLEMAN: All right! "I abandoned my family!" *(Shoots at*

28   *Vietnamese PEASANT and misses.)* My "wife" wanted to stay and

29   fight her precious war. *(Impatiently)* Why am I here?

30 HO: Because you never left.

31 SINGLEMAN: What do you mean?

32 HO: You've been camping out in your aggression for twenty years.

33 SINGLEMAN: Loss creates chaos.

34 HO: Don't be too quick with words, David. You lodge them like

35   shrapnel, in your listeners. In Vietnam we lack verbs. We

1   establish meaning through context. You have no framework,
2   no discipline ... All you "grunts" know is Search and Destroy.
3   SINGLEMAN: And all you "dinks" understand is Find and Kill.
4   HO: Gyrene!
5   SINGLEMAN: Zip!
6   HO: Jarhead!
7   SINGLEMAN: Gook! *(They laugh.)*
8   HO: Real life is immense, David. In my writings I always spoke of
9   "emulation" as a commendable, friendly form of rivalry in
10   the interest of improved behavior.
11   SINGLEMAN: *(Quoting Ho)* "Work transforms the world;
12   emulation transforms man."
13   HO: A man is not a man until he is willing and able to be by
14   himself, be alone with himself. And take care of no one but
15   himself. You must let Tine go. On the path of courage,
16   outward adversity leads inward. We are soldiers, full of
17   strange oaths; jealous of our honor; quick to quarrel; our
18   reputation poised in the mouth of a cannon. *(A bright light fills*
19   *the stage. DAVID steps aboard an imaginary 'copter. Looking*
20   *down, he addresses his Vietnamese wife and baby.)*
21   SINGLEMAN: Give me the baby! ... I said, "Give me the baby!" ...
22   Well, then, if I can't have him neither can you! *(Shoots her and*
23   *the baby. Noise. Chaos. The chopper — the bright light —*
24   *disappears. The jungle becomes an in-patient wing of a VA*
25   *hospital. DAVID sits transfixed before a TV. He watches* 2001: A
26   Space Odyssey. *Hal, the Computer, intones behind the picture,*
27   *"Open the pod doors, Dave. Open the pod doors." Upstage in*
28   *near darkness HO CHI MINH stands.)*
29   HO: Remember, David: you returned here because you never left
30   this place ... you never left this place ... *(Voice fading and light*
31   *fading)* you never left this place ...
32
33   *The End*
34
35

One Evening in Prague
by William Borden

William Borden's plays have won twenty-one national playwriting competitions and have had over two hundred productions. The film version of his play, *The Last Prostitute*, was shown on Lifetime Television and in Europe and is on video. His novel, *Superstoe*, was republished by Orloff Press. A Core Alumnus Playwright at The Playwrights' Center in Minneapolis, he is a playwright with Listening Winds.

One Evening in Prague was produced by P.A.C.T. in New York City in 1996 and by Love Creek Productions in New York City in 1994.

Playwright's Historical Note

Berta Fanta actually presided over a weekly salon in Prague. Einstein and Kafka both occasionally attended, but there is no record of their meeting — except this play.

Address all inquiries concerning performances, readings, or reprinting of this work *or any portion thereof* to William Borden, 7996 S. FM 548, Royse City, TX 75189. For details, see "Part II: Securing Rights for Your Production," pages 183 to 192.

1   The action takes place in 1911 in Prague.

2

3   *CHARACTERS:* BERTA FANTA — about 30, hostess to a weekly

4   Prague salon of intellectuals and artists.

5   ALBERT EINSTEIN — 32, an up and coming physicist.

6   FRANZ KAFKA — 28, a clerk in a state insurance office and a

7   little-known writer.

8   *SETTING:* The foyer of BERTA FANTA's house in Prague.

9

10   **BERTA FANTA:** *(To audience)* **Welcome to Prague. I'm so glad you**

11   **could come. I'm Berta. Berta Fanta. I'm famous for my**

12   **parties. It's a very intellectual crowd — you'll fit right in. The**

13   **greatest minds of 1911 — right here, in my house, every**

14   **Tuesday evening. We spent a year discussing the philosophy of**

15   **Brentano. Lately we've had a few séances. But no ghosts**

16   **tonight. Tonight is a rather special night. A new guest, newly**

17   **arrived in Prague.** *(EINSTEIN enters.)* **There you are, Dr.**

18   **Einstein! How good of you to come! Are you enjoying Prague?**

19   **Are you settled? The weather is usually much warmer — it's**

20   **been a chilly autumn —** *(KAFKA enters shyly, stumbles into*

21   *EINSTEIN.)*

22   **KAFKA: Excuse me.**

23   **BERTA FANTA: Dr. Kafka!**

24   **EINSTEIN: Excuse me!**

25   **BERTA FANTA: Dr. Kafka, how nice to —**

26   **KAFKA: I'm so clumsy.**

27   **EINSTEIN: It was my fault entirely.**

28   **KAFKA: No, no, I'm like an insect — all legs —**

29   **EINSTEIN: No, no —**

30   **KAFKA: I'm guilty.**

31   **EINSTEIN: It's all relative.**

32   **BERTA FANTA: Let me take your hat, Dr. Kafka.**

33   **EINSTEIN: And mine, too, if you please, Mrs. Fanta.**

34   **BERTA FANTA: You're not wearing a hat, Dr. Einstein.**

35   **EINSTEIN: Oh! So I'm not. I must have forgotten it.**

1   BERTA FANTA: Forgive me! My guests are calling! Introduce
2   yourselves! *(To audience)* You too! *(She hangs KAFKA's bowler*
3   *on a hat rack and exits. KAFKA and EINSTEIN look uneasily at*
4   *the audience, uneasily at one another. An awkward moment or*
5   *two. Finally, at the same time, each thrusts out a hand.)*
6   EINSTEIN: Einstein.
7   KAFKA: Kafka.
8   EINSTEIN: Dr. Kafka? *(KAFKA shrugs.)*
9   KAFKA: Dr. Einstein? *(EINSTEIN waves it aside.)*
10   EINSTEIN: *(Making fun of himself)* I could have sworn I wore my
11   hat! *(KAFKA eyes EINSTEIN's unruly hair.)* I suppose I forgot
12   to brush my hair as well. I have my tie! Shoes. *(EINSTEIN pulls*
13   *up his trousers: no socks.)* I don't see the point of socks,
14   actually.
15   KAFKA: Internist?
16   EINSTEIN: Pardon?
17   KAFKA: Surgeon? Eyes? Throat?
18   EINSTEIN: Physicist.
19   KAFKA: I'm sorry.
20   EINSTEIN: Quite all right.
21   KAFKA: I feel so foolish.
22   EINSTEIN: A natural mistake.
23   KAFKA: You'd think I lived in a burrow.
24   EINSTEIN: And you, Dr. Kafka?
25   KAFKA: Yes?
26   EINSTEIN: Physician? Surgeon? Ophthalmology?
27   KAFKA: Doctor of Jurisprudence.
28   EINSTEIN: Now I'm the one who lives in a burrow! See how
29   quickly we change places! With the speed of light!
30   KAFKA: Professor?
31   EINSTEIN: At the university. Not long ago I was a clerk in the
32   patent office in Bern, in Switzerland.
33   KAFKA: Shuffling papers?
34   EINSTEIN: I'm afraid so. And you, Dr. Kafka?
35   KAFKA: Shuffle, shuffle.

1   EINSTEIN: You too?

2   KAFKA: Shuffle shuffle shuffle.

3   EINSTEIN: Oh my.

4   KAFKA: State insurance office. Claims for injuries.

5   EINSTEIN: I had the strangest application for a patent one day.

6   For a torturing machine.

7   KAFKA: I understand torture. Mental torture. My father —

8   EINSTEIN: This torturing device —

9   KAFKA: My fiancé — on again, off again —

10   EINSTEIN: This torturing device —

11   KAFKA: A machine?

12   EINSTEIN: It wrote the guilty man's crime on his body — that

13   was the torture, you see, that was the way he was executed.

14   Said it could be used — what did he say? — in a penal colony.

15   What sort of mind would think of such a device?

16   KAFKA: Did you approve the patent?

17   EINSTEIN: No. The specifications were all confused.

18   KAFKA: But you considered it.

19   EINSTEIN: That was my job. *(BERTA FANTA enters, in a rush as*

20   *usual, carrying a tray with drinks.)*

21   BERTA FANTA: Are you getting acquainted? So good of you to

22   come, Dr. Einstein! I thought maybe your head was always in

23   the clouds! Please, a glass of wine. And Dr. Kafka, you hardly

24   ever come! Are we too good for you? Your friend Max Brod

25   comes every week! And he's a famous writer!

26   KAFKA: Crowds —

27   BERTA FANTA: This isn't a crowd! This is a salon! *(Offering the*

28   *wine)* Please.

29   KAFKA: No, thanks.

30   BERTA FANTA: You see? Too good for us.

31   KAFKA: I don't drink wine.

32   BERTA FANTA: Why didn't you say so? *(Offers him another glass.)*

33   This is mineral water. *(He takes the mineral water.)* Oh — my

34   other guests are calling! *(She exits. Another awkward moment.*

35   *Finally KAFKA and EINSTEIN raise their glasses to one another*

1   *and drink.)*

2   KAFKA: That wine becomes energy.

3   EINSTEIN: Yes, I suppose it does.

4   KAFKA: Things turn into other things.

5   EINSTEIN: Your mineral water — into pee.

6   KAFKA: You eat, say, a cake.

7   EINSTEIN: A whole cake?

8   KAFKA: A little sugar. Suddenly, you're full of energy!

9   EINSTEIN: Coffee!

10   KAFKA: Yes!

11   EINSTEIN: Winds you right up!

12   KAFKA: Matter into energy!

13   EINSTEIN: I never thought of it like that.

14   KAFKA: Boom! Like a bomb! *(Makes a noise like a bomb.)* It would

15   be like taking that drop of coffee —

16   EINSTEIN: The mass of the coffee —

17   KAFKA: — and multiplying it by — I don't know — some big

18   number — some huge number — like — the speed of light —

19   EINSTEIN: More. More.

20   KAFKA: Like the speed of light squared!

21   EINSTEIN: It's a metamorphosis! Listen, Kafka, it's so difficult,

22   let me tell you, trying to figure out — what I'm trying to

23   figure out.

24   KAFKA: What are you trying to figure out?

25   EINSTEIN: I'm trying to figure out the universe.

26   KAFKA: You too?

27   EINSTEIN: You mean you — ?

28   KAFKA: Well …

29   EINSTEIN: How?

30   KAFKA: I scribble.

31   EINSTEIN: Me too!

32   KAFKA: Stories? Characters? Plots?

33   EINSTEIN: Well, no, I've been using mathematics. But if I made

34   up stories … Yes! If I were to imagine myself sitting on a piece

35   of light — and you on another — what would you call it, a

1   piece of light?
2   KAFKA: Well, it's a certain quantity of —
3   EINSTEIN: Quantum! It would be a kind of experiment —
4   KAFKA: A thought experiment.
5   EINSTEIN: Exactly! And if I went at the speed of light, but you
6   stayed here —
7   KAFKA: What if I walked around while you were flying off on
8   your quantum of light?
9   EINSTEIN: Walked around?
10   KAFKA: Well, your speed would be relative to my speed, wouldn't
11   it?
12   EINSTEIN: Good God, you're right!
13   KAFKA: You can't assume that I'm going to stand here forever.
14   EINSTEIN: *(Thinking it through)* We're both moving.
15   KAFKA: That cockroach over there is moving ...
16   EINSTEIN: The earth is moving ... revolving ...
17   KAFKA: Around the sun ...
18   EINSTEIN: That too!
19   KAFKA: And I suppose the whole solar system is moving.
20   EINSTEIN: There's no point that is fixed, as Newton thought —
21   rather, everything is moving — every which way — oh, my —
22   oh, my — it's like — it's like trying to get someplace, I don't
23   know, say, a castle —
24   KAFKA: A castle?
25   EINSTEIN: Say you've been summoned, but you can't find anybody
26   to take you to the castle, and you just wander around —
27   KAFKA: A castle ...
28   EINSTEIN: Or you were — see, if light —
29   KAFKA: If it were like that, Dr. Einstein, you might as well say
30   that space and time are the same thing!
31   EINSTEIN: I wouldn't go that far, Dr. Kafka.
32   KAFKA: Or that gravity —
33   EINSTEIN: Gravity ...
34   KAFKA: — is nothing but —
35   EINSTEIN: Kafka, ideas are flooding my brain!

1   KAFKA: — nothing but —
2   EINSTEIN: Kafka, it's very scary.
3   KAFKA: Gravity is nothing but —
4   EINSTEIN: I feel like a man suddenly accused of a crime —
5   KAFKA: It's as if gravity were nothing but a curvature in space-
6   time!
7   EINSTEIN: — and no one will tell him what his crime is!
8   KAFKA: A trial?
9   EINSTEIN: A relativity? *(BERTA FANTA enters.)*
10 BERTA FANTA: Dr. Kafka, Dr. Einstein! I see you've hit it off!
11 KAFKA: I must be going.
12 EINSTEIN: I must be going.
13 BERTA FANTA: Oh, no —
14 KAFKA: An idea ...
15 EINSTEIN: A problem I've been struggling with ... *(EINSTEIN*
16   *puts on KAFKA'S hat and exits. BERTA FANTA looks at KAFKA.)*
17 BERTA FANTA: Did you forget to wear a hat tonight? *(But KAFKA*
18   *is on his way, pulling a notebook and pencil from his coat, writing*
19   *as he exits. To audience.)* Did you have a good time? *(She looks*
20   *again off, after the departed figures.)* They never returned. I
21   don't think they ever saw each other again. Sometimes people
22   don't hit it off. They're like two particles of light passing in the
23   night.
24
25   *The End*
26
27
28
29
30
31
32
33
34
35

Give Me Your Tired, Your Poor

by Norman A. Bert
In memory of Jia-hua Chin, who walks in light

Norman Bert pastored a church in Indiana and taught school in Zambia before beginning his career as a university theatre teacher. He has led college theatre programs in Pennsylvania, Montana, and Texas. He believes that theatre is more than entertainment and that good plays give their audiences new insights and change the way they live.

The materials in *Give Me Your Tired, Your Poor* were first developed as part of a celebration script written for Montana's centennial in 1989 — *The Montana Times*.

Playwright's Production Suggestions

Use Brechtian techniques to present this sample of documentary drama. Cast the play non-traditionally and against type. Manage exits and entrances without actors ever leaving the stage; actors not currently involved in a scene take positions around the periphery of the stage and observe the action until their next entrance. Seek a happy balance between internal acting that creates believable characters and external techniques that focus attention on the social situation and message of the play. Perhaps above all, have fun with the piece; find the comedy and enjoy the irony.

Address all inquiries concerning performances, readings, or reprinting of this work *or any portion thereof* to Norman A. Bert, 5704 Nashville Avenue, Lubbock, TX 79413-4601. For details, see "Part II: Securing Rights for Your Production," pages 183 to 192.

1   The action takes place in 1889 on a street in Butte, Montana, and

2   in an office in nearby Anaconda.

3   *CHARACTERS:* ACTOR A, ACTOR B, and ACTOR C — three

4   performers of any age, sex, or ethnicity. The named roles are

5   played by these three as determined by the actors or director. They

6   may use costume pieces as desired to communicate character

7   identities.

8   *SETTING:* A street lamp, a desk and chair, an easel holding title cards,

9   and a bench where the actors sit when not involved in the action.

10

11   *(The title card displays the play's title. The ACTORS enter.)*

12   **ACTOR A: Give me your tired, your poor,**

13   **Your huddled masses yearning to breathe free,**

14   **The wretched refuse of your teeming shore.**

15   **Send these, the homeless, tempest-tossed to me.**

16   **I lift my lamp beside the golden door.**

17   **ACTOR B: But if they're black or brown —**

18   **From south the border, Asia, or Mid East —**

19   **They really shouldn't come here to our town.**

20   **We love all human kind and furry beasts,**

21   **But certain types we just don't want around.**

22   **ACTOR C: We're careful how we speak,**

23   **And sure to be politic'lly correct.**

24   **But our ancestors weren't quite so discrete**

25   **As you will in this little play detect.**

26   **Our scene's an Old West copper mining street.**

27

28   *(Title Card: THE CHINAMAN'S FRIEND[1])*

29   *(Two miners, KRIVITSKI and O'MALLEY meet on the street.)*

30   **KRIVITSKI: So, O'Malley, what's up?**

31   **O'MALLEY: "Up?" "Up," he says. Sure an it's nothing't all that's**

32   **up in my neck o' the woods, Krivitski. I'm that far down I'd**

33   **need a ladder to scratch the snake's belly.**

34

35

---

[1] This scene is based on an editorial with this title in *The Butte Daily Miner* (Butte, Montana), 9/27/1889.

1   **KRIVITSKI:** Yeh, I'm with younz. Da old lady's on my back all da
2   time: "Git a job, ya dumb Pollack, whadya wants us to do,
3   starve?"
4   **O'MALLEY:** I'm tellin' ya, it' the damn gold standard that's a
5   doin' it to us, Jan.
6   **KRIVITSKI:** Nah, it's the Irish wat done it to younz, Paddy. Ya
7   gots bumped last week counta brawlin' on company time.
8   **O'MALLEY:** Hey, you'd a done the same if that big Honky'd a
9   stomped on your toe with his damn hobnailed hoofs. I'm
10   tellin' you, the Company should be countin' their blessings to
11   have the likes o' you and myself a workin' their mines.
12   **KRIVITSKI:** Us Pollacks, at least. Don't know about younz Micks.
13   **O'MALLEY:** You be watchin' y'self, Krivitski, or next you'll be
14   tastin' of my knuckles.
15   **KRIVITSKI:** Take a jab at me and I'll rip your damn arm off,
16   Paddy.
17   **BROWN:** *(A Democratic precinct-man, dressed in a business suit.*
18   *He's been listening to their conversation and now steps up and*
19   *hands each a small handbill.)* **So you want your jobs back?**
20   **Here's the problem: the Republican Chinese connection.**
21   **O'MALLEY:** *(Taking the bill)* **Says who?**
22   **BROWN:** Name's Brown, local precinct chairman for the
23   Democratic Party. I'm telling you, the reason the solid,
24   hardworking American Laborer is out of a job is because the
25   Republicans are flooding the country with Chinese coolies.
26   That's why you're out of work.
27   **KRIVITSKI:** How do you figure?
28   **BROWN:** Just have a look at that article from yesterday's edition
29   of Helena's Republican rag. *(He gestures to the handbills.)*
30   **Why, *The Helen Journal* of yesterday practically endorses**
31   Chinese immigration. It indulges editorially in the belief that
32   the free labor of America can stand a few thousand Chinese
33   on the Pacific coast, and a few thousand Italians on the
34   Atlantic coast.
35   **O'MALLEY:** *(Looking at his handbill)* **Is that a fact now?**

1   ²BROWN: The plain English of it is, it licks the scented hand of the
2   Chinaman.
3   KRIVITSKI: Enough to make your blood boil.
4   BROWN: But what else can be expected of a paper owned and
5   controlled by Russell Braggadocio Harrison, son of a father —
6   yes, I'm talking about the President now — who voted
7   nineteen times in the United States Senate to flood this
8   country with the almond-eyed disciples of Confucius who are
9   willing to work for nothing and subsist on rats and swill-tub
10   refuse, to the degradation and pauperism of American labor?
11   O'MALLEY: Go on. We're listenin'.
12   BROWN: If *The Journal* dared, it would be even more outspoken
13   in its sympathy with the Republican monopolies of this
14   country that sooner or later hope to find cheaper labor in the
15   person of the "heathen Chinee."
16   KRIVITSKI: Damn 'em.
17   BROWN: The windows of every Chinese hash-house in Butte
18   today are darkened with Republican posters, showing that a
19   reciprocal affection exists.
20   O'MALLEY: I've noticed that.
21   BROWN: If you vote the Republican ticket, you vote for Chinese
22   immigration, and don't forget it.
23   KRIVITSKI: I won't forget. And thank younz.
24   *BROWN: Don't mention it. And by the way, remember to vote
25   Democrat next Tuesday.
26   KRIVITSKI: Oh, well, I ain't registered.
27   O'MALLEY: Me neither. And the deadline's gone past.
28   BROWN: *(Handing them small tickets)* Don't give it a thought, boys.
29   Stop by party headquarters and give 'em these chits. Tell 'em
30   Brown sent you. They'll take care of everything. Vote
31   Democrat on Tuesday, like real Americans. *(He retires to sit on*
32   *the bench.)*
33
34
35

²From this point until the speech marked *, all of BROWN's words are quoted directly from the source article in *The Butte Daily Miner.*

1   O'MALLEY: Curse on the American laborer, them damn
2   Mongolians.
3   KRIVITSKI: And their Republican stooges. I'm gonna post this
4   notice on the board down to the Polish Legion. Us Americans
5   need to be informed.
6   O'MALLEY: Sure and it's true. I'll be doin' the same at the hall of
7   the Ancient Order of Hibernians. America for the Americans,
8   I say. Till tomorrow, Krivitski. Friend.
9   KRIVITSKI: See younz later, O'Malley. Brother. *(They shake*
10   *hands, pause, then in a fit of patriotic brotherhood, embrace.*
11   *They retire to the bench.)*
12   ACTOR A: And in a neighboring town,
13   Before the moon goes down,
14   An Asian farmer guides
15   A wagon with high sides
16   To peddle corn and greens —
17   The best we've ever seen.
18   ACTOR B: Does this ambitious gent
19   Think his industrious bent
20   Will earn him a good spot
21   Here in our melting pot?
22   ACTOR C: Early to bed and early to rise
23   Watch all our promises turn into lies.
24
25   *(Title card: A CHINESE RANCHMAN[3])*
26   *(A manager, SCHILLING, sits at a desk doing paperwork. A*
27   *CLERK enters.)*
28   CLERK: Excuse me, Mr. Schilling.
29   SCHILLING: *(Not looking up)* What is it, Evans?
30   CLERK: There's a gentleman here to see you, sir.
31   SCHILLING: *(Still not looking up)* Appointment?
32   CLERK: No, sir.
33   SCHILLING: So who is it, Evans?
34
35   [3]This scene is based on an article in *The Anaconda Standard* (Anaconda, Montana), 10/9/1889.

1   **EVANS: Gives his name as Ah Sang Ching, sir.**

2   **SCHILLING: Mongolian?**

3   **EVANS: Yes, sir, a Chinaman.**

4   **SCHILLING:** *(Looking up for the first time)* **Then he can't be a**

5   **gentleman, now, can he, Evans?**

6   **EVANS: As you say, sir. Sorry, sir.**

7   **SCHILLING:** *(Throwing down his pen)* **What the heck. Show him in.**

8   **EVANS: Yes, sir.** *(EVANS ushers in CHING who is dressed as*

9   *described below and who carries a large basket heaped with*

10   *garden produce.)* **Mister Ah Sang Chi —** *(Catches himself.)*

11   **Excuse me, sir. Here's Ching.**

12   **SCHILLING: Well, what have we here? No coolie hat? No**

13   **nightgown? No slippers?** *(Surprised by CHING's appearance,*

14   *he stands and slowly circles CHING who stands still — respectful*

15   *but unbending. SCHILLING fingers the items of CHING's*

16   *clothing as he describes it.)* **Instead an ancient straw hat. A pair**

17   **of overalls with one suspender, and a woolen shirt. And no**

18   **queue?** *(Fingering CHING's hair)* **Hair close-clipped like a**

19   **free-born American citizen.** *(Returning to sit at his desk,*

20   *amused)* **So what does this peculiar article want, Evans?**

21   **CHING:** *(His English carries a mixture of British and Asian accent.)* **I**

22   **have come to express my appreciation to the Anaconda**

23   **Company, Mr. Schilling.**

24   **SCHILLING:** *(He is surprised by CHING's speech; his amusement*

25   *fades.)* **Appreciation, is it. What is the heathen so appreciative**

26   **about, Evans?** *(Each time SCHILLING asks questions of the*

27   *clerk in this manner, EVANS begins to answer, but CHING beats*

28   *him/her to it every time.)*

29   **CHING: I am appreciative of Anaconda Company kindly provides**

30   **my ranch with water for my gardens. The year is a good one,**

31   **and I come to show gratitude. I ask you Mr. Schilling, as**

32   **Utilities Manager of Anaconda Company, to accept from me**

33   **this poor appreciation gift of produce from my garden.** *(And*

34   *he extends the basket toward SCHILLING.)*

35   **SCHILLING:** *(A moment's pause, then he rises and goes to CHING.*

1   *He looks at the basket of produce. He turns and picks up a paper*
2   *knife from the desk top and, with it, skewers a tomato which he*
3   *lifts up to examine.)* **What's the market price of tomatoes**
4   **today, Evans?**
5   **CHING: Three dollar fifty for three pound standard tomato, sir.**
6   **SCHILLING: I see. And would you call this a standard tomato,**
7   **Evans?**
8   **EVANS:** *(When CHING doesn't answer)* **I'd say premium, sir.**
9   **CHING: I sell as standard.**
10   **SCHILLING: Foolish practice, Ching.** *(He tips the knife down and*
11   *the fat tomato slides off and falls back in the basket. He returns to*
12   *his desk, leaving CHING with basket extended. As the interview*
13   *continues, he makes a great deal of business of cleaning the knife*
14   *with his handkerchief.)*
15   **CHING: Yes, sir. Ching do better in future, Mr. Schilling.**
16   **SCHILLING: I bet you will. And we provide this "ranch" with**
17   **water, Evans?**
18   **CHING: Yes, sir. Water reaches me by flume, and by means of hose**
19   **and watering pot I keep plants looking tolerably fresh.**
20   **SCHILLING: Did you know about all of this, Evans?**
21   **EVANS: I've seen the place, sir.**
22   **SCHILLING:** *(Surprised again)* **That so? Describe it for me.**
23   **EVANS: Well, sir, it has a log cabin — one large room — enlarged**
24   **on three sides by sheds for his stock. It has a dove cote on top.**
25   **SCHILLING: A dove cote.**
26   **EVANS: Yes, sir, a dove cote. The garden is maybe a quarter of an**
27   **acre, fenced about with barrel staves.**
28   **SCHILLING: What stock, Evans?**
29   **CHING: Twenty-three swine, two horses, and chickens.**
30   **SCHILLING: Chickens? And do the hens lay China eggs?**
31   **CHING: I'm sorry, sir. I don't understand.**
32   **SCHILLING:** *(He sniggers to EVANS, enjoying his little joke.)*
33   **What's he grow in this patch, Evans?**
34   **CHING: Beets, radish, celery, potato, onion, turnip, and tomato,**
35   **sir. Premium tomatoes.**

1 SCHILLING: And we provide the water, Evans?
2 CHING: Thank you, yes.
3 SCHILLING: Free?
4 CHING: Thank you, yes.
5 SCHILLING: Why free, Evans?
6 EVANS: Agreement of deed for the foothill area south-east of town,
7   sir. To encourage development there.
8 SCHILLING: I see. And how did he come on all this estate, Evans?
9 CHING: My cousin done me up, sir. He sell me the ranch last
10   September while I live in San Francisco.
11 SCHILLING: Price?
12 CHING: One thousand, six hundred dollar, sir. Too much.
13 SCHILLING: I'd say. *(He does some quick figures.)* Would he sell,
14   Evans?
15 CHING: I desire to sell and return to my home.
16 SCHILLING: Prefer San Francisco, huh?
17 CHING: China.
18 SCHILLING: I'll give you fourteen hundred for the place, Ching.
19   That'll get you back most of your price, and you can catch the
20   early boat to "Cathay" and lord it over the other coolies as a
21   wealthy man.
22 CHING: *(Not batting an eye)* Twenty-two hundred.
23 SCHILLING: Fifteen.
24 CHING: Not a penny less two thousand.
25 SCHILLING: Your purchase price, then: Sixteen hundred.
26 CHING: Two thousand.
27 SCHILLING: We could cut off your water, Ching.
28 CHING: Yes, sir.
29 SCHILLING: Sixteen.
30 CHING: Two thousand.
31 SCHILLING: *(A pause while he glares at CHING. Then:)* I have an
32   appointment, I believe, Evans. Show the Chinaman out the
33   back way. *(Gesturing at the basket)* He can leave the truck on
34   your desk. *(And he returns to his work.)*
35 EVANS: As you say, sir. *(CHING gives the basket of vegetables to*

158

1   *EVANS, and EVANS shows him out. After a moment:)*
2   **SCHILLING: Evans!**
3   **EVANS:** *(Re-entering)* **Yes, sir?**
4   **SCHILLING: Put the Chinaman on the billing list for twenty-five**
5   **bucks a month.**
6   **EVANS: As you wish, sir.** *(EVANS exits, and SCHILLING returns to*
7   *his figures.)*
8   **ACTOR A: Now that all happened long ago**
9   **When ignorance and greed were strong.**
10   **Thank God we've seen a better day!**
11   **ACTOR B: Our laws insure that everyone in America has equal**
12   **rights.**
13   **ACTORS A and C: Rights! Rights! Rights!**
14   **ACTOR C: We all agree that ethnic slurs are wrong!**
15   **ACTORS A and B: Wrong! Wrong! Wrong!**
16   **ACTOR A: Discrimination because of ethnic origin, sex, marital**
17   **status, physical disability, or religion is wrong!**
18   **ACTORS B and C: Wrong! Wrong! Wrong!**
19   **ACTOR B: So rest easy. The events and viewpoints depicted in our**
20   **little play would never be encountered in America today. Right?**
21   **ACTOR A: Right!**
22   **ACTOR C: Right!**
23   **ACTOR B:** *(To audience)* **Right?**
24
25   ***The End***
26
27
28
29
30
31
32
33
34
35

Monologs

Does Anybody Want a Miss Cow Bayou?
by Gary Garrison

Gary Garrison is the Artistic Director, Producer, and a member of the full-time faculty in the Department of Dramatic Writing Program at NYU's Tisch School of the Arts. His plays include *Rug Store Cowboy, Cherry Reds, Oh Messiah Me, We Make a Wall, Scream with Laughter, Smoothness with Cool,* and *Empty Rooms.* His works have been featured at Primary Stages, the Directors Company, Manhattan Theatre Source, StageWorks, Fourth Unity, Open Door Theatre, African Globe Theatre Company, Pulse Ensemble Theatre, Expanded Arts, and New York Rep.

Does Anyone Want a Miss Cow Bayou? has been produced at Pulse Ensemble Theatre, New York Repertory Theatre Company, and Double Image Theatre, and was included in Samuel French's Thirteenth Annual Off-Off Broadway Short Plays Festival.

Address all inquiries concerning amateur performances or readings of this work to Gary Garrison, 14 Washington Place #2A, New York, NY 10003. For all other permissions, including professional productions or reprinting of this work *or any portion thereof,* contact Fifi Oscard at Fifi Oscard Talent and Literary Agency, 212/764-1100. For details, see "Part II: Securing Rights for Your Production," pages 183 to 192.

1   The action takes place in an auditorium during the Miss Texas
2   beauty pageant.
3   **CHARACTERS:** JEANETTE — a stocky 19-year-old. She speaks
4   with a very thick, very drawn southeast Texas accent.
5   THREE JUDGES—optional.
6   **SETTING:** A stage with a folding table and three folding chairs in
7   front of it for the JUDGES. The table holds notepads, coffee cups,
8   pencils, etc.
9
10   *(Houselights are full up. Three JUDGES sit at the table with their*
11   *backs to the audience. They look towards the stage. JEANETTE*
12   *walks to center stage carrying her guitar case. She bends down,*
13   *lays the case on the floor, retrieves a note card, looks at it, folds*
14   *it in half, and puts her hands behind her back. She is stiff,*
15   *awkward, and extremely nervous. As her speech begins, the*
16   *houselights slowly fade.)*
17   **JEANETTE:** *(Obviously memorized)* **Hi! My name is Jean Shirley—**
18   **I mean, Jeanette Shirley ... could I start over? ... Hi! My**
19   **name is Jeanette Shirley Bartlett, and I grew up in Vidor,**
20   **Texas, in 1962 ... I, uhm, ...** *(Looking at the note card)* **Okay, I,**
21   **uhm, okay, I went to school at the Vidor High School, home to**
22   **the Mighty Vidor Pirates.** *Go Pirates!* *(She blows a shrill finger*
23   *whistle and improvises a cheerleader's jump.)*
24   **I was a very active member and a proud squad leader of the**
25   **Mighty Vidorettes Drill Team and Marching Xylophone and**
26   **Drum Squad. I was under the direction of Lonnie Thibodeaux**
27   **... the third.** *(A deep sigh)* **I was also involved in other activities**
28   **while in high school. I was, after all, the fourth place winner of**
29   **the Betty Crocker Cooking Award for my Tuna-On-A-Tight**
30   **Budget proposal. I have also been a babysitter, too, in my life.**
31   **After finishin' high school, I spent the next two years learnin' to**
32   **clip poodles and other assorted dogs. I plan to continue my**
33   **education. I thank you ...** *Oh, wait!* *(Clearing her throat, then*
34   *very seriously)* **I am also concerned with world issues.** *(Bouncing*
35   *back)* **I thank you.** *(A loud buzzer sounds, marking the end of the*

1   *interview. JEANETTE takes a few timid steps.)*

2   **Lissun', I know that weren't very good, but I made it up**

3   **'fore I come in here. Aunt Dee didn't tell me you had to have**

4   **a speech for this thang. Miss—Houston—that girl that came**

5   **in before me who kept spittin' on you when she talked—she**

6   **told me out in the hall. Soooooo, I made a speech up the best I**

7   **could.** *(A long, awkward pause)*

8   **Look, 'fore you say anythang, I know what you're a**

9   **thankin'. And hell, you're right. I ain't purdy. I ain't never**

10   **been purdy. Hear tell it, when I was born I looked like the**

11   **north end of a mule's butt.** *(Laughing nervously)*

12   **Anyway, I know I ain't purdy, and I know I talk funny. I**

13   **didn't know you were suppose to be real purdy to be here.**

14   **'Cept I started lookin' at all them Miss … Whatevers out**

15   **there in that lounge, and I thought, "Well, damn, I guess I**

16   **should be lookin' sorta like them, huh?" … Aunt Dee never**

17   **said nothin' about havin' to be purdy for this thang.** *(Another*

18   *long, grueling pause)*

19   **You didn't have to be expecially purdy for the Miss Cow**

20   **Bayou Contest. All you had to do was rope a few calves, and**

21   **hell, I knew I could do that better than anyone, 'cept Mary**

22   **Sue Reinhardt, who thank God met with an unfortunate**

23   **accident prior to the contest. If she'd been there, I really**

24   **woulda had a run for my money.** *(Realizing what she's said)* **Not**

25   **that I wish anyone harm! No! Not at all! I'm a Christian**

26   **woman … sort of. Anyway, I'm off the track now. Where was**

27   **I?** *(Thinking hard)*

28   **Oh! Now I come to this Miss Texas Pageant and find out**

29   **you gotta be purdy to be here. It didn't say that no where on**

30   **the application. Or if it did, I didn't see it.** *(She moves a step*

31   *closer.)*

32   **Hell, I don't even believe that myself. I knew you had to be**

33   **purdy to be here. I seen one of them contests on the TV at the**

34   **Sears store while I was waitin' for them to put a battery in my**

35   **truck. I don't know who I was foolin' when I filled out that**

1	application. *(Another measured step forward)*
2	You just gotta let me on that TV show, though. Aunt Dee —
3	who has always been a real burr in my butt — said I probably
4	ain't got a shot-in-hell's chance of winnin', but you gotta let
5	me on there. My best friend, Darlene Thompson, said you give
6	an award for bein' the most friendly. Well, I been out there
7	shakin' everybody's hand, and tellin' them how nice they look
8	and everything. Go on, go on out there and ask them how
9	friendly I been. They'll tell you. I'm their favorite. I just open
10	my mouth and they bust a gut laughin'. They like me — a
11	whole lot. Most of 'em. *(The buzzer sounds again. The JUDGES*
12	*don't move.)*
13	S'that buzzer mean it's over and done? S'that mean, "get
14	out?" … Is it just the three of ya' decidin' this thang? *(A*
15	*JUDGE coughs.)*
16	S'that some sorta signal to tell the others it's time to get rid
17	of me? Well, I ain't goin'! I'm gonna stay in here 'till you tell
18	me I can be on that TV show broadcast all over this big state.
19	*(The buzzer sounds again. A JUDGE stands to speak.)*
20	*Sit down, Bucko!* Look, if I didn't have no trouble ropin' a
21	two-hundred pound calf in ten seconds, what makes you think
22	I couldn't get you down in three? *(Picking up guitar case)*
23	I brought along my guitar in case you wanted to hear my
24	talent. I dropped my pick in the toilet, though. I was in there
25	rehearsin' before I come in here, and it just fell right through
26	my legs. So I gotta use my fangers. *(Strikes a few cords, then,*
27	*obviously memorized.)*
28	For you, honorable Judges, I have chose a song that I like,
29	and I'm sure you will too. My talent is sangin' "Take the
30	Ribbon from My Hair" in the style of the very beautiful
31	Tammy Wynette. *(JEANETTE sings a beautiful rendition of this*
32	*song. A JUDGE stands to interrupt.)*
33	Hey, wait. I ain't finished yet. I still got another verse. And
34	as my vocal coach, Miss Mimi Lambert, said, "It is chock full
35	of drama." *(This JUDGE begins to leave.)*

1	*Hey! Sit down before I bust this guitar over your pumpkin*
2	*head, boy!* Now look, I don't like bein' mean. It ain't in my
3	nature. But the three of ya are sittin' there lookin' at me like I
4	was crazy or somethin', not sayin' a damn word, and not
5	givin' me a chance to … I gotta be on the TV show! *(The buzzer*
6	*sounds again. JEANETTE drops the guitar on the floor, making a*
7	*loud, distorted clang.)*
8	Please? … Alright, well, I ain't gonna take up no more of
9	your time. *(She turns to exit, stops, and turns slowly to face the*
10	*JUDGES.)*
11	Damn you! … I don't care if I burn an extra day in hell for
12	sayin' it, but *damn you!* You ain't got a heart among the three
13	of ya. No feelin'. None of ya. I worked at Marsh's Body Shop
14	for a solid year, saved every penny I made to come to Odessa;
15	rode on the stinkin' Greyhound Bus to get here 'cause my
16	truck needs a new fuel pump. I come here, and all you can do
17	is cough, and roll your eyes and shake your head — yeah, I
18	seen it — it's all over your face. But I got up the damn nerve
19	to come here. Don't that count for nothin'? … I know I ain't
20	like them other girls. I never thought I had to be 'till I walked
21	into that lounge and seen all that teased hair and crap they got
22	all over their faces to make 'em look better than they ever
23	could be in broad daylight. *(A beat)*
24	Ain't you gonna ask me my "Likes and Dislikes" question?
25	*(Still no response. No one, including JEANETTE, knows what to do.)*
26	You're probably rackin' your brain to figger out what to do
27	with me. Well, you ain't the first, so don't feel too bad. Nobody
28	has ever known what to do with me — Aunt Dee, my momma
29	and daddy. *(A step forward)*
30	See, that's why I got to be on the TV — Aunt Dee told me
31	my momma and daddy didn't know what to do with me when
32	they had me, so they left me at Aunt Dee's Laundromat with
33	a note and a twenty-dollar bill. *(Another step)*
34	I figgered that if I get on the TV show, Momma and
35	Daddy'd see me, and they'd … they'd know what to do with

me now ... I know they watch the pageant 'cause Aunt Dee told me my momma was Miss Texas, 1974. And she was real proud of it. And she watches the show every year, waitin' to see if they ever do her a tribute. *(A beat)*

I wouldn't have to be a finalist or nothin'. Maybe I could hold the theme flag or somethin'. *(The buzzer sounds one last time.)*

Don't make me beg. *(As she's mouthing the word "please," the lights fade out.)*

The End

Fallin' Together

by Madeleine Martin
In memory of Leilani, who walks with angels

Madeleine Martin's works have been published both nationally and internationally. An award-winning playwright, her plays have been produced in educational settings and off-off Broadway since 1993. She received her playwriting education as a private student of Dr. Norman A. Bert. Currently she is working on a children's book centered around a dog with silky white hair and placing the finishing touches on a full-length play about life after being a police officer.

This monolog has had no publications or performances prior to publication in this anthology.

Address all inquiries concerning performances, readings, or reprinting of this work *or any portion thereof* to Madeleine Martin, PO Box 53521, Lubbock, TX 79453. For details, see "Part II: Securing Rights for Your Production," pages 183 to 192.

1   The action takes place in the present.

2   **CHARACTER:** LANI — a young married woman who looks older

3   than she should.

4   **SETTING:** LANI's living room.

5

6   **I fell apart in Wal-Mart today, Bobby.** *(She laughs.)* **"Fell**

7   **Apart." That sounds like something a toaster does when you drop**

8   **it. My arms and legs didn't fall off or nuthin' like that. But my**

9   **stomach fell into my toes.**

10   **See, I was walkin' through the housewares department ... Shut**

11   **up, Bobby! I'm talkin' now!**

12   **I wasn't searchin' for anything to buy because I didn't have any**

13   **extra money to buy anything with. You made sure of that. You took**

14   **all our money to the bar for shots and beer and pool and cigarettes**

15   **and ...** *(Pause)* **And I was jus' killin' time, waitin' for my**

16   **prescription to come up. My pills. Last thing we need around here**

17   **is another mouth to feed and more doctor bills that we can't pay.**

18   **But I was just lookin' around at some of the things I wished we**

19   **had but can't afford and you know, you might find this boring, but**

20   **you will listen, Bobby. This time, you will listen!**

21   **I saw these pretty picture frames — you know, the kind that**

22   **comes with the wedding pictures already in them with the**

23   **handsome grooms and their pretty brides. None of those brides are**

24   **pregnant, have you ever noticed that? Then I noticed this one**

25   **pewter frame that had hearts and bells all over it, and it was so**

26   **beautiful, but someone had taken blood red lipstick and drawn a**

27   **heart on the glass and they had wrote in that heart, "Bobby loves**

28   **Melissa."**

29   **That's when my stomach fell into my toes. That's when I**

30   **remembered those phone calls you been gettin' from some**

31   **"Melissa," and you said they were just silly pranks.**

32   **Don't you look at me like that.**

33   **I remembered all those late nights "with the guys," and all**

34   **those times my friends had been tryin' to tell me about what was**

35   **goin' on with you and that barmaid down there where you spend all**

1   our money. My money, I should say. I'm the one with the job. I
2   know — you have been "tryin' your hardest to find work."

3   That's when I knew, right then and there, in Wal-Mart, holding
4   that pewter wedding picture frame — and the tears just started
5   streamin' down my face.

6   Don't talk, Bobby! I don't want to hear a word you have to say
7   because it's all lies! You may want to believe that I'm some stupid
8   teenager who's so wild-eyed nuts over you that you can do or say
9   anything you want, but no more. *(Pause)* No more.

10   See — I found myself sobbin' louder and louder. It was
11   humiliatin'. But I couldn't stop. All these people were starin' at me.
12   And then ... then out of nowhere there was this big woman who was
13   grabbin' me and holdin' me and huggin' me and she said, "There,
14   there honey, what man are you bawlin' over like that?" She said
15   it had to be a man because only a man could make a woman blubber
16   like that. I buried my head in her giant breasts and just cried like
17   a baby. Go ahead and laugh, Bobby. You can think this is real
18   funny, now.

19   Turns out, her name is Ivy and she works at a place called
20   Women's Services, and we sat and had coffee. Shut up, Bobby. I can
21   have coffee with whoever I want, whenever I want, and you got
22   nuthin' to say about it.

23   She paid. While we were drinkin' our coffee and talkin', they
24   called on the loud speaker that my prescription was ready, and it
25   was right then that I fell together again. Ivy said to me just like this,
26   all cool and calm, she said, "Do you really need those birth control
27   pills?" It was right then I decided I didn't, Bobby, 'cause you got
28   yourself a new bed tonight.

29   See, Ivy asked me about these bruises too. I told her about last
30   night, and she told me about people that can help me. Sit down,
31   Bobby. I'm not afraid of you anymore. *(There is a knock at the door.)*

32   See — your ride is here. They're gonna' take you to your new
33   bed tonight. The flashin' lights are just a bonus. And when you get
34   out, I won't be here.

35   By the way, Bobby. I used the prescription money to buy that

1   **frame, blood-red lipstick and all, to remind myself about men like**

2   **you. And I'm gonna keep it forever just the way it is.** *(Another knock*

3   *at the door.)*

4   **You better get the door, Bobby. It's for you.**

5

6   ***The End***

7

8

9

10

11

12

13

14

15

16

17

18

19

20

21

22

23

24

25

26

27

28

29

30

31

32

33

34

35

Pretenses

by Louise Stinespring

Louise M. Stinespring received her Ph.D. in Fine Arts from Texas Tech University where she subsequently taught in the Department of Theatre and Dance. Prior to moving to Texas, she studied acting with Sanford Meisner at the Neighborhood Playhouse in Manhattan and then pursued a career as a professional actress.

Pretenses has had no publications or performances prior to publication in this anthology.

Address all inquiries concerning performances, readings, or reprinting of this work *or any portion thereof* to Louise M. Stinespring, 4804 77th Street, Lubbock, TX. 79424. For details, see "Part II: Securing Rights for Your Production," pages 183 to 192.

1   The action takes place in the present.

2   ***CHARACTER:*** A WOMAN — mid 20s to early 40s. She is attractive,

3   WASP-y looking, and dressed in totally white tennis clothes.

4   ***SETTING:*** A bare stage.

5

6   *(A WOMAN enters carrying a tennis racket and ball. She starts to*

7   *serve right into the audience; she tosses the ball up but then catches it.*

8   *She speaks to the audience.)*

9   **I can't serve and I don't want to hit you.** *(Flings racket behind*

10   *her and tucks ball in skirt pocket).*

11   **I got hit in the neck with a ball once. It was an accident, I think.**

12   **My sister has a good serve and I was standing too close to the net.**

13   **She apologized and started to serve again. I walked off the court,**

14   **left three women gaping at me, got in my car and drove away from**

15   **Wainscott forever. That was five years ago. It was match point, too.**

16   **A ladies doubles match against Maidstone and the Turner girls were**

17   **about to win, maybe. But, of course, since I left the court we lost.**

18   **Sally, from Maidstone, called me later that day to ask about my**

19   **neck. I was living in Patchogue and Sally must have gotten the**

20   **number from my mother, who was watching with grim despair. I**

21   **caught a glance of her face as I started the engine. But, the Georgica**

22   **women still won the tournament, thanks to my mother who won her**

23   **match. I wish you could see those Georgica clay courts: the green**

24   **clay and the pristine white lines and the windmill that you could**

25   **walk into. The tennis committee always had their annual meeting**

26   **on the Saturday of Labor Day weekend at four p.m. The Windmill**

27   **Party always started promptly at five, and the lawn by the courts**

28   **became beautifully sprinkled with silk and cottons and gauze and**

29   **Pepsi-cola neckties all moving rhythmically towards and away from**

30   **the bar, carefully placed at an acceptable distance from the guests,**

31   **but close enough to get a quick refill when needed. The children's**

32   **table always had better food than the grown-up table: delicious**

33   **gourmet chocolate chip cookies and a creamy vegetable dip with a**

34   **yummy kind of an orange flavor. I miss the dunes the most. You**

35   **weren't allowed to sit on them, but every once in a while, I'd drive**

1   to the beach at dawn and climb on the dunes and gaze at the white
2   waves and pretend that life was easy. But always some car would
3   invariably arrive just in time to spoil my illusion. On a good day, it
4   would be an older, quiet adult. On a bad day it would be that
5   mommy and baby duo: up at dawn, and craving a little quality time.
6   And I would lose my grip on my imaginary easy life, and I'd widen
7   my smile and say, "Good morning, it's going to be a beautiful day,
8   don't you think?"

9

10   *The End*

11

12

13

14

15

16

17

18

19

20

21

22

23

24

25

26

27

28

29

30

31

32

33

34

35

Fear of Falling
by Norman A. Bert

Norman Bert has taught playwriting and script analysis in colleges and universities since the mid-seventies. He has directed over thirty productions and served as an ACTF adjudicator. In addition to the present anthology, his published books include *Theatre Alive: An Introductory Anthology of World Drama, One-Act Plays for Acting Students — Volumes I and II,* and *The Scenebook for Actors.*

A longer version of *Fear of Falling* was published by Heinemann in *Monologues from the Road: Audition and Performance Pieces*, Lavonne Mueller, editor, 1999.

Address all inquiries concerning performances, readings, or reprinting of this work *or any portion thereof* to Norman A. Bert, 5704 Nashville Avenue, Lubbock, TX 79413-4601. For details, see "Part II: Securing Rights for Your Production," pages 183 to 192.

1   The action takes place on a bus somewhere between Arizona and
2   Montana.
3   *CHARACTER:* ALAN NORTH, Ph.D. — in his 30s. His up-scale
4   clothes are badly wrinkled and travelstained. He has a backpack at
5   his feet.
6   *SETTING:* ALAN sits at the window seat on the bus and speaks to a
7   passenger seated next to him on the aisle.
8
9   **So you think he's drunk? The driver up there. Looks like a**
10   **drunk to me. *[1] Oh come on—it's a *joke*. Don't need to worry about**
11   **bus drivers being drunk. They test 'em all the time. They'd fire his**
12   **butt. * OK, just forget it. * It was a *joke*. Didn't mean to scare you.**
13   *(Pause)*
14   **Know what scares me? Heights. I have this fear of falling. ***
15   **No, I'm not worried about falling off the bus. Buses are safe.**
16   **Canyons, now, that's another thing. A whole nuther thang, as we say**
17   **in Montaner. Couple days ago I sat on the rim of the Grand Canyon**
18   **for two hours. Right on the edge. Confronting my demons, you**
19   **know? OK, not *right* on the edge. I'm no dummy. But still,**
20   **something could happen, you know. * All sorts of things. Like the**
21   **rock ledge I sat on could've broken off just then. There I am, riding**
22   **this chunk of rock to the bottom of the canyon. No, it could happen.**
23   **I could see places where other chunks had broken off, and every one**
24   **of them broke off at some unexpected moment. We're not talking**
25   **paranoia here. My rock could break off, too. Some day it will. Why**
26   **not the day I'm sitting there?** *(Pause)*
27   **Man, I'm really pitted out. Sorry. Been sweaty ever since I got**
28   **on the bus. I know I stink. * Well, sorry anyway.** *(Pause)*
29   **Or some weirdo might push me over. * Over the canyon. Try to**
30   **keep up. * Sorry.** *(Pause)*
31   **Or, standing up after sitting there so long, I might get dizzy and**
32   **fall. Or here's one: in a moment of insanity — and we've all got 'em,**
33   **don't kid yourself, but usually they just pass because there's no**
34
35   [1]Asterisks (*) indicate a verbal response from the speaker's seatmate.

1   opportunity, you know? But I could've had this, this "incident,"
2   and just jumped off. 'Course, none of it happened. But any of it
3   *could* have happened. Happens all the time. *(Pause)*
4   Y'know, riding this bus is like sitting on the edge of the Grand
5   Canyon. Only it's not just two hours. A day and a half, headed back
6   to good ol' Billings. A day and a half sitting on this other rim, see,
7   staring into this other abyss. Talk about your *terror. (Pause)*
8   What I mean is, I'm on the *edge.* Here, check out these clothes:
9   Timberland hiking boots. Slates — like on TV? In-style, out-sized
10   cotton shirt. I paid over two hundred dollars for these clothes. Hell,
11   the boots probably cost that much. Never can remember prices.
12   Now they look like I might've got 'em at Goodwill — the whole
13   outfit for fifteen bucks. But underneath the sweat and the wrinkles,
14   I'm solid. Middle-class. Even got a Ph.D. Yeah. A Ph.D. * College
15   professor. That's another story. Actually, it's *this* story. This is what
16   scares me, you see? *(Pause)*
17   What I'm saying is, just riding the bus is degrading. * Oh,
18   relax! *I'm* riding it, right? But you gotta admit, the bus is
19   America's lowest form of transportation. Here we are — the Great
20   Unwashed. And I'm not just *with* them — I'm one of 'em. That's
21   what scares me. Look around. Look at us. We ain't bootiful, friend,
22   we ain't even *purty.* Some of us are old and unwanted. Him, for
23   instance — not a friend in the world; no one'd care if he died on the
24   bus; a pauper's grave and no one at the funeral. Some of us have
25   the shakes or mumble to ourselves. Oh, we have lots of neuroses and
26   character disorders — real visible. But what do we care? We're
27   *down*, see? If people find us unpleasant to look at, they can look the
28   other direction. And one of us is Professor Alan North, solid,
29   respectable, middle-class stock, big family, church folk, well off. But
30   somehow wrong, on the edge. Lousy marriage. Lousy school. Pitted
31   out. Avoiding eye contact. Babbling to a stranger who couldn't care
32   less. * Oh, please. You're stuck here, and you're too polite to tell me
33   to shut up, and I appreciate it, but let's not pretend we care, OK?
34   *(Pause)*
35   What I'm saying is, this is the brink. For me, this is the *edge.*

1   Just look around. These people scare the dickens out of me. I
2   already look and smell like them. What's to keep me from *becoming*
3   them? *(Pause)*
4   Not a guard rail in sight. *(Pause)*
5   Oh well, survived Grand Canyon. I take comfort in that.
6   'Course that's just an analogy. Analogies illustrate. They don't
7   prove diddly. *
8   What's an analogy? It's uh — Umm — Nothing. Forget it. I
9   talk too much. Look, you want this bottle? * Go ahead. Still half
10   full. Lambrusco. No backwash, either. I'm real careful. Yeah. Real
11   careful.
12
13   *The End*
14
15
16
17
18
19
20
21
22
23
24
25
26
27
28
29
30
31
32
33
34
35

Fathers and Sons:
The Dust Chasin' Me Out, The Dark House That Held You, and The Green Time

by Geoffrey Howard

Geoffrey Howard has enjoyed a broad theatre experience as an actor, director, designer, and playwright. He received his M.F.A. in Directing/Acting from Texas Tech University.

These monologs have had no publications or performances prior to publication in this anthology.

Production Suggestions

Originally conceived as three, separate audition pieces, these monologs share a common theme. They can be presented separately or together. The actor will need to analyze the speeches and, on that basis, decide what the situation is and who the speaker is or, if the actor decides they are different characters, who the speakers are. The actor should be as clear and specific about these decisions as possible.

Address all inquiries concerning performances, readings, or reprinting of this work *or any portion thereof* to Geoffrey Howard, 620 E. Escondido, Kingsville, TX 78363. For details, see "Part II: Securing Rights for Your Production," pages 183 to 192.

1   The action of these three speeches takes place in times and places
2   to be determined by the actor.
3   ***CHARACTER:*** A MAN — or MEN — with identities to be developed
4   by the actor.
5   ***SETTING:*** A bare stage.
6
7
8   ***The Dust Chasin' Me Out***
9
10   **What does he want from me? I give him everything I can. You'd**
11   **like to think you learn from your past. You'd like to look back**
12   **someday and see that you are better than how you were raised.**
13   **The day I left, the only farm I saw was somehow compacted**
14   **into an area the size of my rearview mirror. An entire life squished**
15   **into a grimy reflection. Momma cryin'. Her hands knotted in a dirty**
16   **apron. Daddy never changing. He just stood there holdin' that gate.**
17   **His eyes of steel and hard leather hands that never touched me in a**
18   **moment of ... cracked tobacco lips scared to death they might**
19   **whisper a kind word. He just stood there holdin' that gate open**
20   **while I drove away with the dust chasing me out.**
21   **I wanted to be better. I wanted, I vowed that my son would**
22   **know how I felt, that his every step was a moment of pride ... But**
23   **here I sit with him outside and me in here with the best of intentions.**
24   **A person would like to think they learn from the past, that they**
25   **will somehow be better than how they were raised.**
26
27
28
29
30
31
32
33
34
35

The Dark House That Held You

Is he good to you? Does he treat you all right? Good.

I dreamed about you the other night. I think the funny thing about dreams is that anything can happen, but none of it makes sense when you talk about it.

Some other man had taken you. But he lived just across the street from me. I stepped out onto my porch in a cold night wind. I stood in the shadow looking at the dark house that held you. For all you knew, you were a guest.

I began to fantasize the most horrible things. I saw this man in my rifle sights. I saw his face exploding as he held you just outside my grasp.

Then I saw a small shadow creeping outside. It was you. You looked at me, this strange shadow across from you. I began to motion frantically for you to come to me. But of course you wouldn't come to a stranger.

I stepped off the porch, into the streetlights. I waved to you again, in a silent scream to come to me. You saw me. You were so happy to see me. You ran to me as any son would to his father. You ran to me, closer and closer ... Then I woke up ... and so ... so I don't know if you made it back to me or not.

The Green Time

He could say the damnedest things sometimes …

"There is a time in my memory when my age was not measured in years."

"What time is that?" I asked him.

"The green time," he replied. "That time when all I cared for was running. I don't remember how old I was. I only remember running … barefoot. Hot grass, cold stones. Being chased and chasing … "

I sit and smile and wait. Watching half the story being told in his piercing eyes. His cold supper is forgotten before him. He goes away for awhile and comes back with a start.

"Beth!" he exclaims as if finding something lost. He smiles and I see him see her. "I remember chasing Beth. We grew up together, ya know? She lived across Stone Creek. Wonder what ever happened to her."

"You caught her. You married her, Dad." I try and smile again.

He looks puzzled, afraid. I see the fear creep back to reclaim him. No, don't go away, Dad. His big hands, now wrinkled and weak but still showing every day of his life, begin to tremble. He looks at me … that soft whisper betraying his heart.

"Who the hell are you?"

"Frank." I try not to speak too much. They tell me it confuses him. I see him try and accept this. He still has that strength of spirit despite his treasonous mind. He begins to fidget.

"It's OK. You were telling me about Beth." I say.

"Who?"

I look out the window past him and watch Stone Creek trundle along as he looks past me, both of us trying to find the green time.

Part 2
Securing Rights for Your Production

Securing Rights for Your Production

Why Secure Rights?

A play producer's first responsibility is to secure performance rights for the "property," the script. If you do not have a designated producer, *you* should take care of this legal detail. Three reasons make it important for performers to be scrupulous about securing performing rights to the plays they do:

Artistic Reasons: New plays are the lifeblood of the theatre, and playwrights are your fellow artists. Knowing you are performing their plays and (when appropriate) receiving money for your use of their property encourages playwrights to turn out more and better scripts. You owe it to your art and your fellow artists to secure rights.

Ethical Reasons: Using a script without permission is theft. It does not suddenly become theft when you join a semi-professional acting company. As a person of integrity you owe it to yourself to secure rights.

Legal Reasons: It's the law. Neglecting to secure performance rights lays you open to fines, lawsuits, and other sanctions.

How to Secure Rights for Scripts in this Anthology

In order to make it easier for you to secure performance rights, the playwrights of scripts in this book have agreed to special arrangements. These arrangements apply to scripts in this anthology only.

To secure rights for your production:

1. Using the following descriptions, decide which kinds of production you are doing.

2. Fill out the Performance Agreement Form or Performance Report that corresponds to your type of production. You may either tear out the form included in this book or photocopy it.

3. In the case of Competition or Full-Scale Amateur Productions, send the P.A.F. and royalty payment to the address at the end of the introduction to

your script. Do this *at least* two weeks prior to your performance.

4. In the case of Class Projects and Departmental Juries, you may complete and send the Performance Report after the production.

Types of Productions

Class Projects and Departmental Juries. These performances are open only to students and instructors of your institution. There is no advertising outside your institution and no admission is charged. For **Class Projects and Departmental Juries**, no royalties are charged; however, since many playwrights like to know when their property is being used by students, you are encouraged to fill out the Optional Performance Report and send it to the author as a courtesy.

Competition Performances. This category covers performances done for contests sponsored by recognized state, regional, or national organizations; these performances have no production budget, and no admission is charged the spectators. **Competition Performances** must pay a nominal $5.00 royalty and secure permission by filing the appropriate Performance Agreement Form.

Full-Scale, Amateur Productions. These productions have no restrictions in terms of production budget, size of audience, admission charges, or publicity, but the performers are not members of Actors Equity. **Full Productions** must pay royalties ($20.00) for the first performance and ($15.00) for each subsequent performance, and they must secure rights by filing the appropriate Performance Agreement Form.

Other Productions. All other productions, including performances by Equity companies and productions to be broadcast or produced as movies, must negotiate rights and royalties with the playwrights or their agents.

Optional Performance Report for a
Class Project/Departmental Jury Production

of the play _____

by _____, playwright,

as the script is printed in ***New One-Act Plays for Acting Students.***

This is to inform you that we of the _____

department of _____ *(institution),*

at _____

_____ *(address),*

performed the above-named script as a Class Project or Departmental Jury on

_____ *(dates).*

This performance had no audience other than students and instructors of our institution. We did not advertise the performance outside our institution, nor did we charge admission to the performance.

We included the playwright's name in all printed announcements or programs.

If we perform this production of this script under circumstances other than those listed above, we will first negotiate performance rights for those performances in a separate document.

We think the playwright would be interested to know the following details about our production and/or responses to the script:

_____

_____

_____

_____

_____

_____

_____

_____

_____

_____

Signed: _____

Title or Position: _____

Date: _____

At your option, send this completed form, or a photocopy thereof, to the playwright or playwright's agent as indicated in the script's introduction. No royalty payments are required for Class Project or Departmental Jury performances of the scripts in this anthology.

Performance Agreement Form for a Competition Performance

of the play _____

by _____, playwright,

as the script is printed in *New One-Act Plays for Acting Students.*

We hereby request permission to perform the above-named script in competition under the auspices of _____

_____ *(sponsoring organization),* a

recognized LOCAL, STATE, REGIONAL, NATIONAL *(circle one)*

organization, on _____ *(dates)*

at _____
(name and address of performance place).

We hereby certify that this performance has no production budget and that no admission will be charged to attend the performances.

If we perform this production of this script under circumstances other than those listed above, we will first negotiate performance rights for those performances in a separate document.

In consideration of the right to perform the script under the above-specified circumstances only, we enclose herewith the sum of $5.00.

We further agree to include the playwright's name in all printed announcements of the performances and to include in all programs the playwright's name and the following statement: "*(Title of play)* is performed by special arrangement with the playwright."

Signed: _____

Title or Position: _____

Date: _____

Producing
Organization: _____

Address: _____

Telephone Number: (   ) _____

At least two weeks prior to the performance dates indicated above, send this completed form, or a photocopy thereof, along with a check for $5.00, to the playwright or playwright's agent as indicated in the script's introduction.

Receipt of this form and royalty payment by the playwright or agent automatically secures performance rights to this play under the competition circumstances and limitations specified above.

Performance Agreement Form for a Full-Scale, Amateur Production

of the play _____

by _____, playwright,

as the script is printed in *New One-Act Plays for Acting Students.*

We hereby request permission to present _____ *(number)*

performances of a Full-Scale Amateur Production of the above-named script

on _____ *(dates)*

at _____
(name of performance space)

at _____.
(address)

We hereby certify that this is a non-Equity production.

If we perform this script under circumstances other than those listed above, we will first negotiate performance rights for those performances in a separate document.

In consideration of the right to perform the script under the above-specified circumstances only, we enclose herewith $20.00 for the first performance and $15.00 for each subsequent performance, being a total of $ _____.

We further agree to include the playwright's name in all printed announcements of the performances and to include in all programs the playwright's name and the following statement: *"(Title of play)* is presented by special arrangement with the playwright."

Signed: _____

Title or Position: _____

Producing
Organization: _____

Address: _____

Telephone Number: (   ) _____

At least two weeks prior to the performance dates indicated above, send this completed form, or a photocopy thereof, along with a check for the royalties to the playwright or playwright's agent as indicated in the script's introduction.

Receipt of this form and royalty payment by the playwright or agent automatically secures performance rights to this play under the Amateur Production circumstances and limitations as specified above.

Part 3
Rehearsing the Play

The third part of this book provides assistance for actors who are preparing a play without a director. Depending on your experience, you may use this section in different ways. Relatively inexperienced actors should read and use most of the materials as they work at developing their own rehearsal methods. Actors with considerable experience and training may find much of the material unnecessary; even these actors, however, are likely to encounter rehearsal problems for which they have no immediate solutions, and in cases like these, they may find some of the suggestions helpful as trouble-shooting tools.

Scheduling the Rehearsals

Sample Rehearsal Schedules

Here are samples of three approaches to preparing a play. If none of them suit your needs exactly, borrow some ideas from them and construct your own schedule. The "Rehearsal Calendar" that follows the third sample schedule provides a convenient place for you to record your plans.

Sample Schedule A: This loosely organized schedule demands considerable self-discipline and inventiveness from actors.

Learning about the characters and the play using read-throughs, discussion, improvisations, and research. Approximate number of rehearsals: _____.

Session with a coach to check progress and get suggestions.

Dealing with technical details such as blocking and memorization. Approximate number of rehearsals: _____.

Session with a coach to get feedback and suggestions.

Polishing the play for performance. Approximate number of rehearsals: _____.

Performing.

Sample Schedule B: This schedule forms the basis for the rehearsal session guides *(pages 203 to 217)*.

Analyzing the script.
Reading the script together.
Improvising.
Playing the given circumstances.
Investigating character identity.
Playing the intentions.
Rehearsing with a coach to get feedback and suggestions.
Incorporating technical elements.
Repeating earlier concentration points (optional, as needed).

195

Getting off book.
Bringing it all together.
Rehearsing with a coach to get feedback and suggestions.
Repeat of synthesizing rehearsal (optional, as needed).
Final dress rehearsal.
Performing.

Sample Schedule C: This schedule will work best if you have a coach who will give a lot of time and guidance to your project.

Individual script analysis.
Read-through: group script analysis.
Improvisations.
First blocking rehearsal.
Second blocking rehearsal.
Monitored blocking rehearsal.
Revising your blocking.
Characterization: given circumstances.
Characterization: character analysis.
Characterization: objectives.
Memorization: putting down the book.
Memorization: confirming your memory.
Monitored characterization rehearsal.
Characterization: bringing it all together.
First technical rehearsal.
Second technical rehearsal.
Pacing rehearsal (with a coach's assistance).
Final dress rehearsal.
Performance.

Rehearsal Calendar

Play title: _____

Actor's name: _____ Telephone: _____

Actor's name: _____ Telephone: _____

Actor's name: _____ Telephone: _____

First rehearsal. Date: _____ Place: _____ Time: _____

    Concentration point: _____

    Warm-up leader: _____

Second rehearsal. Date: _____ Place: _____ Time: _____

    Concentration point: _____

    Warm-up leader: _____

Third rehearsal. Date: _____ Place: _____ Time: _____

    Concentration point: _____

    Warm-up leader: _____

Fourth rehearsal. Date: _____ Place: _____ Time: _____

    Concentration point: _____

    Warm-up leader: _____

Fifth rehearsal. Date: _____ Place: _____ Time: _____

    Concentration point: _____

    Warm-up leader: _____

Sixth rehearsal. Date: _____ Place: _____ Time: _____

   Concentration point: _____

   Warm-up leader: _____

Seventh rehearsal. Date: _____ Place: _____ Time: _____

   Concentration point: _____

   Warm-up leader: _____

Eighth rehearsal. Date: _____ Place: _____ Time: _____

   Concentration point: _____

   Warm-up leader: _____

Ninth rehearsal. Date: _____ Place: _____ Time: _____

   Concentration point: _____

   Warm-up leader: _____

Tenth rehearsal. Date: _____ Place: _____ Time: _____

   Concentration point: _____

   Warm-up leader: _____

Eleventh rehearsal. Date: _____ Place: _____ Time: _____

   Concentration point: _____

   Warm-up leader: _____

Twelfth rehearsal. Date: _____ Place: _____ Time: _____

   Concentration point: _____

   Warm-up leader: _____

Thirteenth rehearsal. Date: _____ Place: _____ Time: _____

    Concentration point: _____

    Warm-up leader: _____

Fourteenth rehearsal. Date: _____ Place: _____ Time: _____

    Concentration point: _____

    Warm-up leader: _____

Fifteenth rehearsal. Date: _____ Place: _____ Time: _____

    Concentration point: _____

    Warm-up leader: _____

Sixteenth rehearsal. Date: _____ Place: _____ Time: _____

    Concentration point: _____

    Warm-up leader: _____

Seventeenth rehearsal. Date: _____ Place: _____ Time: _____

    Concentration point: _____

    Warm-up leader: _____

Eighteenth rehearsal. Date: _____ Place: _____ Time: _____

    Concentration point: _____

    Warm-up leader: _____

Performance. Date: _____ Place: _____ Time: _____

    Warm-up leader: _____

Approaching Rehearsals

Productive Rehearsal Attitudes

Forming good mental attitudes toward time, performance level work, and characterization will help make your rehearsals efficient and productive.

First, determine to use **time** well. Remember that, in contrast to spatial arts like painting, theatre is a time art. The clock, therefore, is one of your most important tools. Never call off a scheduled rehearsal. Even if you don't feel like rehearsing, do it anyway. Nothing can hurt your performance more than skipping rehearsals. Then, once you start to rehearse, rehearse; don't let yourselves wander off on some conversational by-way. And give it a full shot. If you decide on a 1½-hour rehearsal, rehearse for 90 minutes, not 75; if you can't maintain concentration for 90 minutes, try two 50-minute sessions instead.

Second, commit yourselves to concentrating on **performance-level work**. As Stanislavski said, every rehearsal should be a performance and every performance just another rehearsal. Never permit yourself to "just walk through the scene" — act it. Every time. You will progress farther and faster. And never comment when you make a mistake. Breaking character during rehearsals builds bad habits that may haunt you in performance. Furthermore, once you crack, it takes extra time and energy to get back into character.

Finally, work on **characterization** in every rehearsal. Even if you don't think a particular rehearsal has much to do with characterization (for instance, blocking or tech rehearsals), use the time to create your character. Aim to learn something new about your character in each session, and write down these discoveries to help solidify your gains. If you start getting bored, experiment with giving your character a different voice, posture, or personality. And *never* tell yourself or your partner that you need to wait for costumes (or props, or the "real stage," or the Second Coming) before you can really get into character. This game, called Waiting for Santa Claus, is a device poor actors use to deceive themselves. If a costume or prop item is that important, bring it to rehearsal yourself.

Rehearsal Session Procedures

Begin your rehearsal with about five minutes of vocal and physical warm-ups. Warming up will make your rehearsal more successful. Not only will warm-ups help you prepare your body and voice for the different demands you are about to make on them, but they also will prepare you psychologically. If you notice, for instance, that the second or third run-through of your play is better than the first, there's a good chance you're using your first run-through as a warm-up; this is a bad habit for actors to form. And equally important, warm-ups provide a clear transition from everyday life to the time you will spend in rehearsal; if you don't do warm-ups, you will find it more difficult to stop visiting and start concentrating on rehearsal. Divide the responsibility for warm-ups between you and your partner so that neither one of you have to find and lead them all the time. If you don't know any warm-up exercises, several books in the bibliography will give you ideas. A good warm-up session includes activities to do four things: warm up the body, warm up the voice, loosen up the actors' sense of play, and get the actors into character.

Once you start through a scene, work straight through it without stopping for anything. The scripts in this book are short enough to go straight through the entire play without a break. Your rehearsal will be far more productive if you don't stop to discuss each problem that occurs. Many of these problems ("Should I hold the broom in my right hand or my left?") solve themselves in successive repetitions simply through the magic of doing; stopping to talk about them wastes your time and breaks your concentration on character.

After you finish a run-through, briefly discuss the major things you want to change. Briefly. Spend your time rehearsing, not talking about rehearsing. If you are spending more than one-third of your rehearsal time talking, you're talking too much. And don't try to solve all the problems in any one of these discussion periods; focus on two or three major changes. The other problems will wait, or, more likely, solve themselves.

Conclude your rehearsal by summarizing your progress. Talk briefly and specifically about what you have accomplished and what you need to do next time you rehearse. And before leaving, be sure you've agreed on the next rehearsal time and that you've cleaned up the space.

Rehearsing for Specific Objectives

Analyzing the Script Individually

Objective:

To discover as much about your play as you can on first acquaintance.

Techniques:

Begin by reading straight through the script. Aim during this first reading to discover the life of the script. You may find that reading the play aloud helps you feel its rhythms and get immediately in touch with its characters. Reading a script demands a different approach from reading an essay, short story, or poem. If, like most people, you have not read a lot of scripts, you might want to look over "How to Read a Playscript" *(page 218)* before approaching the play itself.

Immediately after your first reading, without taking a break, jot down your first impressions of the play. Aim at description, not evaluation. If you must evaluate, focus more on the positive than the negative; the point is to accept and understand the play on its own terms. Some sample descriptive statements might be: "The play moves fast/slowly." "It is funny/sad/like a soap opera." "It is realistic/a moodpiece/weird."

Next analyze the play in detail. The "Study Questions for Individual Script Analysis" *(pages 219 to 221)* can help you avoid overlooking important aspects of the play. In order to keep your analysis specific and precise, write down your observations.

When you think you've learned everything about the play that you can in one session, give yourself a short break, and then read straight through the script again; aim to see the play as a whole.

Progress assessment:

Take a few moments to register what you have accomplished: What did you know about the script before your first reading, or even immediately *after* the first reading? How much do you know about it now? Congratulate yourself on the difference.

Two further suggestions:

First, don't start memorizing yet; you've got plenty of time, and memorizing too soon may make it harder for you to experiment freely with the script and your role. Second, you may want to highlight your lines, but you're better off not underlining them; underlining fills spaces you may later want for writing notes, and it makes lines harder to read.

Read-Through: Analyzing the Script Together

Objective:

To agree with your fellow actor(s) about the nature of your script.

Techniques:

Begin by reading through the script together. Don't interrupt your reading in order to correct mistakes or try different interpretations; work for flow and worry about improvements later. During this rehearsal, concentrate on your character but don't push; characterization needs to develop naturally throughout the rehearsal schedule. For instance, if you settle on a particular "voice" for your character at this early rehearsal, you may not feel free to experiment with other, potentially better, voices later.

After the read-through, briefly tell each other how you understand the play. One way to do this is to share your responses to the "Study Questions for Individual Script Analysis" *(pages 219 to 221)*. You may want to discuss your different ideas briefly, but don't let this discussion become heated or lengthy; if you simply register your opinions and then move ahead, you'll save time and your disagreements will begin to solve themselves.

Next, read straight through the script again.

Now, using the "Discussion Guide for Group Script Analysis" *(page 221)*, talk about the play. If you agree, you might write down your responses to the questions. If you don't readily agree, discuss your opinions *briefly*, and then read through the script again. After re-reading the play, see if you can reach agreement. If so, write it down; if not, write down your different responses and let it go at that.

Improvising

Objective:

To trigger your imagination for creative play interpretation.

Techniques:

Prepare for this rehearsal by dividing your script into three segments which are roughly equal in length. If, as suggested on page 220, you already divided your play into episodes, you can base these segments on that work; you may need to group some of the smaller episodes together to provide three larger segments for rehearsal purposes. In order to save rehearsal time, do this work before coming to rehearsal; it may be more efficient to assign this task to one partner rather than spending unnecessary time negotiating segment breaks.

Starting with a lively set of warm-ups will help this rehearsal immensely. You need to approach improvisation with a sense of adventure and playfulness, with the intention of taking risks and making mistakes. Warm-ups will help you tune in to your play impulses. You might conclude your warm-up session by playing Leap-Frog all around the rehearsal area. This game will thoroughly activate your body and will help you get past the fear of looking silly — a fear that can destroy improvisations.

After warm-ups, read through the first segment of your play. Now put down the scripts, and without speaking, pantomime your way through the section. Talk about what happens in this segment: Who is doing what to whom? What is different at the end than at the beginning? Try to decide this without looking at the script. Now pantomime your way through the section again. Still without looking at the script, decide what physical activity is similar to the human event in this part of the play: Boxing? Seduction? Hide and seek? Rape? Ping-Pong? A cat with a mouse? Forget the play for a moment and pantomime that activity, complete with appropriate non-verbal noises such as grunts, screams, or laughter. Now re-read the segment you're working with, and then put down the scripts and pantomime it again, this time incorporating some of the behavior of the physical activity you experimented with. Conclude your work on this segment by reading through the scene while doing the pantomime. Don't worry if it doesn't look "realistic"; right now you're after the primitive, underlying lives and conflicts of the characters, not a realistic performance of the scene.

Before going on to the next part of the script, you may want to do a transitional improv to provide variety and help you move from one section to the next. Some suggestions:

Fight-Dance-Fight. Start a slow-motion, no-contact fight with your partner. Do this in character, and be sure to involve your whole body. Gradually let the fight shift into a slow-motion dance, and then change it back into a fight again. For an interesting and productive variation, try switching characters for Fight-Dance-Fight.

Jungle/Barnyard. Pick an animal that your character reminds you of. Imitate the animal, complete with sound, walk (crawl?), and gesture. Once you've "got it," encounter your partner in his/her "animal state." What happens?

Wake-up. Lie on the floor, and completely relax. Imagine yourself to be your character asleep in the early morning of the day on which the events in your play take place. What is your character dreaming about? Morning comes, and your character wakes up, gets out of bed, yawns, and stretches hugely. Suddenly an idea or image or memory pops into your character's mind and you freeze in mid-stretch. Tell your partner what stopped your stretching.

After the transitional improvisation, approach the second segment of the script using the sequence for the first one. Continue to alternate between script-based improvs and transitional improvs until you are through the play.

Progress assessment:

Tell each other one thing you learned about your own character, one thing you learned about each other's character, and one thing you learned about the play.

Problems? If the improvs seem to fall flat and you're learning nothing about your roles, you probably are not committing yourselves fully enough or going far enough with the exercises. In such a case, you might want to ask someone else to help you by directing your improvisations. The assistant's job would be to tell you what to do next, suggest new moves, and push you to experiment further.

Playing the Given Circumstances

Objective:

To **real**-ize your character's situation in terms of time and place.

Techniques:

Prepare your mind for this rehearsal by scouring your script for every scrap of evidence it can give about the location and time of your play. **Where** the play occurs includes not only the country, city, and immediate surroundings (represented by the set), but also what the location and every part of it *means* to your character. **When** the play occurs includes not only the calendar and clock time, but also the psychological moment in your character's life. Writing down all the information you discover about the place and time will help you be specific and is a good device to help you internalize what you have learned. Prepare physically for the rehearsal by collecting any hand props you will need. From now on, use your props in every rehearsal.

Begin by arranging the rehearsal furniture you think you will need, and then do your warm-ups.

After warm-ups, get in "places" to begin your play, and pause. In your mind, go over all the details you discovered about the time and place of your play. Visualize your set as that place; let yourself, as your character, enter into that time. When you sense that both you and your partner are ready, begin the play. Don't worry if you misjudge each other's readiness to start; you can iron out the details later. Go straight through the play, and concentrate *at every moment* on your character living in the time and place of the play.

After your run-through, talk about the beginning of the play. Which one of you gets the scene underway? How will this initiator know when the passive partner is ready? Once you've settled this detail, share your individual lists of time-and-place data. Don't waste time debating your differences — just listen to each other.

Run through the play again. If your perceptions of time and place had significant differences, you might follow this run-through with a brief discussion of any major contrasts in your ideas.

Once you are in places for the next run-through, pause a little longer before starting the action, and imagine where your character has been and what s/he has been doing immediately prior to the play's beginning. If you can, visualize this "moment-before" in considerable detail, and if you make a habit of going through it like a mental play-before-the-play prior to each entrance, you'll never suffer the embarrassment of coming on stage out of character. Perform the play, and then briefly discuss anything you'd like to change about your scene. If you have time, it would probably be a good idea to go through the play a fourth time before quitting; remember to concentrate on making real the time and place of the action.

Progress assessment:

Conclude your rehearsal by each telling the other one thing you learned about your character or play during the session.

A note on set arrangement and blocking: You will be wise to postpone blocking until you are more familiar with your characters and the play. Many directors pre-block plays before characterization work, but before blocking, they have invested *days* of study in understanding the script; in contrast, as actors without a director, you will be developing your basic understanding of the script through the rehearsal process itself. At this point, then, simply arrange the furniture you need, and let your characters move around the set as the action and their relationships demand. Gradually, you will discover natural, meaningful blocking patterns.

If, however, you do decide to block before this rehearsal, begin by arranging your set. The "Blocking Checklist" *(pages 226 to 227)* has some suggestions for set arrangement. Once the set is arranged, act your way straight through the script, and then discuss one or two changes you need to make in your blocking; again, the "Blocking Checklist" may be of help. Avoid getting picky, at this early stage, about specific gestures or body positions; such fine-tuning this soon will waste your time and may inhibit development of your character. Repeat the sequence of acting and discussing until you are satisfied with the blocking. You'll save a lot of time erasing if you wait until the end of the rehearsal before making blocking notes in the script's margins.

Investigating Character Identity

Objective:

To deepen your acquaintance with your character.

Techniques:

Prepare mentally for this rehearsal by combing your script for every scrap of evidence about *who* your character is. Using the "Character Analysis Questions" *(page 222)* or the "Character Profiles" *(pages 223 to 224)* may help you avoid overlooking important pieces of data. Making written notes will help your memory and attention to details. Prepare for the rehearsal physically by assembling a costume. Resist the temptation to postpone using your costume — especially if the costume is different from what you usually wear in public (for instance, a bathrobe) or less than you usually wear (for instance, a swimsuit). In particular, you should rehearse in the shoes your character will wear during the performance, and if your character will be costumed in a skirt, you should wear one during rehearsals — especially if you don't normally dress that way. These costume items should become a regular part of your rehearsal because they fundamentally affect the way people move and behave.

Begin your rehearsal by arranging your set and doing your warm-ups. Then, aiming for concentration and performance quality, act your way straight through the play.

After the first run-through, take about ten minutes to introduce your characters to each other. Each pretend that your character is an old acquaintance of yours but that your character and partner have never met. Tell your partner the things that are really important for understanding who your character is. You may want to ask some questions about each other's character, using the same premise of never having met the person before. Have fun with this; the more you can enter into the game, the more you are likely to learn from it.

Now, act your way through the play again. Follow this run-through with a gossip session about your characters. Pretend your characters are mutual acquaintances of you and your partner. Give each other the *real* scoop about your characters. Let the gossip get a little catty; after all, it's for your characters' own good.

Follow the gossip session with another run-through. During the moments of concentration before the beginning of your play, visualize yourself as your character.

After this run-through, you might tell each other how you and your character are similar and different. What can you draw on from your life to apply to this character? How do you have to change yourself to become this character? If you have time, follow this talk session with a fourth run-through.

Progress assessment:

Conclude your session by telling each other how you feel about your progress. This might be a good time to check your schedule to be sure you are rehearsing frequently enough to be ready by the performance date.

Other techniques:

If the introduction or gossip exercises don't work for you, or if they work so well that you want more of the same, invent your own games. For instance, you might compose obituary notices for your characters (imagine they died immediately after the end of the play). Or you might play the role of an FBI agent doing a security check on your partner's character who has applied for a position with the Bureau; grill your partner for details about the applicant.

Playing the Intentions

Objective:

To focus on the chain of intentions which make up your role.

Orientation:

If Character A tries to force her will on Character B, and Character B not only resists but also tries to force his will on Character A, the result is conflict and drama. Most plays consist of a lively chain of shifting conflict. The moment one character has no intention at all, drama ceases to exist, the play gets boring, and the actors begin to fall out of character. The following suggestions will help you investigate the intentions of your characters.

Techniques:

The best preparation for this rehearsal is writing out your character's "through line of action." You may want to refer to the "Guidelines for Constructing a Through Line of Action" on page 225. Although writing out a through line of action takes time and hard work, it pays huge dividends.

Start your rehearsal by arranging your set and doing warm-ups. Then act the play, focusing with complete concentration at every moment on what your character is trying to accomplish during that moment, and on the transitions from intention to intention.

After the first run-through, compare your character's super-objective with that of your partner's: What is the overall objective of each of your characters? How do their different objectives bring them into conflict? When and how is the major conflict resolved?

Next, play through the script again. Concentrate on living out your character's through line of action.

After this run-through, you might see if you can help each other with one or two moments when one or the other is not sure about his/her character's intentions. For instance, your partner might say, "I don't really know why I make that first exit." Or you might say, "I get lost during your speech on page fifteen. I don't know what I'm supposed to be doing, and my mind starts to wander. What do *you* think my character is trying to do during your speech?" Remember while you talk, that it is each actor's own business to determine his/her character's intentions; the point of this discussion is not to take away that responsibility and privilege but only to get assistance in problem solving.

Don't let this discussion drag on and on; rehearsing is doing, not talking about doing. If you find you are talking more than rehearsing, you may even want to use the clock to limit your discussion times. Continue your rehearsal by repeating the sequence of acting and discussing, focusing at every moment on your character's intentions.

Objective:

You might conclude this rehearsal by telling each other what moments in the play you each feel especially good about. Celebrate these bright spots and determine to let them spread through the rest of the play.

Incorporating Technical Elements

Objective:

To check the play's set, props, and blocking.

Techniques:

Prepare for this rehearsal by collecting any props and costume items which you haven't already been using. If you've postponed attending to these technical elements, procrastinate no longer. Handling actual props will help you invent characteristic business with them; wearing the actual costume will help you develop characteristic mannerisms.

Begin the rehearsal by arranging your set and props and getting into costume. Using the questions about set arrangement in the "Blocking Checklist" *(pages 226 to 227)*, look at your set from the audience's perspective and make any necessary adjustments.

When you're satisfied with the set, do your warm-ups, and then perform the play. If the presence of new props and costume items or a different set arrangement causes some awkward moments, avoid breaking character; dealing with the problems *after* the run-through will be far more efficient.

After the run-through, critique your blocking using the "Blocking Checklist" *(pages 226 to 227)*. If you begin to find quite a few problems, limit yourself to talking about one or two, and then correct them while acting the play. After the second run, deal with a couple more improvements and put them into effect. Continue by repeating the acting/critiquing sequence.

Progress assessment:

At the end of the session, if you discovered your play is still missing props, decide which one of you will bring them. Take stock of what remains to be done on your play. Do you need another session on blocking and tech? Or do you need to return to the concentration point of an earlier rehearsal? If you are still dependent on the book and you're having a real problem keeping your place in the script while handling the props, maybe you should devote a rehearsal to getting off book. In the midst of considering what you still have to do, remember to notice and celebrate all the progress you've made so far.

Getting Off Book

Objective:

To free your mind and hands from dependence on the script.

Orientation:

If you've rehearsed frequently and with concentration, and if you've made a practice of going over your lines by yourself outside of rehearsal, you may already be very nearly lines-perfect. If so, you might well eliminate this rehearsal or combine it with another one. If you do a memorization rehearsal, be sure to concentrate on acting and characterization along with the memorization. So-called "lines rehearsals" in which actors sit and read lines back and forth without movement and characterization are wrong in theory and inefficient in practice. Such practices reinforce the erroneous idea that the bare words have an importance of their own separate from the characters' lives. Furthermore, by eliminating character and movement, "running lines" cuts off the actors from major aids to remembering the lines.

Techniques:

After warm-ups, begin by putting the scripts down and acting your way straight through the play. Don't stop if you or your partner forget lines. Don't check the script. Don't break character, apologize, or curse yourself, your memory, or the play. If you go up on a line, focus on what your character is trying to accomplish at that moment and ad-lib your way through the spot. If your partner gets lost, don't feed him/her the line; instead either jump ahead to your next speech or ad-lib to call your partner back to his/her character's intention. If both you and your partner get lost, don't stop; muddle through to the conclusion, and stay in character. The goal, of course, is a word-perfect performance exactly as the lines are written. But stopping now in the middle may just train your mind to block up at the same place each time. An ad-lib is better than breaking character.

After the run-through, pick up your scripts and each choose one spot where you lost a line. Go over these two places together several times. Then act through the play without the script again. Continue to alternate between runs-through and work on specific lines until your time is gone or until you've done a performance without memory lapse.

Once you are confident of your lines, check to see that the lines you are speaking correspond to those in the script — that comfortable but inaccurate ad-libs have not crept in. You can do this either by running the play once, script in hand, or else by asking your partner if s/he is aware of any inaccuracies in your lines.

Progress assessment:

If you are word-perfect, congratulate each other and celebrate. If one or both of you still have memory problems, pinpoint them and determine to have those spots learned before the next rehearsal.

Rx:

Persistent memory problems are indicative of concentration problems. Probably the forgetful actors are not concentrating, or else they are concentrating on the wrong things (for instance, their memory problems instead of their characters). If you repeatedly stumble over a particular spot, check your through line of action; chances are you are not clear about your character's intention at the trouble point.

Bringing It All Together

Objective:

To pull the elements of the play together into a satisfying performance.

Techniques:

After arranging the set, do your warm-ups; commit yourself to them so your first run-through will be the best you are capable of.

With full concentration, act the play. Focus on making it performance quality — the best you can do. Remember that when you perform it for your audience, you probably won't have a chance to go through it once "dry" in order to get in the mood.

After the run-through, evaluate your play. Since you are within your own performance, you may find it difficult to view your show objectively; you may realize later (probably after the rehearsal is over, or even after the final performance) that you've given a few aspects of your performance more attention than they deserved while ignoring other important elements. One way to minimize this danger is to have a director watch you and give feedback, but even directors can have blind spots. Another solution is to use some kind of a check list; you might construct your own check list by including the concentration points from your previous rehearsals, or you could use the "Final Performance Feedback Sheet" *(page 230)*.

Remember that rehearsing is doing. Don't talk it to death. Limit yourselves to dealing with one or two points, and then do another run-through.

Progress assessment:

If, by the end of your rehearsal, you still have work to do, return to this concentration point in the next session.

Dress Rehearsal

Objective:

To try out your play under performance conditions.

Techniques:

Prepare for dress rehearsal by scheduling the performance space for your use; if possible, schedule your dress rehearsal at the same time of day as final performance. The reason for this timing is to prepare for events that happen at the same time each day (such as a freight train which thunders past your building daily at an hour which coincides with your performance). In order to provide a "test audience," you might want to invite several friends to watch, and if the performance program will consist of several plays done in succession, you may want to arrange for a couple of other shows to join you.

Meet long enough before the announced time of your rehearsal to do warmups and get into costume. If, at performance, you will have to arrange your set and props in full view of the audience or under some kind of time constraints, simulate those set-up and strike circumstances during dress rehearsal.

Prior to your show, stay backstage or sit in the audience as you will at final performance. Refrain from burning off useful energy by fussing around stage or bantering with your audience.

At the announced time, set your stage, announce your play, and perform it. When you're done, take your bows, strike your set, and exit.

When you see your friends afterward, remember that if you ask them how they liked your play you are trapping them into flattering you. Just thank them for their presence and for being a good audience. If they want to tell you how they felt about the show, they will do it without your prompting.

Progress assessment:

When the audience is gone, evaluate yourselves. How efficient was your set-up and strike? Do you need to run through those procedures once or twice to correct problems? Did you get together soon enough to get your warm-ups and costuming done? Or did you get together too soon and end up with too much waiting time? How did the presence of the audience affect you? Did you crack? Rush? Make inappropriate eye contact with the audience members? Did you fail to hold for laughs or other audience reactions? What might you do to improve the experience for yourselves or your audience?

Assisted Rehearsals

Objective:

To get feedback and advice from a knowledgeable theatre person.

Orientation and preparation:

Since you can't step off stage to watch yourselves perform, you may profit from the criticisms of an experienced observer. If your instructor doesn't include monitored rehearsals as a regular part of the course, look for a helper who has had some experience acting or directing. Decide when you want your "coach" to attend rehearsals; probably two visits will be sufficient. Depending on you and your coach, you may want to specify what you want feedback on. You could use the "Feedback Sheets" *(pages 228 to 230)* or make up your own. Even if you just want general, non-directed feedback, there may be one or two specific details you want comments on; if so, you'll be wise to tell the critic before performance rather than expecting him/her to pick out small details from a plethora of impressions after the fact.

Get together soon enough to do warm-ups, get into costume, and set the stage before the scheduled arrival of your observer. If you are ready before s/he arrives, don't just sit around and get nervous. Some suggestions of what to do until your coach arrives:

- Do a full run-through of your play, and follow it with a normal self-criticism session; you may discover a few last-minute improvements you can make.

215

- Do some of the transition improvs from the rehearsal session titled "Improvising" *(pages 205 to 206)*, or play around with some of the characterization exercises from the session on "Investigating Character Identity" *(pages 208 to 210)*. These activities will give you a fresh look at your characters which will enliven your performance.

As soon as the observer arrives and gives you the go-ahead, perform the play. Resist any impulses to visit with the coach before performing. Excuses, questions, explanations, and introductions at this point are a waste of everyone's time. They are probably a device you use unconsciously to postpone performance.

After the performance, learn all you can from the observer. Realize that learning to deal profitably with criticism is a valuable part of your training as an actor. Some suggestions:

- Write down notes of the coach's observations to help your memory.

- Do not argue or offer excuses or explanations; you can evaluate the criticisms later.

- Do not respond to criticisms with, "Oh, yes, I know"; if you knew, you should have corrected the problem.

- Make sure that you understand the suggestions; if you're not sure what a particular comment really means, ask.

Progress assessment:

After the coach leaves, discuss the criticism with your partner. Be sure you both agree on what the observer said. You may want to decide which comments are useful and which you don't agree with, but don't waste time or energy indulging in self-pity, self-recrimination, or arguments with the absent critic. Instead, decide what you need to do to incorporate the useful observations, and either get to work right away or set up your next rehearsal time. Be sure to end on a positive note; *especially* if the criticism was brutal, tell each other at least one aspect of your performance each of you was happy about.

Performing

Objective:

To share your finished art work for the mutual enjoyment of yourselves and your audience.

Techniques:

Prepare for performance by taking care of yourself. Save partying until afterward, and get to bed on time the night before. Watch what you eat prior to performance; do eat, but refrain from heavy, hard-to-digest foods. Avoid alcohol, uppers, and downers; no matter how these drugs make you feel, their effect is to diminish your rational control. Don't buy a little phony self-confidence at the cost of your ability to concentrate.

Before performance, take care of warm-ups, costuming, and props, and then do what you can to maintain concentration. This doesn't mean going into a trance, but it does mean refraining from loud or physical interaction with others which will burn off energy you should pour into your performance.

When your time comes, perform with all the concentration, energy, awareness, and commitment you can muster.

If your instructor gives oral feedback after your scene, take notes just as you did during monitored rehearsals. The note-writing will help reinforce the learning process, and the activity will help you deal with any negative, post-performance emotions you may experience.

Finally, thank your partner for his/her work, return all borrowed props and costume items, and begin looking for the next show to try out for.

Rehearsal Tools

How to Read a Playscript

A script is a technical document intended for the use of performers and technicians in staging a play. Because of this, playscripts should be read differently than essays, short stories, or poems. The following suggestions will help you be more efficient in reading a script.

1. In your first encounter with a script, read it *straight through.* The novelist expects the reader to read the novel in several sittings with sizable time gaps between; the playwright expects the audience — including you, the reader — to absorb the play in a single, sustained encounter.

2. Read at a rate slightly faster than the spoken word. Don't underline; it slows you down.

3. As you read, imagine the events happening on a stage, not "in real life."

4. Do not focus on word play or symbols. Although these may be present and can add to the enjoyment, they are not what the play is about.

5. Do not focus on philosophical meanings. The ideas in a play add to its power, but they usually are not why the play was written or what the play is about.

6. Focus on character identities and relationships between characters. Changes within and between characters are particularly important, because human change is *action*, and action is what plays are all about.

7. Focus on situations and events. "Situations" are periods of static human relationships; they may contain tension and conflict, but they are unchanging. "Events" are changes in human relationships; they are transitions from situation to situation. Most plays consist of an alternating sequence of situation — event — situation — event — situation.

8. Watch for physical actions and behaviors ("business") which are implied in the dialog. Not all actions are spelled out in the stage directions. For instance, in *A Streetcar Named Desire*, Blanche says to Stella, "Are you deliberately shaking that broom in my face?" To motivate that line, the

actress playing Stella must, immediately before the line, have the broom somewhere in the direction of Blanche's face, even though the stage directions say nothing about the gesture.

9. If you want to take notes on the play (a wise activity), do so after reading the script, not during the reading.

Note: These suggestions will work not only for the short scripts in this book, but also for full-length scripts, scripts by Aeschylus and Shakespeare — any scripts.

For more help in how to read a playscript, see the Book List section on "Script Analysis" *(page 233).*

Study Questions for Individual Script Analysis

As you study your script, seek what is *unique* about your play. Almost all plays show *selfish* characters in *conflict* with each other, and almost all plays keep the audience in *suspense* about what will happen; how is your play different from all other plays? Play analysis is an on-going task. Be prepared, therefore, to learn new things about your play and to change your ideas throughout the rehearsal process.

A. The action of the play

1. In thirty words or less, summarize the story of your play.

2. How are things different at the end of your play than at the beginning? In other words, what changes in the course of the play? (Answer this question in one sentence.)

3. How does the play arouse interest? Sustain interest? Satisfy interest? (Use one sentence for each answer.)

4. What is the primary focus of the play? In other words, what is most important in the script: Telling a story? Depicting a character? Communicating ideas to the audience? Dazzling with spectacle?

B. The characters in the play

1. In twenty-five words or less, describe each character.

2. What is the basic relationship between the characters? For instance, are they lovers? Parent and child? Business associates? Total strangers? Master and servant?

3. What is the central goal, motive, or desire of each character? (One sentence per character.)

4. What obstacles keep each character from accomplishing his/her goal immediately? (One sentence per character.)

5. What is the central conflict? How does it develop? And what is the result? (One sentence per question.)

C. The style of the play

1. What is the dominant mood of the play? Be as specific as possible. Some samples: hilarious, hateful, frightening, silly, mystifying, cerebral, anxiety-producing.

2. Where does the action occur?

3. When does the action occur?

4. How is the world of the play like the real world?

5. How is the world of the play different from the real world?

D. The plot of the play

1. Divide the play into episodes and summarize each episode in one sentence. A typical romantic play, for instance, might have the following episodes: (1) Alvin asks Jane to marry him. (2) Jane rejects Alvin on account of his name. (3) Alvin wins Jane by changing his name to Elmer.

2. What is the relationship between episodes; how does the plot progress from episode to episode? You will probably need to write a short paragraph to cover this. Some sample plot progressions: (i) Chronological and causal: Episode A *causes* episode B. Episode B in turn *causes* episode C. Episode C concludes the play. (ii) Chronological but not causal: Episodes A, B, and C happen first, second, and third in the time of the story, but the earlier episodes don't really *cause* the later ones. (iii) Non-chronological: Episode B is a "flashback"; in the time of the story, the episodes occurred in the order B, A, C. (iv) Other: Some modern plays have no relation to "real" time and arrange their incidents rhythmically, similar to movements in a symphony.

E. The ideas of the play

1. What philosophical ideas or questions does the play suggest? (Use one sentence for each idea or question.)

2. What is the theme of the play? (Limit yourself to one or two sentences.) A theme may be an idea that is repeated until it dominates a play (technology threatens our humanity); or it may be a topic established by varied but related ideas and questions (how people respond to technology).

3. How important are ideas to the play? (Limit yourself to one sentence.) Answers might range from "This play exists for the sole purpose of establishing its theme" to "Any ideas found in this play are purely incidental to the main focus on telling the story."

Further Study:

While the above questions will help you understand your script, they barely scratch the surface of play analysis. To develop your dramatic analysis capabilities, continually read and view plays, and read books such as those listed in the Book List section titled "Script Analysis" *(page 233).*

Discussion Guide for Group Script Analysis

The following questions are intended to help actors talk productively about their script. It's a good idea to write down a summary of the responses to each question.

1. What happens in this play? Try to summarize the action in one sentence, and then, if necessary, expand on it.

2. Where and when does it happen? Deal first with map-and-clock reality: "It happens on June 6, 1942, in a hospital room in southern California." Then deal with socio-psychological time and place: "It happens immediately after their divorce and before the birth of their child, and it occurs on *his* turf."

3. How are the characters involved in what happens? Who makes it happen? Who profits/loses/changes the most as a result? Who is in control at each moment in the play?

4. How does the plot progress? How many episodes or scenes are there and what is the relation of each scene to the ones that precede and follow it? Can you graph the emotional intensity of each scene?

5. What is the play's style?

Character Analysis Questions

1. What do other characters say about your character? Make a *complete* list. For each statement indicate whether you think the speaker is correct, is mistaken, or is lying.

2. What does your character say about himself/herself? Be complete. Again, indicate whether your character is truthful and accurate about each statement, ignorant about himself/herself, or intentionally exaggerating, minimizing, or falsifying.

3. What does your character do, and what do these actions reveal about his/her person?

4. What do the stage directions say about your character?

5. What is your character's super-objective? The super-objective is the one thing your character most wants to accomplish in the play. Compose the super-objective carefully.

   a. Start it with a purpose statement: "I want to … " or "I must … " or "I have to … "

   b. Follow with an **active** verb: "I want **to kill** … " or "I want **to seduce** … " or "I want **to cure** … " or "I want **to tame** … " (Avoid static verbs and verbs such as "to show" as in "I want to show I am honest.")

   c. Follow the second active verb with an object that relates you to others in the play: I want to kill **the king**, I want to seduce **my servant**, I want to cure **my patient**, I want to tame **my lover**.

   d. Be sure the super-objective is specific to the play and at the same time deals with the entire role in the script. In *Oedipus Rex*, for instance, a good statement would be: "Oedipus wants to heal Thebes by punishing the murderer of Laius." An overly broad statement would be: "Oedipus wants to win everyone's admiration." This seems to be a life-long goal of Oedipus but is too general for this single event in his life. A sample of a super-objective that is too small might be, "Oedipus wants to learn his own identity." Actually he doesn't settle on this purpose until well into the play, and after he discovers who he is and blinds himself, the play still goes on for some time.

Sample Character Profiles

To play your character well, you need to know a great many more details about him/her than you will ever share with the audience on stage. Here are three character profile outlines you may use to fill in your character's background. When you add details from your imagination, be sure they fit with the character as portrayed in the script.

Profile 1: Six Traits of Character

This six-trait scheme comes from Sam Smiley's book, *Playwriting: The Structure of Action,* pages 83 to 91.

1. Biological traits: Is the character human or non-human? Male or female?

2. Physical traits: Include here all details about the character's body, voice, costume, manner of walking, and tempo — in other words, everything the audience can *see* and *hear* about the character.

3. Attitudinal traits: What is your character's basic outlook on life? Include such details as characteristic moods and habits.

4. Motivational traits: What are your character's goals, motives, drives, and desires? Also include your character's fears and hatreds.

5. Deliberational traits: What does your character think about? How does your character think? To what extent is your character ruled by mind rather than heart (emotions) or belly (desires)?

6. Decisional traits: What, if any, decisions does your character make? How does s/he go about making decisions?

Profile 2: The Bone-Structure of a Character

This three-part outline comes from Lajos Egri's book, *How to Write a Play,* pages 36 to 38.

Physiology

1. Sex
2. Age
3. Height and weight
4. Color of hair, eyes, skin

5. Posture
6. Appearance
7. Defects
8. Heredity

Sociology

1. Class
2. Occupation
3. Education
4. Home life
5. I.Q.

6. Religion
7. Race, nationality
8. Place in community
9. Political affiliations
10. Amusements, hobbies

Psychology

1. Sex life, moral standards
2. Personal premise, ambition
3. Frustrations, chief disappointments
4. Temperament
5. Attitude towards life
6. Complexes, obsessions, inhibitions, superstitions, manias, phobias
7. Extrovert, introvert, ambivert
8. Abilities, talents
9. Qualities

Profile 3: Identification of a Character

Jim Cash, film writer and teacher at Michigan State University, developed the following profile for his own use and for his students:

1. Name the character. Male or female.
2. Birthdate and birthplace.
3. Education
4. Occupation.
5. Height, weight, eyes, and hair.
6. Marital status.
7. Children.
8. A significant event that happened at the age of ten.
9. At the age of twenty.
10. At a later age.
11. Ten statements of information about this character — what s/he thinks, feels, cares about, hopes for, believes in, the conflicts and harmonies in his/her life, any kind of information that gives the character dimension.

Constructing a Through Line of Action

1. Go through your script and make a mark at every place where your character changes from one intention to another. The time between each mark is a "beat" or "unit of action."

2. In a notebook, write down two things for each beat. First, write down the intention. Use the same format as for the super-objective *(page 222)*. Second, write down what happens to the intention and how it changes to the next one. Typically, intentions are either fulfilled, defeated, postponed, or modified.

3. Don't forget to treat your character's *entrance* as a beat, complete with intention and transition to the next beat.

4. Avoid the following constructions for intentions: "to show ... ", "to express ... " *Especially* if what follows is an emotion.

5. Be sure your statement of intentions includes the *why* behind the physical act. **Wrong:** "He wants to sit down." **Right:** "He wants to infuriate the Emperor by sitting down."

6. As much as possible, make your intentions concrete and specific. Avoid vague intentions.

7. Intentions should all differ from each other. This is especially the case when they follow each other in adjacent sequence; it is also usually the case when two similar beats are separated by several other beats. At the very least, they should build in intensity.

8. Each beat should relate to the character's super-objective. The relationship need not be *stated*, but it should be relatively obvious.

For more details on this technique, see page 234 of the Book List.

Analyzing Your Lines

Every line — every *word* — in your role means something specific to your character. Furthermore, your character wants to accomplish something as a result of every line s/he speaks. These six steps will help insure none of your lines are meaningless or purposeless (in other words, *dead*) when you say them.

1. Look up all words whose definition or pronunciation you are uncertain of.

2. What is the *sub-text* of the line? That is, what does the line mean *to the*

character who says it? One way to discover sub-text is to paraphrase the line. Sample: Line: What time is it? Various sub-texts might be: (a) How long until my execution? (b) You are *really* late! (c) I think I missed my wedding.

3. Decide on the *verbal action* of the line. That is, what is your character *trying to accomplish* by saying the line? Sample: For the sub-texts in item #2 above, the respective verbal actions might be: (a) To discover if I still have time to escape from death row. (b) To insult my "friend." (c) To find out if I've avoided a marriage I really didn't want.

4. Notice all *images* in the line. An image is a verbal expression of a sensory experience or object which the speaker is remembering or imagining. Be sure you are able to visualize, in your mind's eye, the images your character talks about; focus on these images every time you rehearse or perform the role.

5. Don't skip a line. The point of this exercise is to help you deal with lines you've been ignoring (running them over your lips but bypassing your character's head). The line you are tempted to skip as "obvious" is likely the one that most needs work.

Blocking Checklist

A. Arranging the set.

1. Where is the audience in relation to your set?

2. How many entrances/exits do you need, and where are they? Are they located so that they maximize the effect of important entrances or exits? Upstage-center doors, for instance, make it difficult for actors to exit without turning their backs on the audience.

3. Where is the furniture? Where are important props such as telephones? Is your set cluttered with unnecessary furniture? Is the furniture arranged so that it shares the play with the audience? The following arrangement, for instance, will make it difficult for the audience to see the face of an actor in Chair "B" and may hide an actor in Chair "A" behind the downstage actor.

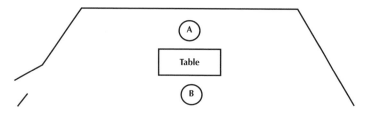

Rearrange the set like this:

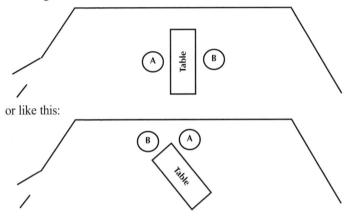

or like this:

B. Checking the blocking.

1. Does the blocking share the play with the audience? Usually minimize blocking which places the actor's back to the audience or which conceals upstage actors behind downstage actors.

2. Does the blocking focus attention on the dominant actor at each moment? In the course of a single scene, the action may belong to one character for a while, then shift to another; at times, two or three characters may share the scene. The blocking should enhance the focus.

3. Is there an appropriate amount of movement in the scene? Begin with the amount of movement the action would seem to demand in real life, and then heighten this by adding crosses and making them larger (don't forget to motivate each cross). Modify your blocking by considering the characters' relative tempos. In *A Streetcar Named Desire*, for instance, Blanche is likely to move often, quickly, and frenetically while Stella probably moves slowly, less often, more cow-like.

4. Does the blocking symbolize relationship by position and movement? For instance, in a scene where two lovers are "growing apart" the actors might gradually move further from each other. In a scene where one actor "talks down" to another, the persecutor might be standing upstage of the victim who might be seated or even lying on the floor. In a scene where two apparently equal characters are "sparring," their movement pattern might approximate that of two circling boxers.

For more details on blocking, check the Book List on page 234.

Feedback Sheet: Characterization

Play Title : _____

Character: _____ Actor: _____

1. Did the actor concentrate consistently?

2. Was the character believable?

3. Are there moments when the character's intentions need to be clarified?

4. Are there other useful comments?

Observer: _____

Date: _____

Feedback Sheet: Tech and Pacing

Play Title: _____

Character: _____ Actor: _____

1. Should any technical elements be changed?

2. Has the actor made progress in believability?

3. Are there sequences that should be faster, slower, louder, softer, etc.?

4. Were there lapses in line memorization?

5. Are there other helpful comments?

Observer: _____

Date: _____

Final Performance Feedback Sheet

Play Title: _____

Character: _____ Actor: _____

Technical considerations

    Were there memorization lapses?

    Were crosses, pictures, and business effective?

    Was projection adequate?

Character portrayal

    Were given circumstances consistent throughout?

    Were intentions clearly and consistently played?

    Did the actor clearly play the character's changes?

    Was the characterization inventive?

    Was there meaningful variety in the performance?

    Was the energy level satisfactory?

    Did the actor avoid over-acting?

Professionalism

    Did the actor cooperate with fellow actors throughout the rehearsal period?

    Did the actor take responsibility for rehearsal and production processes?

    Did the actor maintain seriousness of purpose?

    What did the actor do to help build cast morale?

    Did the actor display willingness and ability to take direction?

Additional comments:

Evaluator: _____

Date: _____

Part 4
Book List

Rehearsal Helps

Rehearsing without a Director

Cohen, Robert. *Acting One.* 4th ed. Mountain View, CA: McGraw-Hill, 2001. "Rehearsing."

Felner, Mira. *Free to Act: An Integrated Approach to Acting.* New York: Holt, Rinehart, & Winston, 1990. "The Rehearsal Process," pp. 232–49.

Warm-ups

Barton, Robert. *Acting: Onstage and Off.* 3rd ed., New York: Harcourt, Brace, Jovanovich, 2002. "Relaxed Readiness," pp. 29–67.

Linklater, Kristin. *Freeing the Natural Voice.* Brooklyn: Drama Publishers, 1976. "Warm-up."

Machlin, Evangeline. *Speech for the Stage.* 2nd ed., New York: Routledge, 1992. "The Actor's Practice Routine" and "The Actor's Warm-up Exercises," pp. 239–43.

Script Analysis

Felner, Mira. *Free to Act: An Integrated Approach to Acting.* New York: Holt, Rinehart, & Winston, 1990. "The Elements of Dramatic Analysis," pp. 157–71.

Thomas, James. *Script Analysis for Actors, Directors, and Designers.* 2nd ed. Burlington, MA: Focal Press, 1998.

Waxberg, Charles. *The Actor's Script: Script Analysis for Performers.* Portsmouth, NH: Heinemann, 1998.

Improvisations

Gronbeck-Tedesco, John L. *Acting through Exercises: A Synthesis of Classical and Contemporary Approaches.* Mountain View, CA: McGraw-Hill, 1991. "Working Across the Given Circumstances," pp. 156–68.

Johnstone, Keith. *Impro: Improvisation and the Theatre.* New York: Theatre Arts Books, 1989.

Spolin, Viola. *Improvisation for the Theatre: A Handbook of Teaching and*

> *Directing Techniques.* 3rd ed. Evanston, IL: Northwestern University Press, 1999.

Blocking

Cohen, Robert. *Acting One.* 4th ed. Mountain View, CA: McGraw-Hill, 2001. "Staging the Scene."

Dean, Alexander and Lawrence Carra. *Fundamentals of Play Directing.* 5th ed. New York: International Thomson Publishing. "Basic Technique for the Actor," and "The Five Fundamentals of Play Directing."

Character Analysis

Abbott, Leslie. *Active Acting: Exercises and Improvisations Leading to Performance.* Belmont, CA: Star Publishing Company, 1993. "Developing Your Characterization," pp. 115–24.

McGaw, Charles and Larry D. Clark. *Acting Is Believing: A Basic Method.* 7th ed. Belmont: Wadsworth Publishing Company, 1995. "Getting into the Part."

Constructing a Through Line of Action

Felner, Mira. *Free to Act: An Integrated Approach to Acting.* New York: Holt, Rinehart, & Winston, 1990. "Defining Beats," and "Building Beats into a Scene," pp. 232–49.

McGaw, Charles and Larry D. Clark. *Acting Is Believing: A Basic Method.* 7th ed. Belmont: Wadsworth Publishing Company, 1995. "Seeing a Part as Units of Action."

Memorization

Barton, Robert. *Acting: Onstage and Off.* 3rd ed., New York: Harcourt, Brace, Jovanovich, 2002. "Memorizing," pp. 238–39.

Cohen, Robert. *Acting One.* 4th ed. Mountain View, CA: McGraw-Hill, 2001. "Memorization Methods."

Dealing with Stage Fright

Barton, Robert. *Acting: Onstage and Off.* 3rd ed., New York: Harcourt, Brace, Jovanovich, 2002. "Stage Fright Substitutes," p. 33.

Cohen, Robert. *Acting One.* 4th ed. Mountain View, CA: McGraw-Hill, 2001. "Stage Fright."

Other Scripts by Writers in This Anthology

Norman A. Bert

Unless otherwise noted, all scripts available from the playwright, 5704 Nashville Avenue, Lubbock, TX 79413-4601.

Breakfast. A ten-minute comedy about a woman trying to cope with too many cold cereal choices. In *Play It Again: More One-Act Plays for Acting Students*, Colorado Springs: Meriwether Publishing Ltd., 1993.

Dr. Dixie Duzzett's Delight. A ribald one-act satire on modern sexual mores and addition therapy.

Phone-call from Sunkist. A coming-of-age drama for three men based on an industrial accident. In *One-Act Plays for Acting Students*, Colorado Springs: Meriwether Publishing Ltd., 1987.

Riders of the Golden Sphinx. A full-length spoof of Western melodramas, incorporating the Oedipus story and laced with classical cowboy songs.

Ucross Junction. A one-hour, site-specific, imagistic play set in an art exhibit that investigates the intersection of art and life. Written with Madeleine Martin.

Denny Berthiaume

All scripts available from the playwright, 12345 El Monte Road, Los Altos Hills, CA 94022.

Between the Darkness. A full-length musical about Abraham Von Helsing, the nemesis of Count Dracula.

Office HRS. A full-length play about healing and recovery after child sexual molestation.

Playtime. A full-length comedy about the director of a Shakespeare repertory company.

She Loves Me, She Loves Me Not. A female monolog about suicide following domestic violence.

Conrad Bishop and Elizabeth Fuller

Full Hookup. A modern tragedy in a trailer park. Available from Dramatists Play Service.

Marie Antoinette. A play about the legendary queen and the contradictory images of history. Available from Word Workers Press.

Mating Cries. A collection of micro-plays about bonding. Available from Word Workers Press.

Rash Acts: Eighteen Snapshots for the Stage. An anthology of short plays from two years of ensemble touring. Available from Word Workers Press.

Seismic Stages: Five Plays for Teens. Three one-acts and two large collections of short plays created with and for teenagers. Available from Word Workers Press.

William Borden

All scripts available from the playwright, 7996 S. FM 548, Royse City, TX 75189.

Garage Sale. A play about Warren, who is selling everything — pajamas, wedding pictures, his past.

I Want to Be an Indian. A play about a liberal who wants to be a Native American and gets his chance one night in a bar on a reservation.

Sakakawea. A musical drama about the legendary guide of the Lewis and Clark expedition confronted by a skeptical reporter who prompts her to tell her story.

Tap Dancing Across the Universe. A play about a college professor who wants to run away from home and gets his chance when he is visited by a would-be shaman, a run away mother, and a hippie.

Turtle Island Blues. A play about five hundred years of American (Turtle Island) history featuring Sitting Bull, Columbus, and others.

Mathew Calhoun

All scripts available from the playwright, 23-51 19th St., Astoria, NY 11105.

Communication Problems. A farce about a man who gets stuck in a job with "the boss from hell."

Life in the Suburbs. The Last Weed in Glen Ellyn and *Conditions.*

Living in Sin. A comedy with tragic overtones about the first family's fall from grace.

Skits-Ophrenia. A comic review: a skit-series about crazy behavior in ordinary situations.

Tortured People. A drama about domestic abuse and human rights.

Gary Garrison

All scripts available from the playwright, 14 Washington Place, #2A, New York, NY 10003.

The Big Fat Naked Truth. Five women — strangers to each other — mysteriously locked in the same room.

Gawk. A ten-minute play about the relationship between two women brought together when a young boy is shot in a drive-by shooting.

Padding the Wagon. A ten-minute play about the World Trade Center crisis.

Tender Salvation. A short play about the exploits of a young man at a video dating service.

When a Diva Dreams. A full-length ensemble comedy for six women set in New Orleans.

Eric Geyer

All scripts available from the playwright, 327 W. Ridgewood, San Antonio, TX 78212.

Anything Will Help. A homeless woman receives more than her fair share of unsolicited advice in this short play about perspective and the nature of charity.

The Bank Errand and Other Boring Stories. A man hires a prostitute to listen to the anecdotes that he would not dare bore his true friends with in this strange story exploring the true meaning of objectification.

The Gift. A comedy about a man who learns valuable truths from a meddling pair of talking ketchup and mustard bottles.

The Vagabond. A college graduate dreams of living life without worldly possessions or obligations — until he wins a very large television.

Julianne Homokay

All scripts available from the playwright, c/o The Fulton Opera House, PO Box 1865, Lancaster, PA 17608.

Dionessa. A one-act about an invalid teen-aged Irish girl who receives a strange visitor out of the wild countryside.

Impeccable Judgement. A ten-minute drama about a father and daughter who struggle to communicate over unmentionable subjects.

Judy Gray. A full-length dark comedy about a teen-aged math and science whiz who builds a pair of wings so she can fly away.

Roscoe's Little Theatre. A one-act about a prodigal son who makes his last stand against the corporate take-over of his heritage, using his family's old theatre building as a battleground.

The Wedding Story. Ten-minute comedy about a storyteller who reveals the gory truth behind the picture-perfect bride and groom.

Geoffrey Howard

All scripts available from the playwright, 620 E. Escondido, Kingsville, TX 78363.

The Bob and Al Show. Developed from *The Well-Made Play*, the characters find themselves dealing with issues of theme and purpose as they are now forced to help their fledgling playwright develop a mystery play.

Green with all the Dents. An aging man comes to terms with loss as he is visited by sometimes altered memories while he attempts to restore life to an old green truck.

The Well-Made Play. Three characters find themselves confronting their own playwright as they are created.

Michael Johnson-Chase

All scripts available from the playwright, 21 S. End Ave., #522, New York, NY 10280.

The Alarm Clock. A play co-written by Luoyong Wang.

Dog and His Master. A play co-written by Luoyong Wang.

The Temple. A screenplay co-written by Luoyong Wang.

David MacGregor

All scripts available from the playwright, 31100 Westfield, Livonia, MI 48150.

Double Blind. Psychological thriller screenplay.

The Good Soldier. A screenplay.

Mainstream. A stage play.

Phobos. A sci-fi screenplay.

Smoker. A stage play.

Madeleine Martin

All scripts available from the playwright, PO Box 53521, Lubbock, TX 79453.

Dodging the Bullets. A monolog featuring a woman who refuses to file assault charges against her battering husband.

Doing the Laundry. A forty-five minute play in which a woman hangs out her bitter memories along with her laundry.

For Better or Worse. A monolog in which a woman makes detailed plans for a wedding she swears she'll never have.

The Patrician Potty. A ten-minute play about a divorcing couple squabbling over who gets custody of an antique toilet.

Swan Song. Written with Norman Bert, this eccentric short satire examines the wormier side of academic awards.

Michael Moore

All scripts available from the playwright, 2234 Patriot Commons Rd., Abilene, TX 79601.

Ellie and the Bear Man. A full-length play about two physically challenged people who fall in love in 1950 West Texas.

The Price of a Woman. A one-act play fictionalizing the final encounter between Biblical King David and his wife, Michal.

Beauty. A one-act play about the last day of the life of Countess Elizabeth Bathory, who allegedly murdered over six hundred young girls and bathed in their blood.

Wisdoms of Pearl. A one-act play about a rural mother's reaction to her teenage son skipping school.

When Valentines Comes. In this one-act play, a grieving teen-age boy gets unexpected help from a ghost that visits him on Valentine's Day.

Robert Patrick

Both scripts are available from Dramatists Publishing Company, Chicago.

Mutual Benefit Life. A young married couple and the girl upstairs try to milk an amnesiac friend of his money.

My Cup Ranneth Over. Two roommates finally fight.

Louise M. Stinespring

"Just Be Yourself: Derrida, Difference, and the Meisner Technique" in *Method Acting Reconsidered.* Ed. David Krasner. New York: Palgrave Macmillan, 2000.

Megan Terry

Approaching Simone. Obie Award for Best Play; a full-length action biography of the great French theologian, Simone Weil. In *Plays by Megan Terry*, New York: Broadway Play Publishing, 1999.

Ex-Miss Copper Queen on a Set of Pills. One act; a former beauty queen tries to live on the streets with other homeless people. New York: Samuel French.

Fireworks. A one-act play in which a young father returning from war tries to reconcile his two children to his impending divorce. In *One-Act Plays for Acting Students*, Colorado Springs, CO: Meriwether Publishing Ltd., 1987.

Hothouse. War stories from herstory, a full-length play dealing with the wars faced by three generations of women. New York: Samuel French.

Mollie Bailey's Traveling Family Circus: Featuring Scenes from the Life of Mother Jones. A double biography in a circus setting, this full-length musical demonstrates the indomitable spirits of two very different but very strong and vibrant women. New York: Broadway Play Publishing: also available from the Omaha Magic Theatre, 2309 Hanscom Blvd., Omaha, NE 68105.

About the Editors

Norman A. Bert and Deb Bert collaborate writing plays and theatre books. Norman earned his Ph.D. at Indiana University, specializing in dramatic theory and criticism. He has taught acting, playwriting, and other theatre courses since 1975. He currently teaches playwriting and dramatic analysis at Texas Tech University. He has been actively involved in the Playwriting Awards Committee of the Kennedy Center American College Theatre Festival and the Playwrights Program of the Association for Theatre in Higher Education. Norman has written over twenty-five play scripts, most of which have been published and/or produced, and has authored several books including *One-Act Plays for Acting Students, Play It Again: More One-Act Plays for Acting Students, The Scenebook for Actors*, and *Theatre Alive!* an anthology of world drama with historical introductions.

Deb earned a B.A. in theatre arts from Montana State University — Billings, where she graduated with high honors. A native of Montana, Deb writes under the pen name of Madeleine Martin. Her scripts have been produced in Montana, Texas, and off-off-Broadway in New York. She is currently writing a children's book as well as continuing her play writing.

When they're not absorbed in theatre-related activities, Norman and Deb enjoy traveling and spending quality time with their good friend and companion Geppetto, a Maltese.

Order Form

Meriwether Publishing Ltd.
PO Box 7710
Colorado Springs CO 80933-7710
Phone: 800-937-5297 Fax: 719-594-9916
Website: www.meriwether.com

Please send me the following books:

_____ **New One-Act Plays for Acting Students** $19.95
#BK-B261
edited by Norman Bert and Deb Bert
An anthology of one-act plays for one to three actors

_____ **More One-Act Plays for Acting Students** $19.95
#BK-B130
edited by Deb Bert and Norman Bert
An anthology of one-act plays for one to three actors

_____ **One-Act Plays for Acting Students #BK-B159** $19.95
edited by Dr. Norman A. Bert
An anthology of complete one-act plays

_____ **Theatre Alive #BK-B178** $49.95
by Dr. Norman A. Bert
An introductory anthology of world drama

_____ **The Scenebook for Actors #BK-B177** $16.95
edited by Dr. Norman A. Bert
Collection of great monologs and dialogs for auditions

_____ **Truth in Comedy #BK-B164** $17.95
by Charna Halpern, Del Close and Kim "Howard" Johnson
The manual of improvisation

_____ **112 Acting Games #BK-B277** $17.95
by Gavin Levy
A comprehensive workbook of theatre games

These and other fine Meriwether Publishing books are available at
your local bookstore or direct from the publisher. Prices subject to
change without notice. Check our website or call for current prices.

Name: _____ e-mail: _____

Organization name: _____

Address: _____

City: _____ State: _____

Zip: _____ Phone: _____

❑ **Check enclosed**

❑ **Visa / MasterCard / Discover #** _____

Signature: _____   *Expiration date:* _____

(required for credit card orders)

Colorado residents: Please add 3% sales tax.
Shipping: Include $3.95 for the first book and 75¢ for each additional book ordered.

❑ *Please send me a copy of your complete catalog of books and plays.*

3 1901 04367 3401